This manual is not just for start-up companies. Established co͟  ͟ to renewing
their product and service portfolio to avoid progressive profit at changes in
customer needs, market segmentation, new technologies and ͟ed leading to
loss of competitive advantage. The ideas contained in this m͟ ͟nge the *status*
quo and develop future strategies which add value and lead to

Dr David Hughes FREng, CDir
Innovation Consultant and former Technology Planning Director
GEC plc and Director General, Innovation Group, DTI, UK

In a world where 92% of start-ups fail within 3 years, the savvy innovator needs to join the 8%. Uday Phadke and
Shailendra Vyakarnam provide an array of new tools and insights. They distinguish themselves by grounding their
work in decades of detailed research; importantly, their sources cover the experience of successful and unsuccessful
ventures alike, across contrasting industry sectors. This is invaluable in three ways: their comprehensive framework
helps entrepreneurs organise their activities into 12 'vectors'; detailed analysis of each vector facilitates the tailored
integration of existing and new methods; and practical research-based tools guide decision-making and priorities,
contingent on the unique circumstances faced by each firm. It should be essential reading for governments, start-
ups and mature companies. This is the real deal.

Paul Doxey, forensic accounting expert and innovator,
founder of Dagger Forensics; creator of the
nirv[KM] suite for harnessing complexity

An interesting and informative read taking start-ups through what is an important process to understand and integrate into their strategies for growth. This is a great follow on from the idea to start up and breaching the chasm. We should all be making plans for growth early in our business plans. This is about planning for success.

Martino Picardo, former CEO Stevenage Bioscience Catalyst
now Independent Consultant

Working at the interface between academic innovation and industry application presents us with a number of challenges. This evidence-based manual provides practical approaches to help fill the void between concept and delivery of a useable product. It is invaluable to understanding the commercialisation journey and pinpointing what is needed to create a successful business.

Dr Kathryn Chapman
Executive Manager, The Milner Therapeutics Institute, Cambridge

Great to see a unified toolkit which helps innovative companies to go beyond the start-up buzz and to scale-up systematically to become commercially successful enterprises — a wide range of case studies bring the tools to life and show how priorities can change with the maturity of the business.

Warwick Hill
CEO-in-Residence and Managing Director,
Microsoft for Start-ups, London

As the founder and leader of a database technology company in the AI space, with applicability across a wide range of markets and applications, our key challenges are in making the right strategic decisions about market focus, product functionality and business models. The detailed vector-based tools have enabled us to shape our strategic priorities, design our business models and make critical decisions about our approach to scaling and commercialising our technology across a wide range of market spaces.

Haikal Pribadi
Founder and CEO of GRAKN.AI

The journey from an idea to a successful product is very challenging, and in this second book the authors have condensed their wisdom into the key issues which entrepreneurs must address. It is now time for this material to be embedded into all MBA courses.

Dr John Baits, CTO DN Capital;
former Worldwide CTO for Cable & Wireless
MD of IT and Research for Telstra
Senior Executive at IBM
Visiting Professor at University of Southampton, UK

This manual builds on *Camels, Tigers & Unicorns* and provides further amazing insights on the factors that affect commercialisation of innovations for economic and social value. Understanding and leveraging these insights could be hugely valuable, not only for innovators and organisations but also for institutions supporting innovators and policy-makers (including governments). I look forward to leveraging these insights for our efforts in supporting deep-science innovations in India.

Dr Taslimarif Saiyed
CEO, Centre for Cellular and Molecular Platforms,
NCBS, Bangalore

The tools and frameworks in *The Scale-up Manual* provide a powerful basis for high-growth firms such as ours to understand where we are in the commercialisation journey, to articulate our strategic objective and to understand how we can shape our priorities using the meso-economic vectors. The market-space mapping tool and the Commercialisation Monitor, in particular, have helped us to position and differentiate our offerings in the complicated healthcare market space.

Dr Lorin Gresser
Chief Executive, Dem Dx

Our new AI-powered gait and movement analytics engine outperforms consultants in diagnosing neurological and musculoskeletal disease in different clinical environments. The tools in *The Scale-up Manual* enabled us to identify and characterise three different types of customers, to shape products, services and pricing to match their needs, and to understand and exploit the different channels for reaching these customers.

Dr Adar Pelah, CEO, Asuuta

Converting ideas into reality requires not only a conceptual framework to understand the overall commercial landscape but also the right tools to build a clear plan for effective implementation. With *Camels, Tigers & Unicorns*, Phadke and Vyakarnam synthesised and extended a broad spectrum of frameworks for converting ideas into innovations. Now with *The Scale-up Manual*, the same authors respond to practitioner demand with a focus on 'how to' tools needed by tech and non-tech entrepreneurs alike to identify their exact location on the scale-up journey, diagnose their dominant requirements at each stage and then execute step-by-step the plan emerging from this detailed analysis. The outcomes of a generation of thinking about the often-confusing realities of business growth have been distilled into a robust, accessible toolkit. The resulting Commercialisation Canvas provides a comprehensive overview of the scale-up journey, tailored to each team's exact requirements.

Dr David Gill
Managing Director of St Johns Innovation Centre, Cambridge

Over the past 20 years, I have seen entrepreneurs struggle with every aspect of innovation from ideation through company start up to subsequent leadership of maturing companies. *The Scale-up Manual* brings together a wealth of knowledge from different models that supports the entire commercialisation journey. The authors develop the tools and models described in *Camels, Tigers & Unicorns* and, through their case-study based approach, provide a pathway to convert theory into practice. *The Scale-up Manual* arrives at a time when governments across the globe are looking to innovation to fuel future economic growth. Whether you are an aspiring entrepreneur, leading an established enterprise or responsible for innovation policy at the national or international level you will benefit from reading this book.

Dr Adrian Ibrahim
Head of Business Development and Technology Transfer
Wellcome Trust Sanger Institute

The Scale-up Manual

Handbook for Innovators, Entrepreneurs, Teams and Firms

The
Scale-up
Manual

Handbook for Innovators, Entrepreneurs, Teams and Firms

Uday Phadke • Shailendra Vyakarnam

World Scientific

NEW JERSEY • LONDON • SINGAPORE • BEIJING • SHANGHAI • HONG KONG • TAIPEI • CHENNAI • TOKYO

Published by

World Scientific Publishing Europe Ltd.

57 Shelton Street, Covent Garden, London WC2H 9HE

Head office: 5 Toh Tuck Link, Singapore 596224

USA office: 27 Warren Street, Suite 401-402, Hackensack, NJ 07601

Library of Congress Cataloging-in-Publication Data

Names: Phadke, Uday, author. | Vyakarnam, Shailendra, author.
Title: The scale-up manual : handbook for innovators, entrepreneurs, teams and firms / Uday Phadke, Shailendra Vyakarnam.
Description: New Jersey : World Scientific, [2018]
Identifiers: LCCN 2018023719 | ISBN 9781786345905 (hc : alk. paper) | ISBN 9781786346261 (pbk : alk. paper)
Subjects: LCSH: New business enterprises--Management. | New products. | Marketing. | Strategic planning.
Classification: LCC HD62.5 .P5185 2018 | DDC 658.4/06--dc23
LC record available at https://lccn.loc.gov/2018023719

British Library Cataloguing-in-Publication Data
A catalogue record for this book is available from the British Library.

For any available supplementary material, please visit
http://www.worldscientific.com/worldscibooks/10.1142/Q0176#t=suppl

Desk Editors: Anthony Alexander/Koe Shi Ying

Typeset by Stallion Press
Email: enquiries@stallionpress.com

Printed in Singapore

For Wendy, Leela and Jamie

For Annapurna, Aditi, Rajesh, Kiren and Aaryan

Origins of this Manual

The idea for this manual came from the extensive feedback we received based on our book *Camels, Tigers & Unicorns* [1], aimed at rethinking how science and technology-enabled innovation is actually commercialised, as summarised in Figure 1. Readers of this rather academic textbook pointed out that our approach to assessing the maturity of a proposition combined with the meso-economic vectors or drivers of change provided a powerful basis for creating practical tools for entrepreneurs, innovators and high-growth firms. The common concern we heard about existing treatments was that most current approaches focused on the early stages of venture creation and that most tools conflated the impact of different variables.

We also heard from readers who recognised that our approach could be used to address the scale-up challenges for all innovative firms not just those enabled by science and technology.

The purpose of this manual therefore is to provide a practical guide which can be used by all those embarked on a scale-up journey, without having to comprehend the intellectual basis of our approach in detail. Our approach builds on, but differs from previous approaches, which have generally been informed by case studies based on a relatively small number of mature firms.

This really is a **how-to book**, which readers can dip into and use, based on wherever they are on their commercialisation journey, confident that they are using a comprehensive and consistent resource based on a unified treatment of the scale-up challenge.

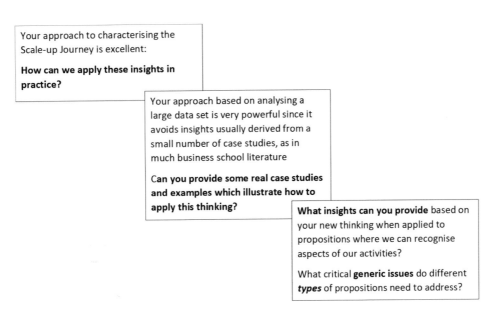

Your approach to characterising the Scale-up Journey is excellent:

How can we apply these insights in practice?

Your approach based on analysing a large data set is very powerful since it avoids insights usually derived from a small number of case studies, as in much business school literature

Can you provide some real case studies and examples which illustrate how to apply this thinking?

What insights can you provide based on your new thinking when applied to propositions where we can recognise aspects of our activities?

What critical **generic issues** do different **types** of propositions need to address?

Figure 1.   Reactions to *Camels, Tigers & Unicorns.*

About the Authors

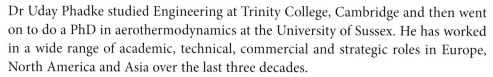

Dr Uday Phadke studied Engineering at Trinity College, Cambridge and then went on to do a PhD in aerothermodynamics at the University of Sussex. He has worked in a wide range of academic, technical, commercial and strategic roles in Europe, North America and Asia over the last three decades.

He has a deep technology background in a number of areas, including aerospace engineering, digital signal processing, remote sensing, electronics, computing and software, medical diagnostics, engineering design, media and telecommunications, financial technologies and digital media.

He has been actively involved in the building of over 100 technology firms over the last two decades as an advisor, mentor and investor, working closely with technology transfer offices, innovation agencies, incubators and accelerators. He has also been part of the founding team at a number of technology advisory and consulting companies since the early 1980s; since 1997, he has been Chief Executive of Cartezia, the technology business builder based in Cambridge, UK.

He was Entrepreneur-in-Residence at the Judge Business School at the University of Cambridge from 2011 to 2016 and is now actively involved in several innovation policy development initiatives in Europe and Asia.

 Dr Shailendra Vyakarnam did his MBA and PhD at Cranfield. He has since combined academic, practitioner and policy interests to provide advice to governments on the development of entrepreneurial ecosystems, technology commercialisation and entrepreneurship education. He has mentored entrepreneurs and held non-executive directorships of small firms in addition to developing growth programmes for SMEs over several years.

From 2003 to 2015, he focused on the development of practitioner-led education for entrepreneurship at the University of Cambridge Judge Business School, where he led The Centre for Entrepreneurial Learning.

Dr Vyakarnam was awarded 'Best Entrepreneurship Professor' at the 2nd Asian Business Schools Awards in 2011. In 2012, he was elected to the prestigious European Academy of Science and Arts. He has held visiting professorships at University of Reading and University of Aarhus, the Indian Institute of Science and the American University of Cairo.

He has taught and mentored hundreds of entrepreneurs in over 20 countries and continues to live his passion for entrepreneurship as founder, director and advisor to several firms. He is now Director of the Bettany Centre for Entrepreneurship at Cranfield University.

Acknowledgements

We would like to thank the founders, leaders and managers of the several hundred innovative firms across Europe, North America and Asia who shared their data, experiences and insights with us as we were developing the tools described in this manual. We have of course been careful to preserve their confidentiality but would like to acknowledge their generosity and time in sharing quite detailed information about their progress and challenges. Many of these leaders and managers also supported us in testing and refining the approaches and tools described in *The Scale-up Manual*.

We would also like to thank the following individuals in particular who reviewed early drafts of this manual and provided detailed commentary, critiques and suggestions for improvement: Peter Collins, David Gill, Cath and Lars Holmgaard-Mersh, Arun Muthirulan, and Andy Walker.

Contents

List of Figures

Part I

Building Blocks

Chapter 1

Who is this Manual for?

The approach used in this manual provides the first **integrated framework** for understanding the journey from research and concept creation to full-blown commercialisation.

The integrated framework is built on explicitly defining the maturity of any proposition and applying the meso-economic vectors which can determine the trajectory and pace of commercialisation.

As a result, this manual can be used by the following key users shown in Figure 1 engaged in different parts of the journey:

- **Researchers and Innovators** working in academic settings, technology transfer teams and innovation agencies whose main focus is likely to be on identifying opportunities arising from new concepts, technologies and processes.
- **'Early-stage' entrepreneurs** focused on transforming early concepts into prototypes which can demonstrate potentially interesting new capability or functionality.
- **'Early-stage' firms,** where one or more individuals have combined to create a formally defined legal entity (the firm) which is actively engaged in creating and developing a prototype or product or service. Our integrated approach means that we are less concerned with how the ownership of ideas and intellectual property and the legal basis of the firm

is manifested; in practice, the point at which an entrepreneur or group of entrepreneurs creates a formal legal entity called the firm can depend on 'local rules' about IP ownership and exploitation, how activities are funded, and the motivations of the key actors.

- **'Growth' firms,** which are focused mainly on converting a prototype product into a commercially sustainable product or service proposition, gearing up for widespread commercial exploitation.
- **'Mature' firms,** which are focused on the full commercial exploitation of sustainable products or services.
- **'Established' firms,** which are typically larger players who have already successfully deployed one or more products or services in the market space. For these firms, this manual can provide an explicit reminder of how they can create new products; it also illustrates the differences between starting this process in the research laboratory, creating new prototypes, or modifying business models.

Others who may find this manual useful are those designing and implementing new industrial policies and strategies and those running intervention agencies, such as incubators and accelerators, who are likely to be hosting the entrepreneurs and firms who are the primary targets for this manual.

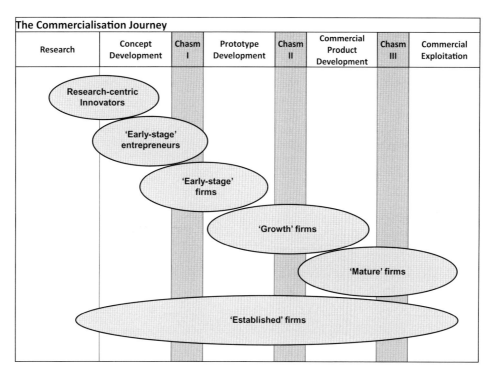

Figure 1. Who should use this manual.

Chapter 2

How to Use this Manual?

2.1 Using Part I of this Manual

All users should read Part I so they can understand the **integrated framework** which covers the complete scale-up journey from concept creation to full commercialisation. Part I explains the basic building blocks for this manual:

- The **scale-up journey** from research and concept generation to reaching the maximum number of customers, as described by the **Triple Chasm Model**.
- The **commercialization readiness** of a technology, innovation or firm, encapsulated by CRL/mTRL values and position relative to the Chasms.
- The meso-economic **vectors and sub-vectors**, which govern the pace and trajectory of growth.

- The **commercialisation canvas**, which integrates these components into a single coherent view against which firms can map their journey.

All these building blocks are relevant for technology and technology-enabled propositions. The same applies **for non-technology firms except in two specific respects**:

- mTRL values are not relevant — users should focus on CRL values only.
- The technology development and conditional deployment vector can effectively be set to zero for these firms.

2.2 Using Part II of this Manual

Users working at the very early stages of growth, for example, in academic research labs or innovation teams, should look in detail at **Sections 8.2, 9.1 and 9.2**.

Users working on converting concepts into prototypes should look in detail at **Sections 8.1, 8.2, 9.1 and 9.3**.

Users who have already developed prototype products and services and are now looking to create sustainable commercial offerings need to study **Chapters 8–10**.

Users who have already developed products with sustainable business models need to look at **Sections 8.3, 8.4, 9.4, 9.5 and 10.1**.

Firms which have already established significant traction with a specific product may now want to build a portfolio of products to build on this position. Users in these firms can use this manual to address three different types of challenges:

- Firms developing additional products aimed at the same market space and the same customers, should look at **Sections 8.1, 8.4, 9.4–9.6 and 10.1**.
- Firms developing new products aimed at different customers in the same market space need to look at **Sections 8.1, 8.4, 9.4–9.6 and Chapter 10**.
- Firms developing new products for different customers in different market spaces should look at **Sections 8.1, 8.3, 8.4, 9.3–9.6 and Chapter 10**.

Firms engaged in *cross-border commercialisation* may need to re-traverse Chasm III, when market conditions in the new market are sufficiently different, for example, different distribution infrastructures.

In some situations, where market conditions are radically different, firms may also need to re-traverse Chasm II, developing different business models in the process.

2.3 Using Part III of this Manual

All users should look at the case studies set out in Part III, and use the **guidance set out in Chapter 13**, to look in detail at the *relevant* case studies.

2.4 Using Part IV of this Manual

All users should read Part IV, which describes how the frameworks and tools described in Parts I and II **can be applied** to diagnose their current status, to clarify the next objective, to understand the gap between the goal and the current situation, and shape the intervention required. This approach can be applied at different points in your trajectory, based on your current situation. This can usefully be combined with insights from relevant case studies identified in Part III.

A detailed description of how to use this manual is given briefly in Figure 1.

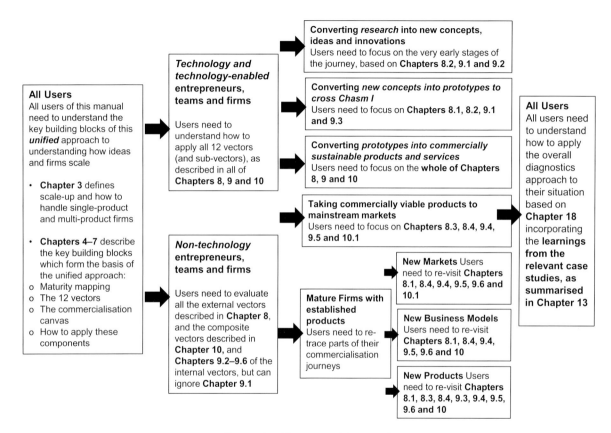

All Users
All users of this manual need to understand the key building blocks of this *unified* approach to understanding how ideas and firms scale

- **Chapter 3** defines scale-up and how to handle single-product and multi-product firms

- **Chapters 4–7** describe the key building blocks which form the basis of the unified approach:
  o Maturity mapping
  o The 12 vectors
  o The commercialisation canvas
  o How to apply these components

Technology and technology-enabled entrepreneurs, teams and firms

Users need to understand how to apply all 12 vectors (and sub-vectors), as described in all of **Chapters 8, 9 and 10**

Non-technology entrepreneurs, teams and firms

Users need to evaluate all the external vectors described in **Chapter 8**, and the composite vectors described in **Chapter 10**, and **Chapters 9.2–9.6** of the internal vectors, but can ignore **Chapter 9.1**

Converting *research* into new concepts, ideas and innovations
Users need to focus on the very early stages of the journey, based on **Chapters 8.2, 9.1 and 9.2**

Converting *new concepts into prototypes to cross Chasm I*
Users need to focus on **Chapters 8.1, 8.2, 9.1 and 9.3**

Converting *prototypes into commercially sustainable products and services*
Users need to focus on the **whole of Chapters 8, 9 and 10**

Taking commercially viable products to mainstream markets
Users need to focus on **Chapters 8.3, 8.4, 9.4, 9.5 and 10.1**

Mature Firms with established products
Users need to re-trace parts of their commercialisation journeys

New Markets Users need to re-visit **Chapters 8.1, 8.4, 9.4, 9.5, 9.6 and 10.1**

New Business Models
Users need to re-visit **Chapters 8.1, 8.4, 9.4, 9.5, 9.6 and 10**

New Products Users need to re-visit **Chapters 8.1, 8.3, 8.4, 9.3, 9.4, 9.5, 9.6 and 10**

All Users
All users need to understand how to apply the overall diagnostics approach to their situation based on **Chapter 18** incorporating the **learnings from the relevant case studies, as summarised in Chapter 13**

Figure 1. How to use this manual.

Chapter 3

Defining Scale-up

3.1 Our Approach

Our **practical** approach to scale-up is based on a detailed understanding of the commercialisation journey described in *Camels, Tigers & Unicorns* [1], which explains how the growth of all firms can be represented by diffusion behaviour interrupted by three discontinuities or chasms.

This enables us to address the scale-up challenge without setting any arbitrary criteria for the current size of the firm or the rate at which it grows, both of which can depend on the environment in which the firm operates. Our approach is distinct from the macro-economic definition proposed by the *OECD* [2] and adopted by others, which provides little if any insight into the actual scale-up process as shown in Figure 1.

Our approach, based on mapping the *meso-economic* vectors, in the spirit of *Schumpeter's approach* [3], on to the commercialisation journey, enables us to provide a practical guide to *understanding and managing* the scale-up process.

It also provides much better evidence-based guidance for those working on strategic policy interventions, without resorting to generalised macro-economic ideas such as market failure, but *our focus here is on the practical challenges of scaling-up.*

Science and technology-enabled innovation can have a significant impact on the scale-up process, but not all firms depend on this for scale-up. We isolate the effect of technology by explicitly defining the impact of the technology development and deployment vector.

OECD Definition:

High-Growth Firms (HGFs)

High growth enterprises, as measured by employment (or turnover) are enterprises with average annualised growth in employees (or in turnover) greater than 20% a year, over a 3-year period, and with ten or more employees at the beginning of the observation period

The Challenge

OECD definition raises interesting questions:

The definition of HGFs may be helpful at a macro-economic level but

- it is arbitrary
- it provides few insights into the *scale-up process*
- observation periods, and when they start and finish, may be inconsistent with the dynamics of different market spaces
- there is increasing evidence of a decoupling between revenue growth and growth in employee numbers
- this appears to endorse notions of the need for special interventions to deal with 'market failure'

Our Approach

We make no *a priori* assumptions about which firms are capable of scale-up based on their current size

We take an Operational view about scale-up potential based on understanding:

- The External environment firms operate in
- The Internal capacity or capability which the firm can harness
- Trade-offs between the External and Internal viewpoints, partially reflected in the motivation of the firm's leadership

Our approach is based on the concept of **meso-economic vectors** which operate in the area between macro-economic drivers and the micro-economic theory of the firm.

Our practical definition enables us to examine the scale-up potential of ALL firms, irrespective of their previous trajectory or current size and formulation

Figure 1.   Defining scale-up.

3.2 Single-product vs Multi-product Firms

The research insights from *Camels, Tigers & Unicorns* [1] confirm that cumulative customer growth at the product level is the best metric to understand the growth of a firm. While most early-stage firms are focused on a single-product proposition, any approach to understanding scale-up also needs to understand how multi-product firms grow.

Our approach to scale-up is based on applying our insights to the growth of single-product firms and extending this to create an aggregated approach to the growth of multi-product firms as shown in Figure 2.

The overall approach in all cases depends on defining and characterising scale-up firms based on understanding the real drivers of growth.

Our approach needs to address the **different starting points for different firms** in terms of firm maturity and complexity.

To do this, we need:

- To understand the **complexity** of the firm's proposition, particularly the product portfolio (single product vs multiple products).
- To describe the **maturity** of each product in the portfolio.

- To **characterise** each product in the portfolio, using the detailed meso-economic vectors.
- To understand how to **aggregate** the impact of multiple products on the overall profile of the firm: this means understanding the target customer and market space for each product.
- To understand the differences in product aggregation at the firm level based on different **approaches to the product portfolio**.

Firms can scale-up in a number of different ways, so we need to understand the commercialisation journey for each type of firm.

Firms can adopt three generic approaches to new product acquisition: Build, Buy or Partner.

Virtually all early-stage firms will typically focus on a single product 'Build' approach.

The very small number of early-stage firms which adopt a product portfolio same approach need to apply the approach as for multi-product firms.

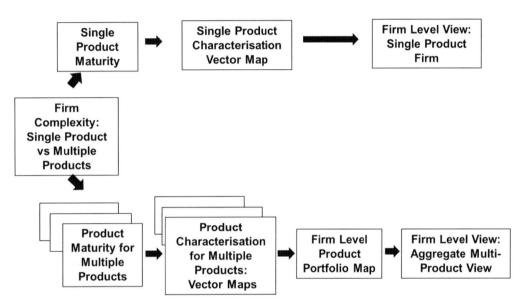

Figure 2. Our approach to tackling single-product firms vs multi-product firms.

Chapter 4

The Product Scale-up Journey

4.1 Defining Maturity: The Triple Chasm Model

The typical product scale-up process consists of periods of diffusion interrupted by discontinuous growth in customer adoption, at the three Chasms.

Chasm I: This describes the transition from the Product or Service *Concept* to a *Working Prototype*.

Chasm II: This describes the transition from an early *Product or Service* to a *fully functional Product or Service with a Sustainable Business Model*.

Chasm III: This describes the transition from early customers to the *main body of customers* as the firm scales significantly.

Figure 1 reprises the Triple Chasm Model described in *Camels, Tigers & Unicorns* [1] and Figure 2 illustrates the cumulative growth profile across the Chasms.

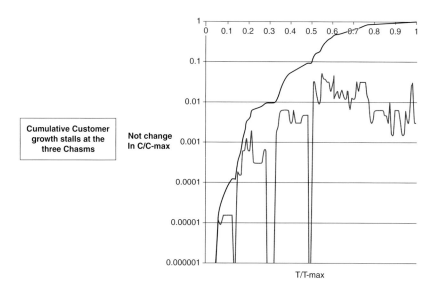

Figure 1. Reprise of the Triple Chasm Model.

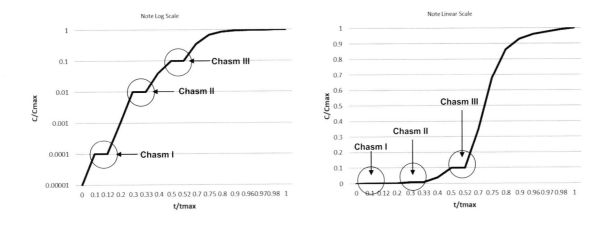

- The early stages of growth take a lot longer than most perceptions-and even longer than most conventional wisdom reported in business literature.
- Typically, half-way through the product journey, cumulative customer penetration will only have reached about 10% of the maximum number of customers.

Figure 2. Cumulative growth profile across the Chasms.

4.2 Defining Maturity: Modified Technology Readiness Levels and Commercialisation Readiness Levels

Technology can be a critical component for many businesses but that is not universally the case.

We are concerned with three main types of businesses, although the boundaries between these three types can often be blurred, as shown in Figure 3:

- Technology firms where technology is an integral part of the product or service provided by the business.
- Firms which are enabled by technology — digital technologies are moving many companies into the technology-enabled category but that does not mean that they are technology companies; for example, most media companies actually belong in this category.
- Non-technology firms where the role of technology, apart from operational IT support, is not important.

Understanding these differences is important because it enables us to define the maturity of a business based on modified technology readiness levels or commercialisation readiness levels as discussed in Chapter 5.

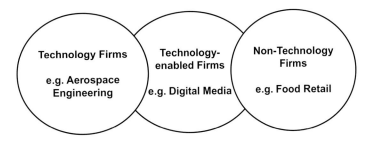

Figure 3. The three generic types of firms addressed in *The Scale-up Manual*.

4.3 Meso-economic Vectors

We use the concept of meso-economic vectors to describe the driving forces which affect the commercialisation journey, especially when crossing the three Chasms. Vectors are usually defined as either a force with magnitude and direction or more generally as a quantity with more than one element. *Camels, Tigers & Unicorns* [1] defined vectors and sub-vectors in the latter spirit. Following this approach, we define 12 vectors, with associated sub-vectors, shown in Figure 4.

External Vectors

- Market Spaces describe areas of activity populated by firms with common goals, structures, processes and dynamics; market space-centric value chains describe the relationships between players in these spaces.
- Proposition Framing, Competition and Regulation describes how the product or service proposition is 'framed' against the value chain; it then identifies partners, suppliers, competitors and regulatory constraints based on this same frame of reference.
- Customer Definition describes the four major types of customers and their characteristics.
- Distribution, Marketing & Sales describes the mechanisms by which products and services reach customers including channels, approaches and methods.

Internal Vectors

- Technology Development & Contingent Deployment covers how technology is described and addresses the different ways in which technology can be packaged to take it to market.
- Product and Service Definition & Synthesis describes how concepts are synthesized into products and services accessible to customers.
- Manufacturing & Deployment provides a broad description of how products and services are made, assembled and delivered where continuous service delivery is part of the proposition.
- Intellectual Property Management provides a wider description of the intellectual value, including brands and know-how, not just patents.
- Talent, Leadership & Culture describes the wider human variables which affect the commercialisation process, including talent, teams and leadership.
- Funding & Investment describes the different forms of funding.

Composite Vectors

- Commercialisation Strategy addresses how firms describe the strategic trade-offs between the internal and external vectors.
- Business Models describes how the firm makes money from a particular product or service.

Vector Type	Vectors	Sub-vectors
External	Market Spaces	Defining Market Spaces
		Market Space-centric Value Chains
		Characterising Market Spaces
		Estimating T-max
	Proposition Framing	Proposition Framing
		Competition
		Regulation
		Differentiation
		Partners & Suppliers
	Customer Definition	Customer Typologies
		Consumers
		Affinity & Knowledge-centric Users
		Governments
		Businesses
		C-max & Market Sizing
	Distribution, Marketing & Sales	Generic Challenges
		Overall Priorities
		The m7Ps Model
		Channels to Market
Composite	Commercialisation Strategy	Approaches to Strategy
		Vector-based Approach
		Priorities vs Maturity
	Business Model Development	Business Models Deconstructed
		Potential Revenue Sources
		Metrics
Internal	Tech. Development & Deployment	Base vs Application Technologies
		Technology Platforms
		Application & Tools
		Products & Services
		Managing Technology Deployment
	Product Definition and Synthesis	Approaches to Product Development
		Voice of the Customer Approaches
		Technology Mapping Approaches
		Approaches based on Synthesis
		Proposition Decomposition
	Manufacturing & Deployment	Components
		Supply Chains
		Processes
		Deployment
		Integrated Operations
	IP Management	Overall Priorities
		Registered Rights
		Un-registered Rights
		Open Rights
	Talent, Leadership & Culture	Talent
		Teams
		Organisational Structure
		Leadership
		Culture
	Funding & Investment	Sources of Funding
		Funding vs Maturity
		Customer Funding
		Firm Valuation

Figure 4. Defining meso-economic vectors and sub-vectors.

4.4 The Commercialisation Canvas

We combine the Triple Chasm Model with the 12 vectors to create a unified framework for evaluating the overall commercialisation process. We then integrate mTRLs and CRLs into this overall framework to characterise maturity more precisely. This overall commercialisation canvas enables us to systematically explore and calibrate the key drivers affecting the scale-up journey.

The canvas in Figure 5 explicitly shows two key factors which change over time:

- The three chasms along the commercialisation journey: the transitions from concept to prototype, from prototype to working product with a commercially viable business model, and then to full commercial deployment. Success depends on successfully crossing the three chasms as shown at the top of the canvas.

- The change in mTRL or CRL as the commercialisation journey proceeds, with these readiness values increasing from 0 to 9, with discontinuities at the three chasms, as shown at the bottom of canvas.

This systematic framework provides a powerful way of analysing the 'maturity' of any product or service: the precise level of maturity can be positioned on this grid.

The framework also shows the relevance of the 12 vectors and their sub-vectors for the commercialisation journey.

The relative importance of these 12 vectors and their sub-components varies with the 'distance travelled' from left to right, which broadly describes maturity of the firm. We can use this canvas to explore and map typical commercialisation trajectories.

> **Scale-up firms can map their current status and desired trajectory against this canvas.**

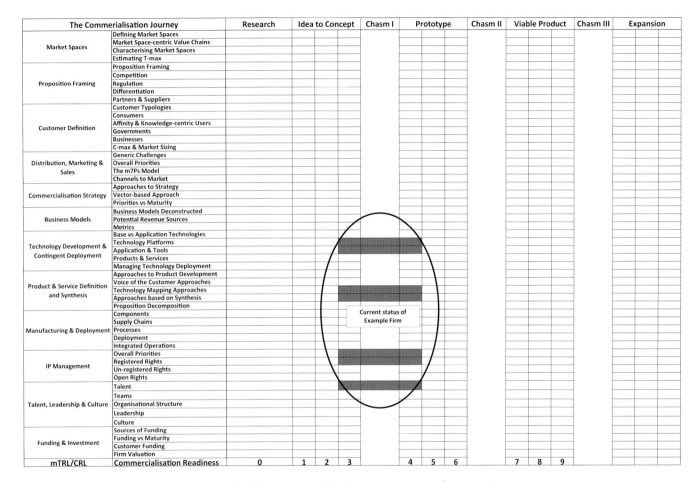

The Commerialisation Journey		Research	Idea to Concept	Chasm I	Prototype	Chasm II	Viable Product	Chasm III	Expansion
Market Spaces	Defining Market Spaces								
	Market Space-centric Value Chains								
	Characterising Market Spaces								
	Estimating T-max								
Proposition Framing	Proposition Framing								
	Competition								
	Regulation								
	Differentiation								
	Partners & Suppliers								
Customer Definition	Customer Typologies								
	Consumers								
	Affinity & Knowledge-centric Users								
	Governments								
	Businesses								
	C-max & Market Sizing								
Distribution, Marketing & Sales	Generic Challenges								
	Overall Priorities								
	The m7Ps Model								
	Channels to Market								
Commercialisation Strategy	Approaches to Strategy								
	Vector-based Approach								
	Priorities vs Maturity								
Business Models	Business Models Deconstructed								
	Potential Revenue Sources								
	Metrics								
Technology Development & Contingent Deployment	Base vs Application Technologies								
	Technology Platforms								
	Application & Tools								
	Products & Services								
	Managing Technology Deployment								
Product & Service Definition and Synthesis	Approaches to Product Development								
	Voice of the Customer Approaches								
	Technology Mapping Approaches								
	Approaches based on Synthesis								
	Proposition Decomposition								
Manufacturing & Deployment	Components								
	Supply Chains								
	Processes								
	Deployment								
	Integrated Operations								
IP Management	Overall Priorities								
	Registered Rights								
	Un-registered Rights								
	Open Rights								
Talent, Leadership & Culture	Talent								
	Teams								
	Organisational Structure								
	Leadership								
	Culture								
Funding & Investment	Sources of Funding								
	Funding vs Maturity								
	Customer Funding								
	Firm Valuation								
mTRL/CRL	Commercialisation Readiness	0	1 2 3		4 5 6		7 8 9		

Figure 5. The commercialisation canvas-mapping firm maturity.

4.5 Mapping a Typical Journey on the Commercialisation Canvas

We can map the typical trajectory for a single-product firm from start-up to maturity on the commercialisation canvas. This can help us to understand where the vectors involved in the commercialisation journey play critical roles which can impact the trajectory of a typical firm. For example, the technology development and deployment vector can be strategically important early on at Chasms I and II. Strategic missteps at these early stages can have serious consequences later in the commercialisation journey. At the early stages of growth, around Chasm I, broad awareness of the market space is important, but detailed insights into customer behaviour and targeting become much more important at Chasm II.

The biggest challenges are around Chasm II, where the key vectors concern the synthesis and precise definition of the product or service and the associated business model which will enable sustainable business operation by the firm; this includes a detailed understanding of the key business model metrics. The commercialisation trajectory leading up to Chasm II also highlights the critical importance of having the right funding and talent to increase the likelihood of crossing Chasm II successfully. Distribution, marketing and sales becomes important around Chasm II and beyond because this can control the ultimate growth trajectory of the firm.

> Overall, the key observation to make about this commercialisation trajectory shown in Figure 6 is the 'patchy' nature of the coverage of the canvas, which suggests that firms can focus and apply resources more effectively instead of assuming that all things matter all the time.

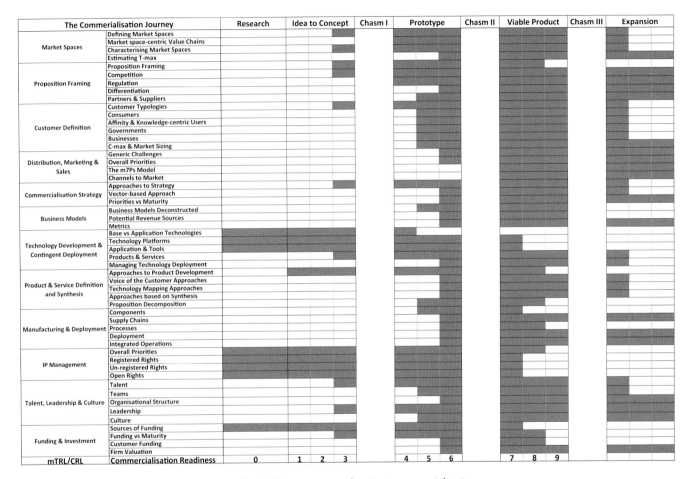

The Commerialisation Journey		Research	Idea to Concept	Chasm I	Prototype	Chasm II	Viable Product	Chasm III	Expansion
Market Spaces	Defining Market Spaces								
	Market space-centric Value Chains								
	Characterising Market Spaces								
	Estimating T-max								
Proposition Framing	Proposition Framing								
	Competition								
	Regulation								
	Differentiation								
	Partners & Suppliers								
Customer Definition	Customer Typologies								
	Consumers								
	Affinity & Knowledge-centric Users								
	Governments								
	Businesses								
	C-max & Market Sizing								
Distribution, Marketing & Sales	Generic Challenges								
	Overall Priorities								
	The m7Ps Model								
	Channels to Market								
Commercialisation Strategy	Approaches to Strategy								
	Vector-based Approach								
	Priorities vs Maturity								
Business Models	Business Models Deconstructed								
	Potential Revenue Sources								
	Metrics								
Technology Development & Contingent Deployment	Base vs Application Technologies								
	Technology Platforms								
	Application & Tools								
	Products & Services								
	Managing Technology Deployment								
Product & Service Definition and Synthesis	Approaches to Product Development								
	Voice of the Customer Approaches								
	Technology Mapping Approaches								
	Approaches based on Synthesis								
	Proposition Decomposition								
Manufacturing & Deployment	Components								
	Supply Chains								
	Processes								
	Deployment								
	Integrated Operations								
IP Management	Overall Priorities								
	Registered Rights								
	Un-registered Rights								
	Open Rights								
Talent, Leadership & Culture	Talent								
	Teams								
	Organisational Structure								
	Leadership								
	Culture								
Funding & Investment	Sources of Funding								
	Funding vs Maturity								
	Customer Funding								
	Firm Valuation								
mTRL/CRL	Commercialisation Readiness	0	1 2 3		4 5 6		7 8 9		

Figure 6.   Typical journey mapped against commercialisation canvas.

Chapter 5

The Overall Approach

5.1 Estimating Maturity

The first step in understanding the scale-up challenge is to understand the maturity of your product or service.

This is not an exact science, but a number of different measures can be used to assess relative maturity as shown in Figure 1:

- Where you are relative to the three Chasms.
- Your modified technology readiness level, if technology plays a role in your proposition.

- Your commercialisation readiness level, if technology does not play a direct role in your proposition.

We integrate the maturity relative to the Chasms and the mTRL/CRL values into a simple grid to articulate the estimated maturity for a product. Maturity estimation is critical in understanding and managing scale-up because it has a direct impact on the relevance of the different growth vectors: this of course has a direct impact on funding and resourcing requirements.

mTRL	CRL	Readiness Level from exploitation perspective
0	0	Research in progress
1	1	Validated Research: start concept definition (early impedance matching)
2	2	Initial Concept Defined
3	3	Working Prototype or Demonstrator
Chasm I		
4	4	Product or Service Testing and Concept Refinement
5	5	Proven Product or Service
6	6	Deployment with early customers in real commercial environment
Chasm II		
7	7	Product or service ready for testing in real user environment
8	8	Refinement of Product or service
9	9	Ready for Commercial Deployment with Real Customers
Chasm III		
Adapted from NASA TRL Approach		

Figure 1.   Approach to estimating maturity.

5.2 Vectors: The Building Blocks

At an aggregate strategic level, understanding the relative importance of the vectors is critical when assessing the scale-up challenges.

The vector impact depends on understanding the relevance and execution effectiveness for each vector, based on the judgement of the entrepreneur or manager, corroborated by any reviewers and mentors.

The impact of all vectors can be assessed using **qualitative** judgement; for some vectors, this can be augmented by additional **quantitative** criteria.

The qualitative and quantitative insights at the level of each vector should be used to provide deeper insight and guidance on areas which need to be addressed, not treated as mechanical values.

This approach enables us to address different vectors differently, which is critical given that we may need to deploy different 'currencies' for the different vectors. The aggregate view on the 12 meso-economic vectors is explained briefly in Figure 2.

The vectors are grouped as follows:

External Vectors: Market spaces, Proposition framing, Customer definition, and Distribution, Marketing & Sales.

Internal Vectors: Technology Development and Contingent (conditional) Deployment, Product & Service Synthesis, Intellectual Property Management, Manufacturing & Deployment, Talent, Leadership & Culture and Funding and Investment.

Composite (Trade-off) Vectors: Commercialisation Strategy and Business Models.

The Aggregate View: The 12 meso-economic Vectors
Quantitative Relevance & Execution Scores

External Vectors	**Composite Vectors**	**Internal Vectors**

Tech Dev & Contingent Deployment
Qualitative articulation based on market space insights & analysis

Market Spaces
Qualitative articulation based on players & relations:
Market space-centric value chains

Commercialisation Strategy
Qualitative Approach based on Strategic Mapping Tool
Quantitative approach based on Relevance & Execution Scores

IP Management
Qualitative focus on management choices

Proposition Framing, Competition & Regulation
Qualitative Mapping versus market space centric value chain

Product & Service Synthesis
Qualitative articulation based on approach to synthesis

Customer Definition
Qualitative Focus on Market Typology
Quantitative Estimates of customer numbers

Business Model
Qualitative Approach based on defining business model architecture and components
Quantitative approach based on building detailed spreadsheet model covering revenues, costs, funding and cash flow

Manufacturing & Deployment
Qualitative Approach to Options
Quantitative Relevance & Exec.Scores

Talent Leadership & Culture
Qualitative Approach to Options
Quantitative Relevance & Exec.Scores

Distribution Marketing & Sales
Qualitative focus on channel selection
Quantitative assessment of relative impact of the m7Ps

Funding & Investment
Qualitative Approach to Options
Quantitative approach to valuation and amounts raised

Figure 2. The aggregate view — How we apply the 12 meso-economic vectors.

5.3 Vector Relevance along the Commercialisation Journey

The relative importance of the different vectors changes with maturity along the commercialisation journey as shown in Figure 3. The key insight is that firms need to recognise that **not all vectors matter all the time**.

The key patterns displayed by the 12 vectors are:

Market Spaces: Understanding the nature of the market space starts to become important when constructing the first prototype and this continues to be the case, especially when crossing Chasms II and III.

Proposition Framing: This is critical when crossing Chasms I and II but matters less in between, and much less after Chasm II has been crossed.

Customer Definition: Starts becoming important once Chasm I has been crossed and then remains important for the rest of the journey.

Distribution, Marketing & Sales: This vector only becomes important around Chasm II but then remains consistently important.

Commercialisation Strategy: Starts to become important once Chasm I has been crossed but is most critical around Chasm II.

Business Models: Grow in importance approaching Chasm II and are critical to successfully crossing this Chasm; they can be important around Chasm III, especially when tackling new markets.

Technology Development and Deployment: Critical from the very early stages in the research lab, crucial at Chasm I but declining slowly in importance subsequently.

Product & Service Synthesis: Starts to matter around Chasm I, is critical for Chasm II crossing but then declines towards Chasm III.

Manufacturing & Deployment: Starts to become important approaching Chasm II and then remains important for the rest of the journey.

IP Management: Starts to matter early on, growing in importance around Chasm I and Chasm II, before falling away slowly.

Talent, Leadership & Culture: Grows gradually in importance with maturity becoming critical around Chasm II and beyond.

Funding & Investment: Grows gradually becoming most critical around Chasm II before falling off as commercial sustainability is achieved.

In overall terms, firms need to recognise the behaviour of the vectors at the three Chasms:

- At **Chasm I**, the two key vectors are proposition formulation and technology development and deployment, with product synthesis and IP management also becoming relevant.
- At **Chasm II**, all 12 vectors are critical, which highlights why this is the most difficult part of the commercialisation journey for most firms.
- At **Chasm III**, the key vectors are: market spaces, customer definition, distribution, marketing & sales, commercialisation strategy, business models, manufacturing & deployment and talent, leadership and culture.

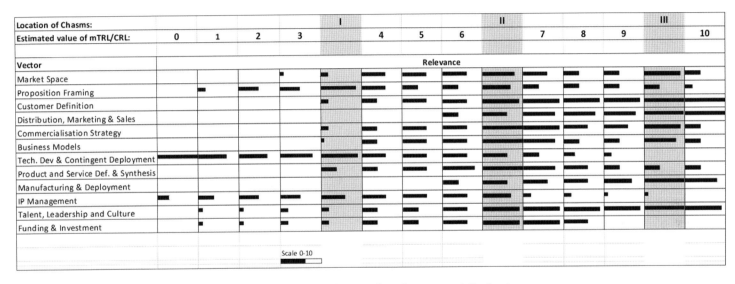

Figure 3. Typical vector relevance along the commercialisation journey.

Chapter 6

Applying the Vectors

6.1 Estimating Vector Impact

The vector-based impact assessment is not intended to provide precise values for specific vectors but to provide a basis for the **comparative impact assessment** of the different forces which affect the pace and trajectory of commercialisation. The goal is to enable management teams (or even the single researcher or entrepreneur) to assess where they are on the commercialisation journey and to compare that judgement with assessments made by mentors and reviewers, **using the same assessment metrics**.

The overall approach works as follows:

- Select an appropriate set of vectors and components based on the specific requirement.
- For any individual vector, use the sub-vectors and components which comprise each vector.
- For each vector or component, assign a score to each vector (or component) based on a linear scale as shown in Figure 1.
- For an overall assessment captured in the commercialisation monitor, apply this approach to all 12 of the meso-economic vectors.

6.1.1 *Guidance on scoring*

- It is important to note that this is a subjective score assigned by an individual or collectively by a team; it can be corroborated by a mentor or reviewer.
- Major differences between scores assigned by different respondents should serve as a trigger for discussion about a chosen approach, strategy or tactics.
- Scores depend very strongly on maturity: the relative importance of the vectors or components changes as firms cross Chasms I, II and III.
- Scores can also be different for different market spaces (but this effect is smaller than maturity relative to the Chasms).
- Using the large body of survey data collected when researching and writing *Camels, Tigers & Unicorns* [1], we can provide some guidance on typical values for the relative importance of the vectors at different levels of maturity.
- You can use this to guide **your own assessment** and to understand how the relative importance of these vectors can affect the growth of your firm.
- But you should see this as a guide: you know your business best!

Our approach to estimating execution performance is based on your assessment of how well you are executing a vector or a component.

Your own score may be different from that determined by a mentor or reviewer.

Any differences in scores should form the basis for a discussion on the divergence rather than seeing these as absolute scores.

Relative Importance	Score
	0
	1
Low Importance	2
	3
	4
Average Importance	5
	6
	7
	8
High Importance	9
	10

Execution Performance	Score
	0
	1
Low Performance	2
	3
	4
Average Performance	5
	6
	7
	8
High Performance	9
	10

Figure 1. Approach to estimating vector impact.

6.2 Aggregate Vector Performance

Aggregating the relative importance and the execution score can provide a powerful indicator of the current status of your firm: the example shown relates to the relative importance of all 12 vectors for a single-product firm around Chasm I for a technology-enabled firm in a specific market space.

The approach is based on the following steps:

- Assess the relative importance of each of the 12 vectors for the firm at the chosen level of maturity.
- Use the typical relative weights derived from Figure 3 of Chapter 5 as a guide but the assessment should also reflect your knowledge, experience and expertise appropriate for the firm being evaluated.

- Assess the execution capacity of the firm for each vector.
- Compute the weighted performance score for each vector (which simply = relevance weight × execution score).
- Explore the vector strategic importance distribution using the polar plot, as illustrated in Figure 2.

This approach, using different polar plots, can also be applied to individual vectors and their components, enabling this analysis to be applied at a more detailed level.

Guidance on typical scores for individual vectors at the different Chasms, based on data from *Camels, Tigers & Unicorns* [1] is provided later when discussing each individual vector.

> **Figure 2 shows a typical strategic assessment at Chasm I for a single-product firm, showing how scoring is applied to understand the relative importance of the 12 meso-economic vectors.**

	Scoring range: 0-10		
Vector	Relevance Score	Execution Score	Weighted Impact (Relevance x Execution)
Market Space	7	5	35
Proposition Framing	9	7	63
Customer Definition	4	4	16
Distribution, Marketing & Sales	1	2	2
Business Model	1	1	1
Commercialisation Strategy	2	1	2
Tech. Dev. & Contingent Deployment	10	9	90
Product and Service Def. & Synthesis	4	1	4
IP Management	6	5	30
Manufacturing & Assembly	1	1	1
Talent, Leadership and Culture	5	5	25
Funding & Investment	1	1	1

Figure 2. Example of vector-based approach.

Chapter 7

The Typical Scale-up Journey

7.1 Crossing Chasms I, II and III: Changing Priorities

Chasm I is the first hurdle on the commercialisation journey. The challenges of stimulating innovation and generating new conceptual ideas should not be underestimated. There is rarely a shortage of innovative ideas: the big challenge is in turning them into something viable, even when the generation of new ideas and testing of prototypes can be done relatively quickly and cheaply. At Chasm I, the biggest focus is on framing the overall proposition in the context of the competitive environment. Understanding potential customers and defining the product in outline terms can be important at this stage. Funding requirements at this stage are relatively small compared to the next stages of the commercialisation journey.

Chasm II is the most complex part of the commercialisation journey: there is insufficient understanding of the existence of this chasm and Chasm II corresponds to the highest area of commercial risk, which is reflected in the reluctance of most investors to fund firms at this stage. This difficulty is reflected in the importance of all the vectors at this point in the commercialisation journey. Product or service iteration in virtually all cases includes development of the right business model: even when the product or service is stable, it can take several iterations of the business model and usually involves several rounds of market testing. Patient funding for Chasm II is a critical issue.

Once Chasm II has been crossed, the **Chasm III** challenge is primarily about expansion, with success dependent on clarity of objectives, understanding and focusing on the right priorities, and deploying the right level and volume of resources. Crossing Chasm III requires precise definition of target customers and users. Talent, leadership and culture of the firm are now critical for success. Figure 1 illustrates how these priorities change across the 3 Chasms.

> **Firms need to be clear where they are on this commercialisation journey and which Chasm is the next challenge.**

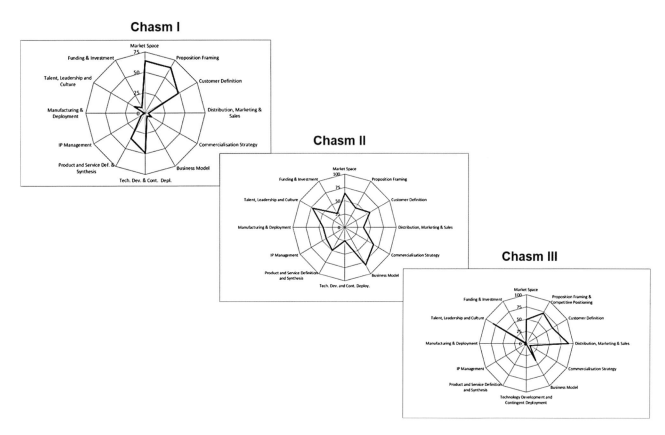

Figure 1. Variation in vectors across the chasms.

Part II

Shaping Your Proposition

Chapter 8

Intervention Shaping: *External* Vectors

Firms typically have less influence in *shaping* the external vectors because they are governed by the economic and structural characteristics of the environment in which the firm operates. These opportunities and constraints can be shaped by national and international policies and decisions usually outside the control of the firm, which is why we refer to them as *external* vectors. Figure 1 provides an overview of the external vectors.

However, firms can exploit the opportunities and constraints of external vectors, to shape their own commercialisation strategies:

Market Spaces: We define market spaces, distinct from market segments, because conventional market segments have become blurred, especially under the impact of digital technologies. The objective in defining a market space is to identify the key relevant players, and the relationships between these players, as defined by market space-centric value chains. This builds on the approach developed by *Porter* [4] and others but turns their approach 'inside out', enabling new players, relationships and the dynamics of interactions to be explicitly modelled; in some industries with dominant mature players, the Porter approach based on case studies with large mature corporations with stable supply chains may still work, but for most growing firms this approach is not very helpful.

Proposition Framing, Competition and Regulation: Building on the new market space-centric value chains, this vector enables firms to position the focus of their propositions on a specific part of the value chain, and to understand three different aspects mapped against the same view:

- the position and roles of competitors, which enables firms to understand how to differentiate their propositions.
- the impact of current and future potential regulation in this market space.
- potential commercial relationships with partners and suppliers.

Customer Definition: Many firms struggle with defining their customers precisely. Our customer definition vector depends on a new typology described in *Camels, Tigers & Unicorns* [1] which distinguishes between governments as customers, business customers, consumers and knowledge and affinity-centric groups, which all behave in different ways. Customers constitute an external vector: although firms may sometimes try to change customer behaviour, this kind of capacity is usually beyond the reach of most firms. Understanding the structure and behaviour of customers can help firms to make the right strategic choices.

Distribution, Marketing and Sales: There are hundreds of books, approaches and tools about the subject of marketing and sales, and our objective here is not to replicate or supplant them. The point of this external vector is to enable firms to understand the critical issues for taking their propositions to market, and to make the right strategic judgements, particularly in terms of channel selection and understanding the key challenges using a modified 7Ps model.

Market Spaces

Qualitative articulation based on defining existing and new players in the market space and the relationships between them, including an explicit connection with customers.

Mapping these relationships to create Market space-centric value chains, where the generation, distribution and transfer of value between the players is explicitly captured.

Proposition Framing, Competition & Regulation

Qualitative Mapping of all the Actors versus the market space centric value chain. The objective is to explicitly define the operations of the firm relative to this value chain, and to **map the activities of competitors, partners and suppliers against the same view**. This same value chain can then be used to assess the impact of current and future regulation on the chosen proposition.

Customer Definition

Qualitative Mapping of the customers of the firm explicitly against the new Customer Typology. The objective is to understand the type and typical numbers for the target customers for the firms proposition. The typical numbers serve as a check of the attractiveness of the new proposition.

Quantitative Estimates of customer numbers based on a simple bottom-up model which avoids the use of top-down estimates using generic data on market segments

Distribution Marketing & Sales

Qualitative focus on channel selection based on understanding potential channels to market and the trade-offs between them.

Quantitative assessment of relative impact of the m7Ps, based on simplified scoring criteria for the importance of each of the mPs. This approach allows a gap analysis based on current performance vs desired objectives

Figure 1. Overview of the external vectors.

8.1 Market Spaces

8.1.1 *What are market spaces and why do we need them?*

The conventional approach to understanding markets depends on *market segmentation.*

This can provide useful data on the overall structure and size of a market opportunity but does not always provide sufficient insight into the real nature of the market opportunity — the dramatic escalation in the number and range of new technologies also creates problems with using conventional segmentation and market measurement techniques. Conventional methods may not adequately describe market segments because technology often creates new categories of activity. For example, how do you distinguish between markets for biotechnology-enabled products and services targeted at plant, animal and human targets, which have all historically been part of entirely different industries? Do we treat these as distinct markets when it may make more sense to treat them in a new aggregate category?

Market segmentation typically reflects *existing* supplier-based industry value chains, so that firms in current delivery systems are seen as being part of that segment. How do we deal with new firms which radically reshape value chains but may be active across multiple conventional markets? Communications technology firms, for example, may impact markets in telecommunications, energy, lighting and healthcare: how do we decide which market category they are best associated with?

Digital technologies have dramatically blurred the boundaries between market segments. For example, media, publishing and telecommunications firms are now competing for the same customers, sometimes with the same product sets. Should a new digital media firm be treated as a content firm or a telecommunications firm in terms of market segments?

This lack of clarity even allows some investors to classify social media network firms as technology firms when they are simply users of ubiquitous technology products also used by other firms across the entire marketplace. The move from products to services, with different business models, also creates difficulties in using conventional market segmentation. For example, innovative new firms may provide technology-enabled services to both healthcare and publishing markets. In this case, which market segment do we assign them to?

We need ways to characterise the qualitative and quantitative nature of potential markets for new products and services. We need a practical and consistent approach which enables us to understand the relative importance of the major factors at work in the market spaces of interest to us; and critically we need an approach which demonstrates how **value is generated, distributed and transferred** to the user and customer. Figure 2 illustrates our approach.

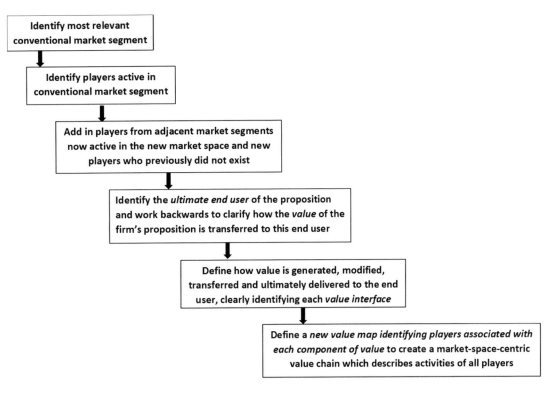

Figure 2. How do you define your market space and the market space-centric value chain.

8.1.2 *Market space-centric value chains*

Porter [4] first introduced the concept of value chains in 1985 with a strong **focus on the firm** and its relationship with suppliers and customers. This firm-centric value chain has been used extensively to understand the structure and organisation of well-established firms. It works well where the firm operates in a well-established market and the locus of interest is internal to the firm.

Firm-centric value chains have several important limitations:

- They usually present a static, 'backward-looking' historic perspective on the role of the firm within the existing market space.
- Processes and roles are defined by the *existing paradigm*, which reduces their potential value in understanding how technology or other factors can generate new processes and enable new players.
- They provide limited insight into the reshaping of relationships with existing and new players and the creation of new business models.

Starting from an *external* perspective, we first visualise the new broader set of processes and the relationships between all the players. We then identify potential roles for players in this new market space, which can be fulfilled by existing players, new players, or players who can morph to fulfil new and different roles. This approach allows us to identify gaps, potential opportunities, competitors and threats; it can also provide insights into future commercial, resource and regulatory challenges.

> **We turn *Porter's* approach 'inside-out' to define market space-centric value chains.**

8.1.3 *Unpacking market spaces*

We illustrate this approach to market space-centric value chains by looking at value chains describing several different market spaces:

- Media & Entertainment
- Electronics & Computing
- Healthcare
- Agri-cereals
- Industrial Bio-tech
- Smart Energy.

These examples highlight how a market space-centric value chain can provide insights into markets which are not available from conventional market segmentation.

The key point to note is that these are *not generic value chains* for any specific market space: firms can construct *unique value chains,* using the approach described, to create detailed insights into how value is created, transferred and delivered to users in their own market space. While these examples can provide useful insights for all firms, it is critical that firms adapt or create value chains which precisely characterise their proposition(s) and the other players in this environment, including partners, suppliers and competitors. Well-constructed value chains can also enable firms to understand regulatory constraints and opportunities.

These value chains can be used to understand the impact of different commercial strategies and business models. They can enable firms to make strategic decisions about *where in the value chain they should focus their energies* and where it might be better to find partners. For example, some firms may take on roles where they manage end-to-end-customer relationships without having a strong position in any single part of the overall value chain.

8.1.4 *The media & entertainment market space*

Digital technologies are dramatically re-shaping the media, publishing and entertainment market space as shown in Figure 3. Firms historically focused on the creation and packaging of content now have to understand and deal with a much wider set of activities including electronic devices and new communications infrastructures. Firms which design, produce and sell devices now have to deal with new business models which might include indirect revenues from advertising and promotion.

Firms operating in this new market space need greater strategic clarity about where they focus and the implications for which vectors they focus on. With the exception of a few big players, most firms are likely to focus on one or perhaps two components of the overall market space-centric value chain, choosing from the five key areas:

- Content Creation and Packaging
- Advertising & Promotion
- Content Distribution and Access Management
- Devices and Applications
- Managing the Delivery of Content and User Experience.

8.1.5 *The electronics & computing market space*

The Electronics and Computing market space has seen a fragmentation of how value is created, transferred and delivered, with the cost and complexity leading to increasing specialisation of activities as illustrated in Figure 4. Although this has led to the emergence of a small number of consolidated global players, there are many opportunities for specialist players, but they are likely to only focus on part of the overall value chain:

- Chip-level design activities
- Foundries
- Integrated devices
- Computing platforms
- Usage environments.

For example, a typical firm in this market space may focus entirely on providing tools for chip design or software operating systems which can run computing platforms.

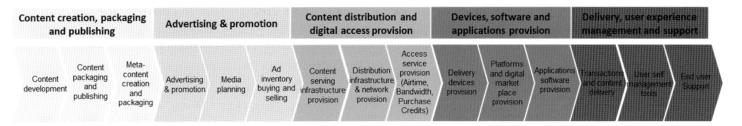

Figure 3. Market space centric value chain for media & entertainment. Adapted from *Camels, Tigers & Unicorns* [1].

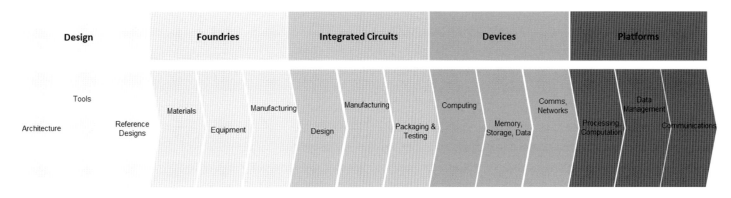

Figure 4. Market space-centric value chain for electronics & computing.

8.1.6 *Healthcare market space*

The healthcare market space is changing radically as new technology developments at the level of genes and proteins create the potential to develop and deliver new diagnostic and therapeutic capabilities at patient level. The opportunities created are tremendous, but success depends on understanding the way in which the value created by gene-level advances can be converted into value at the level of primary healthcare, for example. Addressing this translation challenge requires a detailed understanding of the five major value chain components, as shown in Figure 5:

• Fundamental advances in the life sciences
• The historic medical focus based on structures, systems and the complete body
• Medical interventions in terms of measurement, diagnosis and therapy
• Measures associated with well-being
• The conventional approach to healthcare delivery divided into primary, secondary and tertiary healthcare
• Care in the community enabled by new technologies, for example, digital communications.

Most firms will need to focus on a part of the value chain to address the translation challenge.

8.1.7 *The agri-cereals market space*

The agri-cereals market space illustrates the new challenges in food production, packaging and delivery, particularly the opportunities for firms to play new roles in the 'upstream' part of the overall value chain, before getting to the 'farm gate', as illustrated in Figure 6.

Firms active in this space need to understand whether they are focusing on a part of this value chain such as the development of new seed varieties or whether they straddle many parts of the value chain, such as firms involved in the monitoring and tracking of products all the way through from experimental production to the retail shelf. Firms need to understate the relative importance of the different vectors in deciding where they play:

• Research
• Experimental Production
• Commercial Production
• Processing and Packaging
• Distribution and Delivery.

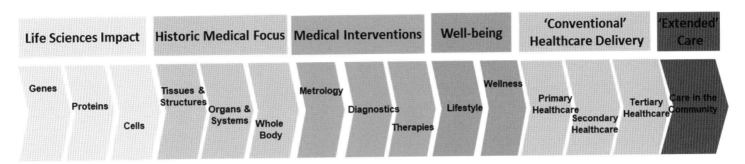

Figure 5. Market space-centric value chain for healthcare.

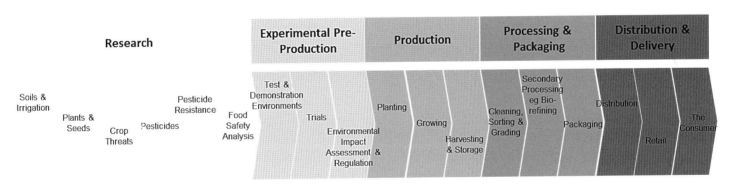

Figure 6. Market space-centric value chain for agri-cereals.

8.1.8 *The industrial bio-tech market space*

The complexity of the bio-tech market space requires the different types of activities to be treated separately, segmenting this market space into red bio-tech (which covers animal biology), green bio-tech (which covers plant biology), white bio-tech (which covers industrial bio-tech) and blue bio-tech (which covers marine biology).

The industrial bio-tech market space focuses on how fundamental technologies can enable the creation of industrial plants where bio-chemical processes can be applied at scale to generate new compounds with different properties, as shown in Figure 7.

Firms operating in this space need to understand how to focus on the development of new chemistry, or how to scale-up processes or to design, build and run industrial scale plants. Very few firms are likely to straddle all parts of this value chain:

- Fundamental research & development
- Product development, for example, the creation of new enzymes
- Scaling-up lab-level results into full industrial processes
- Design and construction of new plants, for example, for ethanol production
- Running large-scale production facilities.

8.1.9 *The smart energy market space*

Delivering on the vision of 'Smart Energy' requires a clear understanding of the overall value chain consisting of the following components as illustrated in Figure 8:

- The generation and storage of energy from a number of sources coupled with the ability to actively manage the response to changing demand.
- The infrastructure for transmission and distribution of power.
- Smart metering of energy utilisation.
- The ability to actively manage consumption, based on new business models.
- To understand and address needs in the customer environment.

Firms trying to exploit this new market space need to know where to focus their efforts and how their success depends on understanding and working with the right players in other parts of the value chain. It is very unlikely that a single play can play all the roles in this extended and complex value chain. For example, just the design and building of a smart meter is likely to involve multiple players.

Research & Development | Product Development | Process Development and Scale Up | Engineering and Construction | Operations and Maintenance

Basic Research · Applied Research · Technology Development · Concept Development · Prototype Product · Bench Scale Product · Pilot level Scale-up · Techno-Commercial Modelling · Commercial-scale Process Development · Plant Design · Fabrication · Installation · Ongoing Operations and Maintenance · Monitoring and Optimisation · Improvements and Enhancements

Figure 7. Market space-centric value chain for industrial bio-tech. Adapted from *Camels, Tigers & Unicorns* [1].

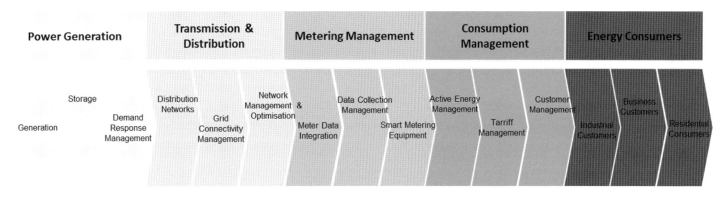

Figure 8. Market space-centric value chain for smart energy.

8.1.10 *Characteristic times for market spaces: The concept of T-max*

Market spaces can vary significantly in structure and complexity but a key factor during scale-up is understanding **how long it will take to reach the maximum number of customers**.

Following *Camels, Tigers & Unicorns* [1], we define this as the **Characteristic time, T-max**, for a market space.

The value of T-max is important because it determines not just the time to maturity for a new product or service but also significantly affects the level of resources required for success. Market spaces with high values of T-max typically require more patience and investment than those with smaller values of T-max, which can scale faster.

We compare values of T-max for 12 market spaces of high interest in Figure 9, based on analysis over the last decade — but one of the tasks when defining a market space is to **estimate the value of T-max for the market space you are operating in**.

We illustrate here how T-max can vary between 5 years and 12 years for the market spaces discussed in *Camels, Tigers & Unicorns* [1]. For some social media market spaces we have studied recently, T-max can be as low as 2–3 years, while in the nuclear industry, for example, T-max can be as high as 25 years.

Your assessment of T-max for the market space you are operating in can have a significant bearing on your success. Market spaces with high values of T-max clearly need longer periods of development, which clearly impacts the resources required, the quantum and types of funding, and the overall risk profile of the enterprise. This also raises interesting questions about overall sustainability of the market space, the firm and the prevailing macro-economic investment environment — firms need to be aware of these constraints.

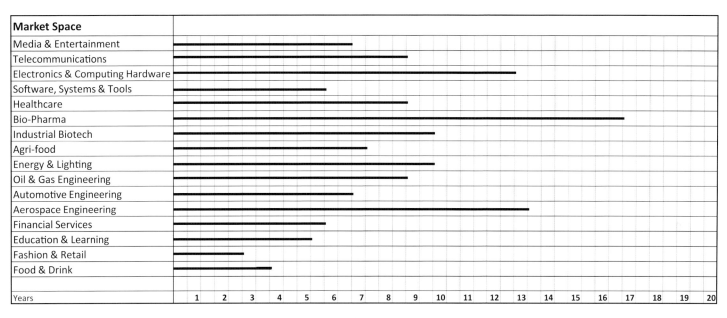

Market Space	1	2	3	4	5	6	7	8	9	10	11	12	13	14	15	16	17	18	19	20
Media & Entertainment																				
Telecommunications																				
Electronics & Computing Hardware																				
Software, Systems & Tools																				
Healthcare																				
Bio-Pharma																				
Industrial Biotech																				
Agri-food																				
Energy & Lighting																				
Oil & Gas Engineering																				
Automotive Engineering																				
Aerospace Engineering																				
Financial Services																				
Education & Learning																				
Fashion & Retail																				
Food & Drink																				
Years	1	2	3	4	5	6	7	8	9	10	11	12	13	14	15	16	17	18	19	20

Figure 9.   Typical variation in average values of T-max for different market spaces. Adapted from *Camels, Tigers & Unicorns* [1].

8.2 Proposition Framing, Competition & Regulation

8.2.1 *Framing*

Framing your overall proposition is not the same as defining the product or service in detail.

It is about *positioning* the proposition in the *context of the market space-centric value chain*.

Framing depends on first defining the market space-centric value chain relevant to your proposition, identifying the key players in the market space, their precise roles and the relationships between the players.

You start by mapping your proposition against this value chain, showing the sources of value important for your proposition.

You map the current and potential impact of regulation against the value chain, for each component, and critically, also where regulation can impact multiple components.

You can then map competing products and services against this aggregate picture, which can provide powerful insights into the differentiation of your proposition.

This strategic framing of your proposition can also guide you on the potential importance of other vectors and how you can shape your strategy and business model.

Finally, you can map potential collaborators, partners and suppliers against this same market space-centric map. Figure 10 illustrates this approach.

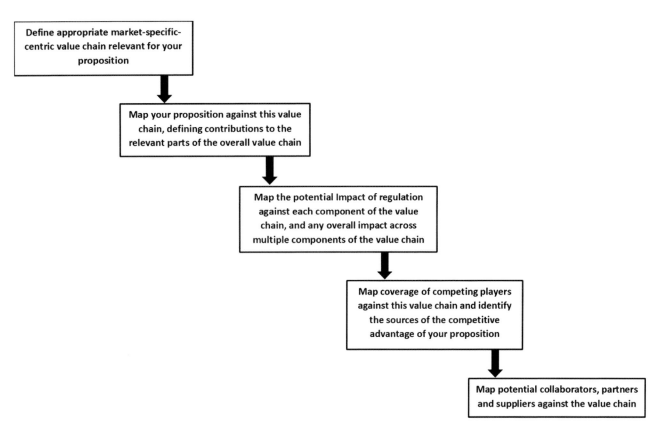

Figure 10. How to frame your proposition against the market space-centric value chain.

8.2.2 *Proposition framing, competition & regulation: An example*

We illustrate this approach in Figure 11 by showing how the media and entertainment market space-centric value chain can be used to frame products and services for a smartphone device provider.

This approach to framing not only allows the device provider to focus on its core competences, but to understand other players in the market space, their roles and positioning, and the opportunities and challenges associated with offering new products and services.

This framing approach also enables firms to understand if and how they can provide a wider range of products and services or change their positioning radically.

For example, device manufacturers can use this to assess the potential for becoming providers of content-based services.

The approach can be applied to a very wide range of market spaces, particularly where technology is changing the nature of products, services and business models.

For example, a very similar approach can be applied to the generation, distribution and delivery of renewable energy products and services or the delivery of new therapeutic interventions in healthcare.

Some of the most disruptive innovations often depend on changing the *frame of reference.*

The new *framing* can sometimes dramatically influence the business model more than the *direct* impact of a new technology.

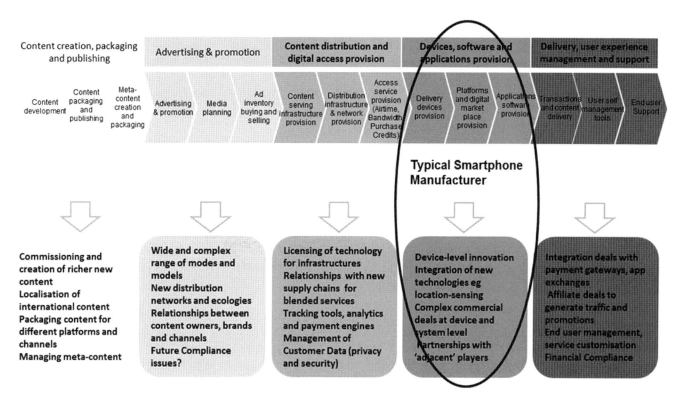

Figure 11. Proposition Framing — An example from the media & entertainment market space. Adapted from *Camels, Tigers & Unicorns* [1].

8.2.3 *Competition & regulation*

Taking a new product or service to market requires clarity about the broader commercial environment, in particular, the potential competition and an understanding of any regulatory constraints.

This is critical for a wide range of market spaces, from telecommunications to biotechnology and healthcare.

We illustrate this in Figure 12 for the sample proposition in the media and entertainment market space by examining the 'populated' value chain from three different perspectives. We use a composite view based on a number of new products and services from different firms in the media and entertainment market space, so we can illustrate the power of this approach.

In practice, of course, a single firm will typically be mapped into a smaller number of areas, but this approach can enable you to understand exactly where you play relative to others in the market space.

Specific features worth observing in this example include the following:

Market Drivers: Positioning and roles of new content creators, new intermediaries, and new distribution players; changes in the behaviour of users as they 'consume' new services.

Technology Drivers: In this market space, new content and meta-content formatting approaches, new data transmission techniques, platforms and infrastructures, and new payment technologies have the potential to redraw the competitive landscape.

Regulatory Drivers: Regulations governing data storage, transmission and delivery, including the licensing and allocation of radio spectrum for distribution, rules around privacy and cyber-security, and regulations around content copyright and advertising.

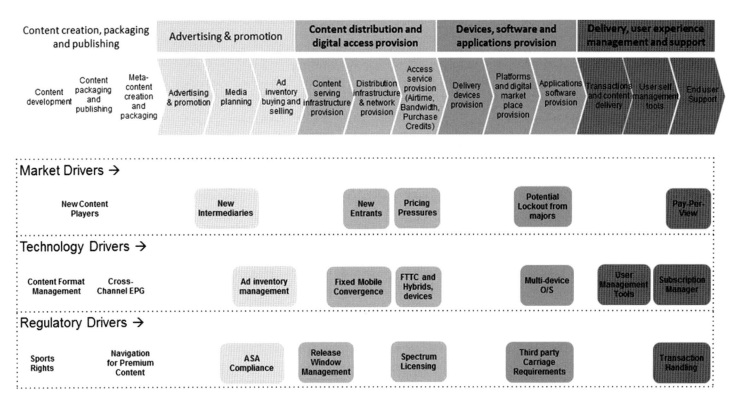

Figure 12. Example — Mapping competition and regulation for the media & entertainment market space. Adapted from *Camels, Tigers & Unicorns* [1].

8.2.4 *Differentiation*

Mapping propositions, competition and regulation onto the same market space-centric value chain provides a powerful way of shaping and refining new products and services — but it can also provide powerful insights into competitive differentiation for new products and services, as illustrated in Figure 13.

- **Differentiation based on focusing on a single or on adjacent parts of the value chain**
  New products and services can be differentiated on the basis that they provide new or different *functionality*, the way or *form* in which this is provided, whether this functionality is delivered more effectively, or whether it is provided more efficiently. This is consistent with conventional ways of describing product or service differentiation.
- **Differentiation based on overall value chain impact**
  Competitive differentiation based on this approach depends on the product or service occupying new or broader parts of the value chain, the effect of which is to deliver integrated functionality for users and customers, often with improved effectiveness and efficiency. The ultimate expression of this kind of competitive differentiation is for the new product or service to assume a *gatekeeper* role in the value chain, which controls the provision of other products and services. This can enable strategic dominance based on controlling a key part of the value chain.
- **Differentiation based on *reframing* the value chain**
  The most radical competitive strategy for a firm is to effectively reframe the overall value chain which governs relationships between the various players in the market space. This can lead to the creation of new types of customers, new types of market space players and the need for new roles in this new environment. It can be used to create new products and services, new business models and to change the rules for competition.

Differentiation based on focusing on a single or on adjacent parts of the value chain

A new type of medical diagnostic product may measure a property not previously measured, or may do it differently (for example non-intrusively), or do it more efficiently so that it does not require specialist staff to operate the equipment, or it may do this at a lower cost.

Differentiation based on overall value chain impact

Smart phone providers can provide additional services such as music on the phone or enable real-time mapping and navigation services using the same device. This can be used to differentiate the core product from competitors who do not provide these additional services. A good example of a *'gatekeeper'* role is the role played by conditional access systems in television, where the provider can control access to content and associated services from other players, based on controlling the distribution system.

Differentiation based on reframing the value chain

An example of this kind of redrawing of the market space and the associated market space-centric value chain is what is happening in the energy and lighting market space: the previous market space based on concentrated power generation in conjunction with an integrated power distribution system is being supplanted by a market space in which power generation, storage and distribution are highly distributed. This is radically changing the nature and role of the firms engaged in the market space, their business models and the nature of competition and regulation.

Figure 13. Types of differentiation — Some examples.

8.2.5 *Partners, suppliers and collaborators*

Analysis based on market space-centric value chains can provide a powerful basis for framing the overall customer proposition and the opportunities for 'co-creation' with partners and suppliers to deliver an integrated proposition for the customer.

We can use the media and entertainment market space to illustrate this, as shown in Figure 14.

In this scenario, customers may want the provision of an integrated product and service offering, which includes the device, content (for example, music or digital maps), and applications which provide navigation capability on the device. Making this more affordable to the end user may require the integration of advertising functionality on the device, which enables brand advertisers to effectively subsidise the provision of other services.

One strategic option for the firm providing the device in this case may be to expand its capability to provide all these services. An alternative strategic option is to collaborate with other firms with the relevant expertise to deliver the full functionality of interest to the end-user and customer.

The collaboration can take two obvious forms: a partnership where the complementary firm shares in the commercial risk and reward in offering the broader service to the customer, or a more conventional supplier arrangement where the device firm procures the additional services from another firm on a commercial basis. In some market spaces, this type of collaboration may be based on a mixture of partner and supplier arrangements. Arrangements may also be made between firms who are otherwise competitors, leading to situations where the 'collaborate–compete' relationship is quite dynamic and changes with types of customers or geographic territories.

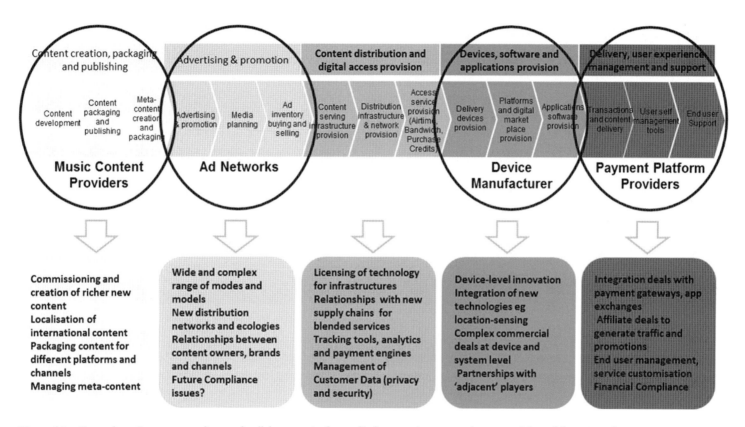

Figure 14. Example — Partners, suppliers and collaborators in the media & entertainment market space. Adapted from *Camels, Tigers & Unicorns* [1].

8.3 Customer Definition

8.3.1 *Customer typology*

Defining the customer clearly is critical when scaling any proposition. While this seems an obvious statement to make, in practice, there is often confusion in defining the customer for a product or service clearly. Figure 15 illustrates our approach to customer typology.

Customer targeting depends on understanding two parameters: the **nature** of the customer and the **potential number of customers** for a product or service.

There are **four** distinct types of customers, based on how customers **decide** to use the product or service, how they **use** it, how they **benefit** from it and how the product or service is **paid** for.

- **Business customers** are firms or businesses who buy and use a product or service. These firms will typically use the product or service in two ways: it may be incorporated into their own product or service or be used to run their own businesses.
- **Governments** and other related organisations are typically buying products for use in their own activities. Their buying behaviour is often characterised by a large disconnect between those making the buying decision and the actual users of the product or service. This can lead to long purchasing timescales, and complex and sometimes opaque decision criteria; but governments can be powerful 'charter' customers.
- **Consumers** are individuals who buy and use a product or service in different ways, ranging from entertainment to carrying out specific tasks. In some situations, products and services used by consumers may be provided free or paid for by third parties, such as advertisers.
- Members of **knowledge or affinity-based groups or communities** who use products or services based on the sharing and use of knowledge within the group. Knowledge or affinity-based users may act as individuals, but their behaviour is shaped either by a group affinity or a need to access specific knowledge. For example, a clinician in a hospital is a knowledge-based user, even though the clinician may operate in a corporate environment. Social media users in 'closed' groups also display similar behaviour.

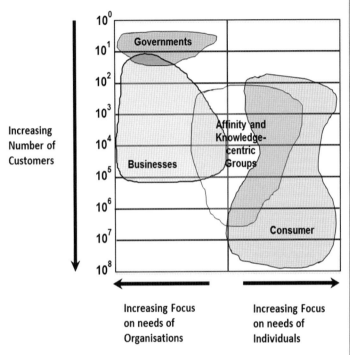

Increasing
Number of
Customers

10^0

10^1 Governments

10^2

10^3

10^4 Affinity and Knowledge-centric Groups

Businesses

10^5

10^6

10^7 Consumer

10^8

Increasing Focus on needs of Organisations

Increasing Focus on needs of Individuals

Products aimed at consumers have the largest number of customers, followed by products and services targeted at knowledge and affinity centric groups; products aimed at governments have the smallest number of aggregate customers. Typically, the 'yield' per customer is smallest for consumers, rising for knowledge-based groups and highest for business customers. This has significant implications for product design, branding and positioning, channels to market and business models.

The business models deployed with different customer groups are quite different. Products and services delivered to other businesses or firms typically deploy several types of business-to-business (**b2b**) models; where these business customers then sell these products and services on to end consumers, the business models may reflect the business-to-business-to-consumer (**b2b2c**) chain. Products and services delivered directly to consumers will deploy business-to-consumer (**b2c**) business models and the pricing reflects the value perceived by the actual user of the service. Products and services delivered to knowledge-based or affinity-centric groups of users are likely to have complex (**b2k**) business models because users of these products may be different from the customers who pay for them. Products and services sold to governments depend on (**b2g**) business models, which can have very different structures, based on the end-use case. These business models may display aspects of all the other types of models. These distinctions between the four major types of customers matter, particularly when business models depend on indirect funding, for example, based on sponsorship or advertising

Most products and services are usually aimed at one of these customer types but sometimes the same product or service may be delivered to different customer types, so clarity is very important.

Figure 15. Customer typology. Adapted from *Camels, Tigers & Unicorns* [1].

8.3.2 *Consumers*

There are many different approaches to segmenting and profiling consumers: the trick is to use the method best suited to a specific proposition. The main approaches depend on three different attributes, as shown in Figure 16:

- Approaches based on user behaviour, which rely largely on survey data.
- Psychographic approaches based on values, attitudes and lifestyles, which includes focus group data.
- Socio-demographic methods which depend on demographic segmentation, social groups and location.

For a long time, the conventional approach to profiling consumers was based on socio-demographic categories which segmented consumers into groups based on social class and spending power. As digital technologies gained traction in the late 1990s, this was augmented by techno-demographic categories which augmented socio-demographic categories based on the willingness to use new technologies.

In the last decade, generational ideas of behaviour have become more prevalent, with frequent references to millennials (where unfortunately this definition can refer to individuals with a range of birth dates from 1980 to 2000, depending on the source!), Generation X and Generation Y.

There have also been attempts to resurrect socio-demographic categories by recasting and extending the older categories. While these different approaches can provide useful insights, firms need a practical way of profiling target customers and estimating potential markets and revenues.

Our integrated approach is based on combining three ways of describing consumers.

The first component of this integrated approach is the weighted behavioural average, which is based on the behaviour of existing users or customers when consuming similar products or services: start with usage behaviour, then add in purchase behaviour (so you get some idea of propensity to buy) and then add in information about the typical benefits desired by the customer when making the buying decision.

The second component is the weighted psychographic profile which integrates information on values (derived from focus group discussions), attitudes (also derived from focus groups) and lifestyles (based on archetypes generated from historic consumption of similar products and services). This second component is similar to the VALS-type approach developed by *Mitchell* [5] and others.

The third component is the weighted socio-demographic average profile: start with socio-demographic descriptors, which cover demographic approaches based on age, gender and generational descriptors; then add descriptors based on socio-demographics; and then geo-location data, which is increasingly important with the wider availability of location information, especially from location-aware mobile devices.

Integrated Consumer Profiling		
Behavioural	**Psychographics**	**Socio-demographics**
Usage Behaviour	Values	Demographic
Sample-based Usage Data	*Focus Groups*	*Age, Gender, Gen X, Gen Y data*
Purchase Behaviour	Attitudes	Social Groups
Sample-based Purchase Data	*Focus Groups*	*Conventional Socio-demographic Data*
Benefits Sought	Lifestyles (typical Archetypes)	Geography
Survey Data	*VALS Types*	*Geo-Location Data*
Weighted Behavioural Average	Weighted Psychographic Average	Weighted Socio-demographic Average
WBA	**WPA**	**WSA**
Weighted Aggregate Consumer Profile		
WCA		

You can ascribe the relative contributions of these three components when describing the typical target consumer, which can be very useful when shaping products and services, deciding on the best business model and choosing the right distribution channels.

The chosen consumer profile can then be used when estimating the size of the potential market.

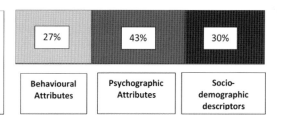

Figure 16.   Characterising the consumer profile.

8.3.3 Business customers

Two key variables determine the behaviour of business customers: the **size** of the target business customer, and the way in which the new technology, product or service is **deployed** by the corporate customer.

We can use a simple model for segmenting firms by size, based on the number of **employees** in the firm-this is the best measure of the size of a firm because it affects the organisational behaviour of the firm, its capacity to absorb new products and services, and its ability to 'deploy' the product or service purchased.

Firm size based on the number of employees is a much better indicator of the buying behaviour of a firm than its turnover or profitability. We use **five** categories because this is consistent with most published national data; the smallest firms, classified as micro-companies employ less than nine staff, the very largest employ more than 500 staff. This segmentation is also consistent with the organisational behaviour of firms based on size.

The way in which a product or service is deployed in a business can have a significant impact on buying behaviour and volumes, based on the potential business impact. This impact depends on whether the target customers intend to **integrate** what they buy into their core products and services, whether they are using the product to **enable** new ways of working, or whether the focus is on more **efficient** operation.

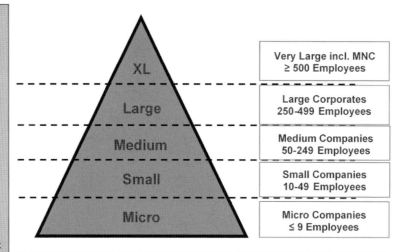

XL	Very Large incl. MNC ≥ 500 Employees
Large	Large Corporates 250-499 Employees
Medium	Medium Companies 50-249 Employees
Small	Small Companies 10-49 Employees
Micro	Micro Companies ≤ 9 Employees

Types of Business Impact created by new products or services:

- Improvement in Business Effectiveness or Efficiency
- Change in a Customer Production Process
- Integration into Customer Product
- b2b distribution impact
- b2b2c distribution impact

Understanding how your product meets the needs of a business customer. Adapted from *Camels, Tigers & Unicorns* [1].

Type of Impact ↓ Size of Firm →		Micro	Small	Medium	Large	Very Large
Improvement in Business Effectiveness or Efficiency	e.g. CRM and Sales process					
Customer Production Process change or Intervention	CNC, Real-time Tracking					
Integrated into Customer Product	Advanced battery technology					
b2b Distribution Impact	Supply chain tracking and Monitoring					
b2b2c Distribution Impact	Integrated Customer Support and Returns					

Example Focus of Product or Service

Figure 17. Mapping impact versus firm size.

8.3.4 *Affinity & knowledge-centric groups*

Most customer research has focused on consumers, with less data on business customers, but there is very little understanding of affinity and knowledge-centric groups. This customer group displays some attributes found in both consumers and businesses but also exhibits some unique characteristics.

This matters in a wide range of knowledge-centric industries which have been transformed by digital technologies, for example, medical publishing, new affinity groups enabled by social media, or members of private clubs or communities with business models distinct from conventional business paradigms.

There are three different types of knowledge and affinity-centric groups, as shown in Figure 18:

- **Knowledge and expertise-mediated groups**, which can be sub-divided into 'deep knowledge', 'practicing knowledge' and 'shallow knowledge' groups. Sophisticated knowledge users are moving from consuming 'data only' products to demanding 'value-added' services, as many media and technology firms have experienced. There is significant pressure on pricing and service levels as the number of suppliers proliferates and some large knowledge publishers make efforts to adopt 'gatekeeper' roles, and to occupy wider roles in the value chain.

- **Affinity-based groups** have grown dramatically, especially as a result of digital technologies, including internet and mobile voice and data services. Customers can be grouped into three sub-categories: peer-to-peer groups, curated groups, for example, professional membership associations and special interest groups. Many of these customers are behaving in new ways which affect service delivery, management and pricing.

- **Hybrid groups** combine the characteristics of knowledge-centric and affinity-based groups, with sub-groups characterised by their primary interest in content, transactions or special areas of interest.

Type of Group ↓ / Size of Groups →			Micro	Small	Medium	Large	Very Large
Knowledge and Expertise Mediated Groups	'Deep' Knowledge	e.g. Researchers, Scientists					
	'Practising Knowledge'	e.g. Clinicians			Eg Clinicians in Health Practices		
	'Shallow' Knowledge	e.g. Patients and Carer groups					
Hybrid Groups – combining Affinity and Knowledge	Content centric	e.g. Music fan clubs, Football					
	Transaction centric	e.g. Discount clubs					
	Interest centric	e.g. Reading clubs, Learning Groups					
Affinity based Groups	Curated Groups	e.g. Private 'clubs', Professional Assn.					
	Peer-to-Peer Groups	e.g. Student and Alumni groups	Eg Local Tennis Club				
	Special Interest Groups	e.g. Community Action, Activity Groups					

Figure 18. Understanding how your product meets the needs of knowledge and affinity centric groups.

8.3.5 *Unpacking customers*

We need to understand how customer behaviour reflects the maturity of a new product. Early buyers of products may be more tolerant of issues than mainstream customers. Using a diffusion model based on a constant rate of innovation, *Rogers* [6] proposed a customer classification based on segmenting users into five categories, the first three of which are relevant to scale-up firms.

Rogers defined these three categories as follows: Innovators, Early Adopters and the Early Majority. Using segmentation criteria based on 1st and 2nd standard deviations from the mean in his model, Rogers suggested that the first two categories in his model accounted for about 35% of all customers, which most researchers agree is a highly optimistic estimate of this early behaviour.

Our research for *Camels, Tigers & Unicorns* [1], based on a large volume of *real data*, suggests a different way of segmenting customers as follows:

- **Proto-customers:** very small number of early customers engaged in crossing Chasm I.
- **Charter customers:** small number of customers engaged in crossing Chasm II.
- **Normal customers:** engaged on full commercial terms post Chasm II.

This approach based on the Triple Chasm Model provides a more realistic estimate of the rate of early customer growth, which typically shows that the first two customer categories account for only 10% of total customer numbers.

This customer definition does not make any *a priori* assumptions about what customers *pay* for the proposition. In reality, the research shows that the behaviour of these customers can be characterised as follows:

- Proto-customers do not usually pay but in a few circumstances may contribute towards product development costs.
- Charter customers will typically pay less than normal customers, based on the contribution they make towards proposition refinement and business model testing.
- Normal customers, post Chasm II, will pay on the basis of the established business model.

8.3.6 *Users vs Customers*

It is critical to distinguish between **Customers** and **Users**, especially given the increasing complexity of business models.

Customers are typically those who pay for a product or service, based on the established business model (although this may be discounted for proto-customers and charter customers in the early stages of a new product launch).

All **customers** typically engage in assessing the commercial value of a product, paying for it and monitoring its value in use, even though they may not actually be using it.

Users may not be involved in assessing, paying for and monitoring the value of a product, but will always be involved in **actually using the product**.

This distinction is important because we need to understand the relationship between customers and users when developing new products.

In most cases, the number of users will typically be a multiple of the number of customers:

No of users = $N\text{-}ucr$ × No of customers, where $N\text{-}ucr$ is the user–customer ratio, which can vary between 1 and larger numbers based on the customer typology and market space.

For business customers, N-ucr may be in the range 100–1000, based on the number of users in the firm.

For Consumers, N-ucr may be in the range of 1–10, depending on whether individuals buy and use a product (say a smartphone) or whether the head of a family buys a product used by several people in the family (say a TV set).

For knowledge and affinity workers, N-ucr can have a very wide range (for example, a hospital acting as a customer may provide the product to thousands of users).

For governments as customers, a small number of customers actually enable thousands of users (for example, a software planning tool).

In all cases, the N-ucr ratio may affect product pricing, based on the perception of value delivered.

8.3.7 *Estimating C-max*

Estimating C-max is not an exact science: for most firms; estimating C-max for a new product can present a significant challenge, especially where the product may be providing new functionality, but this estimation is critical for successful commercialisation.

This estimate of C-max may change as the firm grows, but at any level of maturity, the successful deployment of the right resources can depend on a realistic view of the potential maximum number of customers for the product. Even simple order-of-magnitude estimates can provide powerful insights into priorities and constraints.

Our approach to estimating C-max consists of six key steps, as shown in Figure 19:

- Define the *geographic focus* of the first product, irrespective of broader global ambitions; this enables us to characterise the market space and to understand the linkages between users, buyers and sellers.
- Clarify the *type of customer* for the product, based on the customer typology vector, so we can distinguish, for example, between business customers and consumers.
- Use the customer typology template numbers to determine the potential range of customers, which provides useful guidance on minimum and maximum customer numbers; this insight can sometimes alter thinking about the customer typology.
- Understanding the target customer in the typology model can then be used to understand the relationship between the number of users and the number of customers: for knowledge and affinity centric customers, for example, a single customer such as a hospital, maybe buying a product which is used by several hundred clinician users; even in the consumer market, a single customer (for say a television set) may be buying a product on behalf of several users; business customers are often buying a product for use by many users, and we are of course interested in the number of paying customers, not users.
- Based on understanding the geographic focus, the typology, typical customer ranges, and the ratio of users to customers, we can estimate C-max more robustly than simply working with proxy data.
- Finally, we can test the value of C-max versus real data for C based on the maturity of the product; for example, if a firm recognises its relative maturity, it can use the Triple Chasm Model to check whether the C/C-max ratio is within the expected limits.

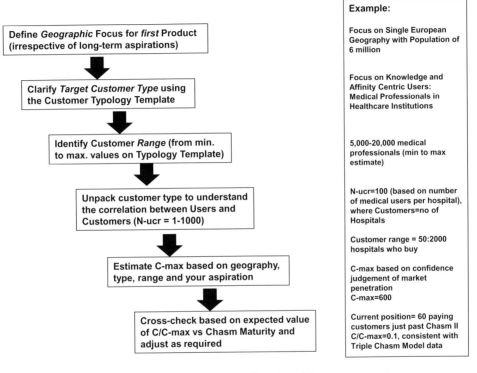

Figure 19. Estimating the value of C-max.

8.3.8 *Estimating potential market*

Successful commercialisation depends on identifying the right markets, customer segments and building a realistic estimate of the market potential for the technology, product or service. Estimating C-max for a single product is a good starting point but may not be adequate in estimating the total potential market.

For some products and services, the addressable market may include all four types of customers discussed above, albeit with different product and service packaging and business models. For example, audio recognition technologies are used to provide music recognition services to consumers: but they can also provide copyright management tools for businesses and organisations who want to extract maximum value from their music rights portfolios.

Where **markets exist already for similar or relevant products**, it is possible to use well-structured data based on actual market measurements.

When it comes to estimating market potential for some new products, the problem is that you may be trying to estimate the size of **markets which do not yet exist**. Where the new market is not dramatically different from current markets, you can make estimates by treating these as **derivative markets**, based on understanding where the key differences lie and how they might affect customer behaviour. For example, some of the early estimates for online digital content channels were based on treating them as derivatives of existing print magazine products. This is not always possible, especially where you are looking at the market potential **of entirely new markets with no obvious proxies**. For example, when in-vehicle satellite navigation systems were first created, there were no obvious parallels to guide estimation of how big this market would become, or indeed to appreciate that the biggest group of customers would eventually be individual consumers.

For all three types of markets, **existing, derivative and completely new markets**, you need to use a structured approach to market estimation, as shown in Figure 20.

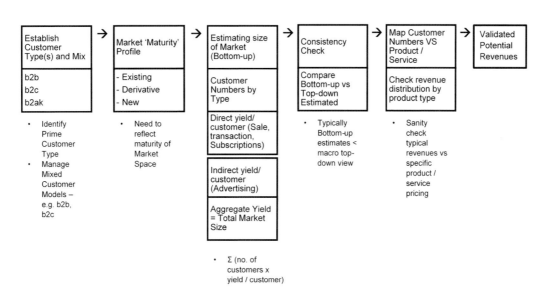

Figure 20. Systematic approach to market size estimation. Adapted from *Camels, Tigers & Unicorns* [1].

8.4 Distribution, Marketing & Sales

8.4.1 *Go-to-market challenges*

Firms face five generic challenges in taking their products and services to market but the relative importance of these challenges depends on the specific circumstances and maturity of the firm, as illustrated in Figures 21 and 22.

Product & Service Management	Category Management
	Portfolio Management
	Life-cycle Management
Pricing	Pricing Strategy
	Pricing Tactics
	Dynamic Pricing
Product Marketing & Sales	Positioning & Branding
	Marketing & Promotion
	Demand Generation & Sales
Channel Management	Channel Mix
	Resource Management
	Performance Management
Post-sales Management & Support	Customer Support
	Customer Management
	Product & Process Improvement

You need to understand the relative importance of these variables for your proposition

Figure 21. The go-to-market variables. Adapted from *Camels, Tigers & Unicorns* [1].

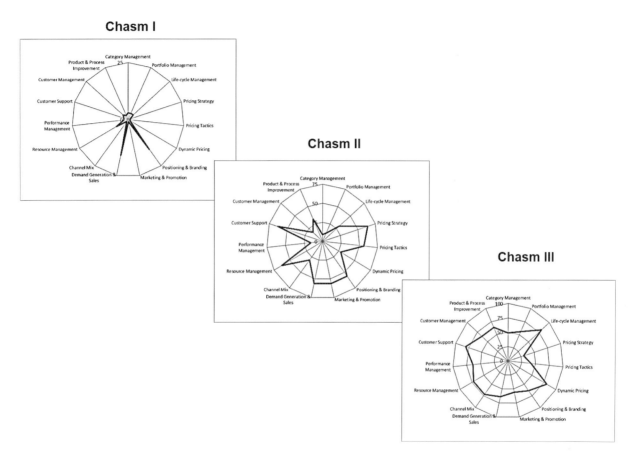

Figure 22. The importance of go-to-market variables changes with maturity.

8.4.2 *The modified 7Ps model*

The go-to-market variables can provide useful **overall insights**, but we use the modified 7Ps model to understand the **specific challenges associated with product positioning, packaging, pricing and promotion**.

The challenges around positioning, branding and promotion have been well described for firms in general — the specific issues have been captured using simplified models, starting with the 4Ps, now extended to 7Ps. We prefer a modified version of this approach which we characterise as the m7Ps model illustrated in Figure 23 defined as follows:

Product: This defines the wider product and service envelope, the core of the product, and the key components of the overall product offer.

Positioning: This defines the overall positioning of a product or service, clarifying the value added and differentiation compared to competing products and services.

Price: This defines 'baseline' pricing for the product core as well as the pricing for additional components, including additional services and add-ons such as maintenance.

Place: This describes how and where product or service is delivered, for example, for physical products such as electronic devices, this might be retail stores, but for media and content-based products, this could include locations such as online stores and e-commerce platform.

Promotion: This covers how products and services are promoted, including advertising, marketing campaigns and digital promotions across a wide range of media.

Process: This includes how the product or service is delivered and consumption processes for users but covers all the processes associated with taking products and services to market, for example, the sales management process. Defining process can be especially important for value-added service delivery of software and computational products and services.

Partners: For many products and services, the role of partners can be critical for go-to-market; this variable is concerned with defining the types of partners and the associated commercial implications.

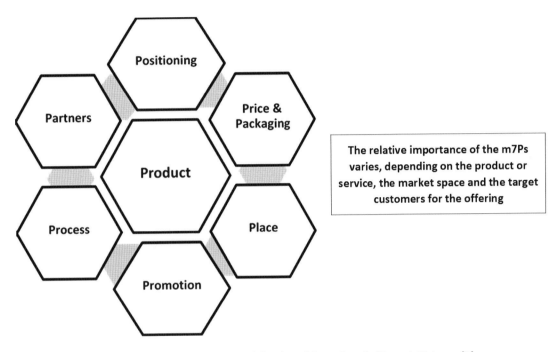

Figure 23. The modified 7Ps model. Adapted from *Camels, Tigers & Unicorns* [1].

Firms can use the m7Ps model to understand how the Distribution, Marketing & Sales Priorities can change with the maturity of their proposition, as illustrated in Figures 24 and 25.

The research discussed in *Camels, Tigers & Unicorns* [1] shows how the relative importance of each of the mPs varies on average with firm maturity.

This research reveals the following broad patterns:

- The m7Ps are not very relevant early in the commercialisation journey, around Chasm I, with Product and Process the only variables which need to be assessed.

- Around Chasm II, all the m7Ps matter, with particular emphasis on the Product and Pricing.
- By the time firms are crossing Chasm III, all the m7Ps are critical, with only a slight decrease in the importance of product.

Firms need to make their own assessment of the importance of each of the mPs, based on a judgement of their relative maturity, guided only generally by the research data.

Firms then need to assess their execution capacity for each component in order to build an aggregate view of their weighted performance score.

| Variable | Scoring ranges: 0-10 | | |
	Relevance Score	Execution Score	Weighted Impact Score (Relevance x Execution)
Product	9	9	81
Positioning	6	7	42
Price	7	7	49
Place	8	6	48
Promotion	7	7	49
Process	10	9	90
Partners	8	8	64

Figure 24. Understanding distribution, marketing & sales priorities using the m7Ps model.

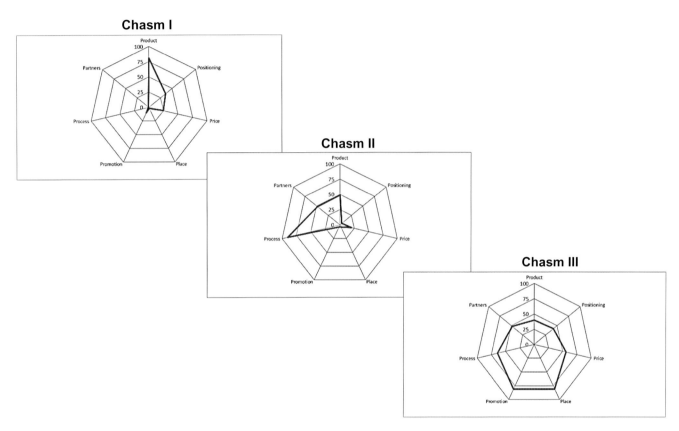

Figure 25. Typical variation in m7Ps across the three chasms.

8.4.3 *Channels-to-market*

The generic challenges surrounding channels-to-market have been extensively discussed but firms scaling-up need a clear understanding of the different channels and their comparative advantages and disadvantages.

The two basic approaches are to go to market **direct** or to harness a range of potential **channels** with different business models.

Channel choices are characterised by who actually **performs the following roles**, as shown in Figure 26:

- Product or service packaging
- Business model implementation, especially revenue collection and cost allocation
- Product or service pricing
- Promoting the product or service
- Making the sale
- Distribution of the product or service (physical, electronic, and 'blended')
- Product and service maintenance and ongoing support.

Working with strategic channel partners typically requires the greatest flexibility because the partner can be involved in all the roles, but this flexibility can bring important benefits in terms of customer knowledge, shared risk and bigger rewards.

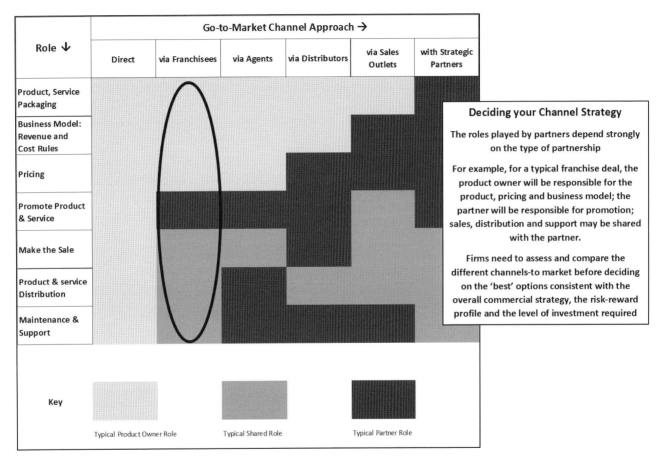

Figure 26. Typical roles for different channel strategies. Adapted from *Camels, Tigers & Unicorns* [1].

Chapter 9

Intervention Shaping: *Internal* Vectors

Firms typically have far more control over the internal vectors which can shape their growth. The relative importance of these vectors can of course depend on the market space that a firm is targeting but we can characterise these vectors and their components explicitly, as summarised in Figure 1.

Technology Development and Contingent Technology Deployment: Technology firms in particular need to understand the relative maturity of their technology and to understand the best strategic approach to deploy their technology commercially. This depends on the hierarchical technology classification model we developed and articulated in *Camels, Tigers & Unicorns* [1]: the approach to commercialisation depends on exploiting the right level in this hierarchy contingent mainly on the market space, customer typology and business model vectors.

Intellectual Property Management: We adopt a much wider definition of intellectual property than the narrow view based on patents. We define registered, un-registered, and open rights which enables us to identify the different sources of IP and how their importance changes with maturity. Our approach covers not just key technologies but also content, meta-content and design rights.

Product and Service Synthesis: Shaping the product proposition is critical in understanding in detail the precise functionality available to end-users. The product decomposition framework enables us to define precisely the technology, content and meta-content components which contribute to the ultimate product or service provided to customers.

Manufacturing, Assembly and Deployment: The way in which a product is manufactured, assembled and deployed is a key internal vector which can determine the success of a product. In our approach, we distinguish between components, supply chains, processes, deployment options and integrated manufacturing methods.

Talent, Leadership & Culture: Our treatment of this critical internal vector is based on a broad approach which separates the contributions of talent, teams, organisational structures, leadership and culture. This structured approach enables us to understand how the human capital requirements change with firm maturity and how to optimise their contribution to the scale-up process.

Funding & Investment: We unpack this key vector to identify the different sources of funding and how these change as firms grow. Our approach allows us to understand the importance of customer funding, in particular, as a key source of financial capital in supporting scale-up. This vector also defines a systematic approach to firm valuation when raising equity finance.

Tech Dev & Contingent Deployment

Qualitative articulation of the technology options for a firm based on market space insights & analysis can be critical for the commercial success of firms enabled by science and technology enabled innovation. For these firms, the technology focus and deployment choices are usually contingent on the applicable Market Space and the nature of the firm's Proposition

Intellectual Property Management

Qualitative focus on how Intellectual Property is described, managed and exploited can be a critical internal vector for many firms, not just science and technology enabled firms. We incorporate a wider definition of intellectual property in defining this vector, which includes brands, trademarks copyright, and 'open rights' not just a narrow definition focused on patents.

Product & Service Synthesis

This critical internal vector provides a *Qualitative* articulation of how a product or service is synthesized and how the components of the product can be explicitly characterised using the Product Decomposition Framework: in a sense this internal vector is the counterpart to the external Proposition Framing vector which positions the offering in the context of the external Market Space.

Manufacturing & Deployment

Qualitative Approach to characterising manufacturing, assembly and deployment enables the critical issues in making and delivering products into the market to be made explicit, which firms sometimes ignore, Different components of this vector can be analysed, and the *Quantitative* Relevance and Execution capacity of the firm can be assessed using normalised scoring techniques

Talent, Leadership & Culture

Qualitative Approach to the human capital issues is based on a systematic assessment of the key components which a firm can shape actively: Talent, Teams, Organisational Structures, Leadership and Culture. Striking the right balance between these components appropriate to the maturity of the firm can have critical impact on the firm's growth trajectory. *Quantitative* Relevance & Execution Performance of these components can be assessed using normalised scoring techniques

Funding & Investment

Qualitative Approach to Funding & Investment is based on identifying the different sources of capital available at different levels of maturity of the firm: this Vector provides a way of profiling and characterising the options. The *Quantitative* extension to this enables firms to assess their current valuation and how it can affect the nature and amount of money raised to drive a chosen strategy.

Figure 1. Overview of the internal vectors.

9.1 Technology Development & Contingent Deployment

9.1.1 *The approach*

Technology can be a critical component of many new product and service propositions, but the commercialisation process depends on three key factors, as illustrated in Figure 2:

- **Technology Characterisation:** this is based on segmenting the technology into six different levels, starting with fundamental building blocks based on base science and technologies, and then aggregating this with other technologies, tools and approaches to create increasing levels of functional capability. This fundamental understanding is critical in assessing commercialisation pathways.

- Using this understanding, we assess the 'optimum' approach to exploiting the technology based on using the most appropriate packaging strategy in the context of the market space the firm is trying to address: this **'contingent' or 'conditional' approach to technology deployment** depends on understanding the dynamics of the target market space, including customer typology, business models, the cost, time and complexity of deployment. **This is a key strategic choice in the early development of a firm with potentially far-reaching implications**.

- The actual **technology delivery** depends strongly on the contingent (or conditional) choices made, but then follows the typical development pathways dictated by the specifics of the technology under consideration; this includes the usual challenges such as performance, usability, reliability and resilience. Some execution pathways can be more complex and expensive than others, so several strategic iterations maybe required before a firm settles on a particular contingent deployment approach.

Technology *Characterisation*

Understanding how technology can be 'packaged' into usable components before it can be taken to market; we describe a 6-layer technology characterisation model to describe the different ways in which technology can be packaged

***Contingent* (or conditional) Technology Deployment**

deciding on the most appropriate type of component(s) for a specific proposition, contingent on the market space, competition, regulation and business model; we provide data, based on research done for *Camels, Tigers & Unicorns (1)*, which illustrates the choices made by different firms

Technology *Delivery*

developing the chosen component(s) to increase the technology readiness level (mTRL/CRL) consistent with crossing the three Chasms; this relies on development activity which increases the maturity of the chosen technology deployment option

Figure 2.   Approach to technology development and deployment.

9.1.2 *Characterising your technology*

Our approach is based on the **different ways** in which a technology can be taken to market, as shown in Figure 3.

We start with **base technologies**, the initial 'building blocks' based on fundamental developments in a particular scientific or technology area. This requires detailed understanding of the precise features and granularity of the technology under consideration. Base technologies may have applications across a wide range of market spaces, but the way in which they are 'packaged' into application technologies reflects the types of applications.

The next layer in our technology deployment model is based on **application technologies**, which are typically an aggregation of one or more base technologies with additional components which may facilitate commercial exploitation: they usually reflect the requirements of the market space.

The **platform** layer can be critical in deploying novel new technologies: it consists of platforms and infrastructures where application technologies are integrated in order to provide new functionality for users in a number of different ways. This integrated functionality also enables new business models for commercialising the technology. Apart from the integrated functionality, it can also play an important role in hiding underlying technology complexity from users where this would be an impediment to adoption.

Users often interact with technologies at the level of **applications and tools**, which depend on an underlying platform which enables the delivery of value to end users. The applications and tools layer depends strongly on the data and metadata associated with the application area.

The **product** layer is where a new technology can be most explicitly perceived by end-users and customers, based on the functionality the product provides. New technologies may form the core of a new product, for example, a new drug based on a new compound or a new display technology which enables a new form of projection system; it may only form part of a new product, which has important implications for how technology is commercialised.

The **service** layer typically builds on the product layer and is concerned with how technologies can be deployed to deliver services to customers. Technologies associated with services can have very wide market application: for example, algorithms associated with data visualisation or analytic tools can be applied in many market spaces, ranging from healthcare to media and entertainment, where large data sets create opportunities for analysis, inference and interventions.

Technology Layer	Characteristics
Base Technologies	Fundamental 'Building Blocks' with applicability across multiple market spaces
Application Technologies	Aggregation of different base technologies
Platforms	Integration of different application technologies to enable new functionality
Applications & Tools	Functionality aimed at end users based on application technologies and platforms
Products	Integrated functionality for users based on base and application technologies, data, meta-data and applications & tools
Services	Integration of products and associated services, including on-boarding, usage and support

Figure 3. Technology characterisation — The key to understanding optimum deployment of your technology. Adapted from *Camels, Tigers & Unicorns* [1].

9.1.3 *Contingent deployment: Why does this matter?*

Firms and innovators focused on commercialising their technologies need to understand the ways in which their intellectual property can be commercialised and the advantages and disadvantages of each deployment approach.

Most firms do not address this systematically: most identify potential opportunities for their technologies in a broad market context and then proceed to develop solutions based on their best instincts. While this approach may work, there are many situations where the initial deployment strategy needs to be modified once the scale and complexity of the challenge becomes apparent.

Choosing the wrong deployment strategy can have dramatic consequences for a firm.

Making the right decisions about technology deployment strategy is particularly important where major new technologies have been developed with one or more of the following features:

- the potential to disrupt a supply chain

- the ability to significantly alter the shape of the overall market space
- to change the nature and roles of players within the space, and also how they interact with each other.

Firms can make different decisions based on the material conditions affecting them at different points in time, as shown in Figure 4. They can also change their approach over time, driven mainly by execution and funding implications. Firms may also pursue alternative approaches in parallel, for example, developing products at the same time as licensing the base and application technologies to other firms designing their own products. There are no intrinsic advantages based in choosing any particular strategy for technology deployment, but the choice can have significant implications, particularly in terms of *depth of technology expertise required*, the *need for complementary technologies*, the *commercial expertise* required, the *cost and speed to market*, *business model flexibility*, and the *trade-offs between risk and reward*.

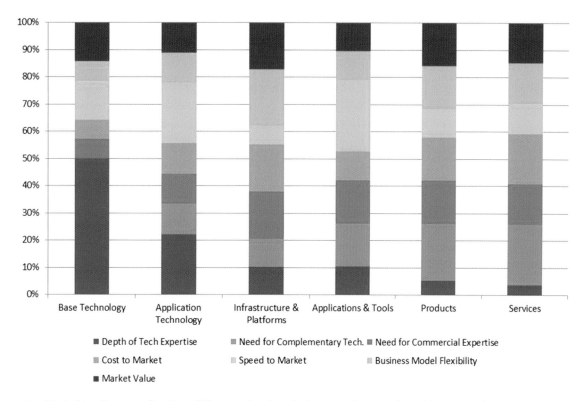

Figure 4. Typical implications of making different technology deployment choices. Adapted from *Camels, Tigers & Unicorns* [1].

9.1.4 *Deployment choices-some observations*

Firms need to understand the implications of the different potential deployment strategies, in particular for the cost and complexity of their commercialisation strategies. The research underpinning *Camels, Tigers & Unicorns* [1] provided the following insights:

- The depth of technology expertise required, relative to the other attributes, declines gradually as the deployment strategy become more market-centric.
- The need for complementary technologies: this matters very little where the commercialisation approach is based on licensing or selling the base technology directly to other firms, but increases gradually as the deployment strategy involves greater integration with other product and service components.
- The need for broader commercial expertise is highest for situations where platforms, products and services are delivered to end-customers: the approach requires greater affinity with the end-customers than for strategies based on selling base or application technologies.

- The cost of technology deployment is the highest for platforms, products and services, given the need for not just complementary technologies but also the need for much broader commercial expertise.
- The speed-to-market is the quickest where the technology is encapsulated in applications and tools.
- Deployment strategies based on complete end products and services are slower given the complexity associated with product development and packaging.
- Approaches to licensing or selling base technologies are also much slower because of the need to choose the right application spaces and educate potential customers.
- Platform deployment typically has the slowest speed-to-market but infrastructures and platforms provide the greatest flexibility in business models, especially based on new service-based delivery. The overall complexity is highest for strategies based on platforms compared to all other technology deployment strategies.

9.1.5 *Some examples*

New technologies with significant potential impact can present serious strategic dilemmas when it comes to making the right decisions on contingent technology deployment. In these situations, the choices will usually reflect the balance between risk and reward as assessed by the leadership of the firm.

Two specific examples illustrate these dilemmas:

3D Printing Technologies

- Potential to fundamentally transform the activities of materials, manufacturing and distribution firms, creating opportunities to provide new products and services.
- The challenge is to maintain focus and to understand the practical constraints when deciding on a single or on multiple deployment strategies.

Quantum Engineering

- Very wide potential impact, across multiple market spaces.
- Lack of clarity of base vs application technology status.
- The challenge is to understand the relative maturity and readiness of the technology for real deployment, and the cost and complexity of establishing market traction.

Firms need to match the chosen strategy to market conditions, to understand their capacity to execute based on the availability of appropriate resources, and to be aware that hubris can be a serious risk especially where they believe they are inventing a new future.

9.1.6 *Understanding base vs application technologies*

The key to understanding how base technologies can be deployed for maximum impact is to understand the linkage between base and application technologies, as illustrated in Figure 5.

This linkage depends strongly on the market space where the application technologies will be applied. The coupling between base and application technologies is different, even for the same base technologies, for different market spaces.

For example, a base technology concerned with computer architectures will be manifested in different application technologies when applied in media and entertainment applications vs 'smart' grids for power management.

Even within the same market space, base technologies can act in different ways to impact on different functional areas. We illustrate this by mapping base vs application technologies for the media and entertainment market space. It shows how a wide range of base technologies can be reflected in different application technologies. The same base technologies may be packaged differently to provide application technologies applicable to different market spaces, for example, in the energy and lighting market or in regenerative medicine.

> If Base Technologies are a critical component of your proposition, you need to build a map like this to understand its impact.

Base technology \ Application technology	Creation, manipulation & packaging	Content storage, retrieval & management	Transaction & customer mgt	Distribution & delivery	Usage	Research, planning & promotion mgt	Integration & process mgt
Input/output	●●●	●●	●	●	●●●	●●	●●●
Processor	●●●	●●●	●●●	●●	●●●	●●	●●
Storage	●●	●●●	●	●	●●●	●●●	●●
Software languages & tools	●●●	●●●	●●●	●	●●	●●	●●●
Software engineering	●●	●●●	●●●	●●	●●	●●●	●●●
Compression	●	●●	●●	●●●	●	●	●●
Encryption	●	●	●●●	●●●	●●	●	●
Communications	●	●	●●●	●●●	●●	●●	●●
Authentication	●	●●	●●●	●	●●●	●	●
Agent technology	●	●●●	●●●	●	●●●	●●	●

Key: ● Low impact   ●● Medium impact   ●●● High impact

Figure 5. Example of base vs application technologies for media & entertainment market space. Adapted from *Camels, Tigers & Unicorns* [1].

9.1.7 *Technology development & contingent deployment: Platforms, applications & services*

Application technologies can be deployed in many ways, but the ability to **integrate** these technologies into a coherent platform can often provide a very powerful way to deploy enhanced functionality for customers, with a more sustainable business model.

Some of the application technologies identified for the media and entertainment market space, for example, can be combined to provide a platform which enables dynamic real-time rights management for the music industry.

Integrated platforms can exhibit three different levels of complexity:

- **Integration of technology functionality** which can **also** enable synchronised **management of content and data.**

- **Functional integration** which can deliver a wide set of functions in a seamless way.
- **Commercial integration** which enables functionality with an integrated business model.

In a variety of market spaces, technology deployment via platforms can create the potential for new classes of defensible, sustainable, and powerful services. This can enable firms to occupy powerful new roles in previously fragmented markets.

We illustrate this in Figure 6 based on a platform which enables the management of loyalty schemes over multiple digital distribution channels. The platform shown can deliver integrated functionality to a set of customers who would otherwise have to use a wide range of technologies to achieve the same functionality.

Service Platform

Cloud-based solution for consumer brands to create, deliver and manage loyalty programmes over multiple channels.

- Create powerful multimedia content for promotions
- Develop and manage tailor-made Offers on selected products & services
- Create, distribute and track Tokens/coupons seamlessly
- Publish and effectively promote your Offers through promotion campaigns
- Track token delivery, usage and redemption in real time
- Review, monitor and modify promotions online
- Share results with partners and suppliers
- Track, analyse end user behaviour and develop key insights

Integrated Technology Platform

| Raw Data Feeds | Customer Behaviour Data | Partner and Supplier reports | Web Pages | Mobile Apps | Interactive experiences |

Technology Components

| Campaign Mngt | Inbound /Outbound SMS/Email | Data storage and Mngt | Identity Mngt | Mapping, LBS, Geo-fencing | Ratings Tools | Content Mngt | In-Store Identity proximity system |

Figure 6. Example of a platform for delivery of a multi-channel loyalty management service.

9.2 Intellectual Property Management

9.2.1 *Understanding IP*

All firms face the same challenges when it comes to managing intellectual property: how to define, protect and actively exploit their IP. In theory, all Intellectual property can be bought, sold, or licensed. The IP owner is the person entitled to commercially exploit it, hence, it is important to establish ownership to avoid disputes.

Provisions regarding ownership of IPRs can be complex and vary depending on the type of right. This means that a creation can give rise to different rights and the owners of each may not be the same person or entity.

Exploitation usually depends on

- **Incorporating** the IP into the firm's products or services.
- **Assigning** the IP which transfers effective ownership to another entity.
- **Licensing** the IP to another entity for incorporation into their products and services.

IP is critical for building sustainable business models, although most financial balance sheets do not usually quantify the value of IP explicitly. IP is often seen as being synonymous with patents, but in reality, patents constitute only a part of the overall picture. Our wider definition of IP covers registered rights (including patents), unregistered rights and 'open' rights. This broad view of IP can underpin the development of robust business models: for example, strong copyright protection or design rights can sustain higher pricing of licenses or the pricing of products and services. This can also constitute a key element of competitive differentiation.

Firms can map and understand the true nature and coverage of their intellectual property, using the IP mapping grid shown in Figure 7.

	'Registered' Rights				'Un-registered' Rights					'Open' Rights		
Component	Patents	Trademarks	Design Rights	Copyright	Trade Secrets	Know-How (Technology and Process)	Algorithms and Software	Specialised Customer Knowledge	Value of Brands	Open Source	Creative Commons Licensing	Fair Use Rights
Customers								Detailed Insight into Customer Behaviour				
Services		Service Trademark	Registered Service Design				Service Algorithms		Service Brand			
Products	Product Patent	Product Trademark	Registered Product Design	Product Copyright			Product Algorithms		Product Brand		Rights to Use & limitations	
Meta-Content			Format Rights	Meta-content Copyright							Rights to Use & limitations	Content Use & Limitations
Content			Format Rights	Content Copyright							Rights to Use & limitations	Content Use & Limitations
Apps, Tools & Processes	Process Patent	Process Trademark	App and Process Design	App Copyright	Knowledge of Apps and Tools take-up	Process Know-how	Process Algorithms			Software Code, Tools and Applications	Rights to Use & limitations	
Platforms & Infrastructures			Registered Platform Design				Infrastructure Code eg workflow tools		Infrastructure Brand	Software Code, Tools and Applications	Rights to Use & limitations	
Application Technologies	Application-based Patent		Application Design				Software Applications		Powered by eg Linked In			
Base Technologies	Base Tech Patent								Powered by eg Dolby			

Where is your IP focus?

Figure 7. Defining intellectual property relevant for your proposition.

9.2.2 Changing IP priorities along the journey

The wider definition of IP leads directly to the need to appreciate the relative importance of the different types of IP at different stages of your commercialisation journey and the related maturity of your firm.

For example, an early emphasis on the generation and protection of patents may give way to the need to protect design rights, copyright protection of algorithms and software, or meta-data which enables the functioning of new devices or processes.

- At early stages of commercialisation, around Chasm I, there are only 3–4 key IP variables of importance, led by patents, copyright and algorithms.
- Around Chasm II, a wider number of IP variables become relevant with this number falling slightly once Chasm III has been crossed.
- Firms need to understand the broader IP issues at stake as commercialisation proceeds: an approach focused solely around the core technology patents and algorithms is unlikely to harness the full commercial value of the innovation.
- Unregistered rights in the form of technology and process know-how can be a critical component of differentiation which improves the likelihood of successfully crossing Chasm II.
- Enforcing content copyright and using specialised customer knowledge in a 'protected' way can significantly improve customer scaling around Chasm III.

9.2.3 Mapping your IP priorities

Your intellectual property priorities are likely to change with maturity — but it is important to understand where you need to focus at any particular point in your journey, as illustrated in Figure 8.

Variable	Sub-variable	Relevance Score	Execution Score	Weighted Impact Score (Relevance x Execution)	
		Scoring ranges: 0-10			
Registered Rights	Patents	9	7	63	
	Trademarks	3	7	21	
	Design Rights	7	7	49	
	Copyright	3	5	15	
Unregistered Rights	Trade Secrets	2	2	4	
	Know-how (technology & process)	7	6	42	
	Algorithms & Software	8	8	64	
	Specialised Customer Knowledge	2	2	4	
	Value of Brands	2	3	6	
Open Rights	Open Source Code	8	7	56	
	Creative Commons Licensing	2	2	4	
	Fair Use Rights	1	1	1	

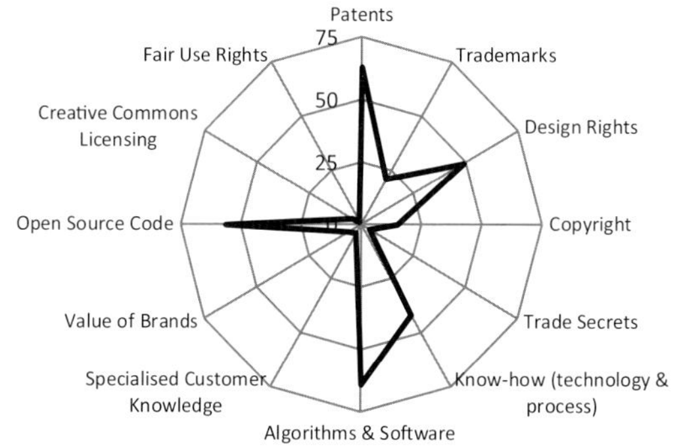

Figure 8.   Map your IP priorities for a given level of maturity.

9.3 Product Definition & Synthesis

9.3.1 *Approaches to product and service design*

The key to commercial success of course is to create a product that customers want to use and pay for — but the challenge lies in deciding which drivers affect customer behaviour. Even though technology can play a key role in the design of some products, for all products and services, there are three generic approaches to the synthesis of new capabilities, as shown in Figures 9 and 10:

- Customer-centric approaches where the product or service strongly reflects the 'voice-of-the customer'.
- Technology-centric approaches where the new product or service depends on mapping the new functionality offered by technology versus customer needs.
- Approaches based on synthesising customer, technology and broader business drivers: synthesis approaches can be strongly influenced by the complexity of new and emerging market spaces.

Customer-centric designs, where the voice-of-the-customer dominates, have a long pedigree, although the precise approach can vary: the design literature provides details of how to use either customer research, focus groups or key user analysis, and we do not propose to replicate this here but note that firms need to be clear about why and how they use one of these approaches.

Technology-centric approaches have also been described in the literature, based on functional or application drivers, but more recently, this has given way to a design focus based on value chains, which provides a broader approach to design.

While both these approaches have been applied successfully, recent approaches have taken a more integrated view to product design, which incorporates customer and technology trade-offs and can re-frame the deployment environment. Design thinking is the most popular of these approaches and has been widely used over the last decade in particular. The outcome-driven innovation approach also focuses on the desired outcomes. We prefer an approach based on *creative synthesis*, which explicitly addresses trade-offs between users, technology and business models.

Firms need to choose an approach to product and service synthesis best suited to their needs.

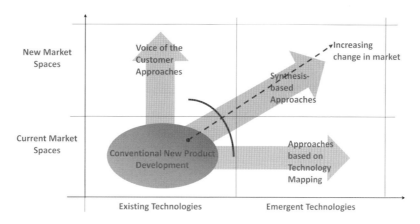

Figure 9. The three broad approaches to product and service design. Adapted from *Camels, Tigers & Unicorns* [1].

Voice of the Customer Approaches	Customer Research & insights
	Customer Focus Groups
	Key User Analysis
Synthesis-based Approaches	Outcome Driven Innovation
	Design Thinking
	Creative Synthesis
Technology Mapping	Functional Focus
	Applications Focus
	Market Space-centric Value Chain Focus

Firms creating new products and services need to be clear about the design approach best suited to the target market space and customers.

Figure 10. Different methods for product and service design. Adapted from *Camels, Tigers & Unicorns* [1].

9.3.2 *Voice of the customer approaches*

- Methods based on detailed research into the **behaviour of consumers** can guide thinking on the functions and features of new products or services.
- Approaches based on customer **focus groups** can enable deeper insights than conventional consumer research. The effectiveness of these approaches depends on the way in which the members of the focus group are chosen and the way in which the groups are curated.
- **Key user analysis** relies on the idea that there are key groups of users for any product or service, and that engaging with these groups will yield the best insights on functions, features and benefits. This technique is of limited value for significantly new products where, for example, it may be very hard to identify key potential users; the technique has been quite effective in driving changes to existing products where the customers are well known.

> Voice-of-the-customer approaches can be very effective where the behaviour of existing customers can be 'extrapolated' into their behaviour towards new products and services.

9.3.3 *Technology mapping*

Approaches based on technology mapping are quite different from voice-of-the-customer approaches, since they focus on the capabilities and potential of technology to shape new products and services, as shown in Figure 11. In particular, new and emerging technologies can enable new functions, features and benefits. In broad terms, there are three types of technology-mapping approaches:

- Techniques based on a strong **functional focus**, which explore how a single technology, or a group of technologies, can enable new functionality in products and services; this functionality may be targeted at existing customers or at new customers attracted by the enhanced functionality.
- Approaches with a strong **application focus**, where technologies do not just enable new functionality but offer the potential to create new applications for customers.
- Techniques based on understanding how technologies can **impact all or parts of market space-centric value chains** offer the potential for innovations greater than techniques based on functional and applications foci. This approach, based on mapping detailed market spaces, can be used to conceive and design radically new product and service concepts.

> Product and service design based on mapping technologies against market space-centric value chains can enable very competitive products with strong differentiation.

Content Creation, Manipulation & Packaging	Content Storage, Retrieval & Management	Processing & Computing Technology	Transaction & Customer Management	Research, Planning and Promotion Management	Messaging, Distribution & Delivery Technology	Usage Environments
Capture	Databases	Processing Architectures	Rights Management	Monitoring Tools	New Voice technologies	Print
Simple Synthesis	Logical Structuring & Tagging	Computing Platforms	Micro-payment Technologies	Sales and Transaction Tracking Tools	sms and derivatives	Mobile Phones & Other Personal (Wearable) Devices
Virtual Worlds	Semantic Tools	New Algorithms	Transaction Management Technologies	Analysis & Modelling Tools	e-mail and related technologies	Large format Computing Devices
Transformation	Search			Media Buying and Selling Technology	Broadcast radio & TV	New Digital Displays
Authoring	Standardisation	Simulation	Billing and Payment Systems	Promotion Management	Narrowcast including IPTV	Re-profiled Consumer Equipment
				Ad-serving Technologies	m2m technologies	
Editing & Proofing	Maintenance & Optimisation				Small cell & related technologies	Operating Systems & Tools
Resource Optimisation & Management						
Workflow technologies						
Security						
Platform Technologies						
Technology Integration Tools						

Overlay labels: Very Low Cost Data; Semantic Technologies; Micro Transactions; Social Media; Mobile Devices; IOT; Virtualisation

Figure 11. Example of a typical technology mapping approach applied to the media & entertainment market space. Adapted from *Camels, Tigers & Unicorns* [1].

9.3.4 *Creative synthesis*

There have been several attempts to understand the importance of creativity and to suggest how this could be systematically integrated into product and service design. Most of these attempts, however, have a very strong abstract focus which makes it difficult to apply them in any practical context. There is general acceptance that new product and service *creation needs to be rooted in a creative and entrepreneurial mindset.*

Synthesis of new products and services depends on clarity of market needs or value sought, as illustrated in Figure 12. Situations where the value creation capability is not clearly identifiable require creative and entrepreneurial approaches to match the two and create new value.

There are three levels of synthesis, consistent with increasing levels of market-space complexity and impact:

- Outcome-driven innovation is built around the theory that customers buy products and services to get jobs done. The approach is based on identifying important but poorly served outcomes, with a focus on customer-desired outcomes rather than demographic profiles, to segment markets and offer well- targeted products.
- Methods based on design thinking where design thinking is used to invent, prototype and test radically new ideas, where there is not a clearly defined user need in the beginning or only a technology concept.
- Creative synthesis approaches, which build on design thinking, but critically integrate potential business models with customer and technology perspectives when creating new products and services.

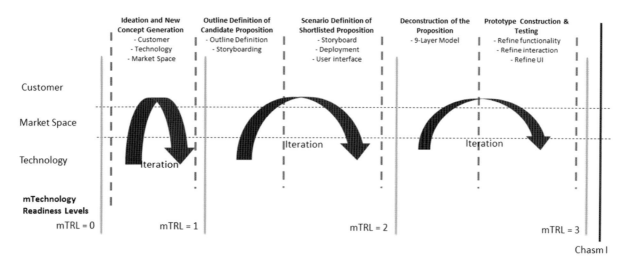

Figure 12. Creative synthesis applied to early stage product design before Chasm I. Adapted from *Camels, Tigers & Unicorns* [1].

9.3.5 *The proposition framework*

Once a product or service has been designed, the proposition framework enables a firm to *'deconstruct'* a new product or proposition into the nine key components, as shown in Figure 13:

- **Base technologies** provide the 'building blocks' which may have applications across a wide range of market spaces, but this layer defines whether and how they impact your product.
- **Application technologies** are typically an aggregation of one or more base technologies with additional components which facilitate commercial exploitation: this layer reflects how they contribute to your product or service.
- The **platform** layer consists of platforms where application technologies are integrated to provide new functionality for users in different ways: this defines whether a platform is part of your product or service.
- The **applications and tools** layer depends on data and metadata; it is particularly important in content and data-centric market spaces but this layer defines whether applications and tools are part of your overall proposition.
- The **data** layer consists of the content, either highly structured data, for example, clinical data describing a disease pathology, or lightly structured data such as a video feed of a musical concert; this layer defines whether and how data is important for your proposition.
- The **metadata** layer forms a *look-up table* which provides a guide to the content layer but may also cover information which enables the functioning of a platform provided directly to customers; this layer defines the importance of meta-data for your proposition.
- The **product** layer is where a new technology can be most explicitly deployed in the minds of customers. Technologies may form the core of a new product, but most products are an aggregation of the layers preceding it; this layer reflects this functional integration.
- The **service** layer usually builds on the product layer and is specifically concerned with how products are deployed to deliver services to customers; services may sometimes be delivered to customers without any product being involved.
- The **customer** layer is critical because it helps clarify who uses the product, service or component of a product or service; for example, this layer can illustrate the impact of focusing on consumers vs corporate customers vs knowledge-centric customers.

> **Not all nine layers are relevant for all products and services.**
> **Non-technology firms can ignore the first two or three layers and start with applications & tools.**

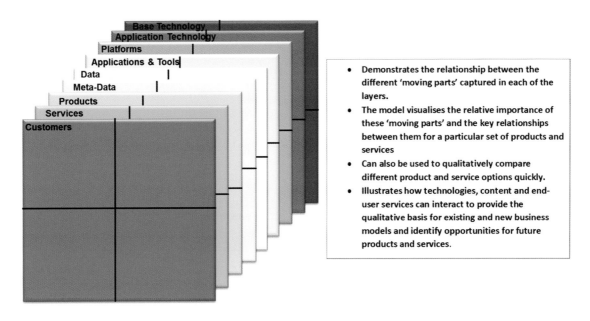

Figure 13. How to deconstruct your proposition using the 9-layer model. Adapted from *Camels, Tigers & Unicorns* [1].

9.4 Manufacturing & Deployment

9.4.1 *Unpacking manufacturing*

Systematic deconstruction of the manufacturing challenges shows five key areas that firms need to assess before they can decide the key issues that matter for them, as illustrated in Figure 14:

- **Manufacturing Components:** New products may sometimes require the creation of new tools and techniques, and in some cases, the development or exploitation of new materials. Some new products may be enabled by new materials which require new processes. Firms need to understand the potential importance of these components for their commercialisation journey.
- **Supply Chains:** Most firms are aware of the need to understand manufacturing supply chains, but for some new products, they may need to identify and work with new players who are not active in the current market space. Understanding the linkages between different players in the supply chain and how to manage them can have a critical impact on the business model; and understanding the resilience of the supply chain can also impact on the firm's decision-making.
- **Processes:** In many cases, the manufacturing and deployment of new products may only require a focus on process optimisation; in some situations, however, taking a product to market cost-effectively may require the creation of new manufacturing processes. Where this needs to be done from scratch the impact on the commercialisation strategy and business model may be significant, although in some cases that can be mitigated by 'cross-fertilising' processes from one market space to another.
- **Deployment:** Products and services which involve on-going relationships between the provider and the customer, for example, in computing platforms, create additional manufacturing challenges based on how products are assembled, installed and set-up. In some cases, the product or service may require active monitoring of components and systems, including dynamic management and maintenance.
- **Integrated Operations:** Advances in manufacturing and deployment, including mass customisation are changing some of the manufacturing challenges for firms. For example, the Industry 4.0 initiative, which builds on the potential for dynamic tooling, supply management and customised manufacturing and deployment, requires firms to understand the relative importance of inter-operability, data transparency and exchange and automated decision-making.

Key Manufacturing Challenges

Manufacturing Unpacked	
Components	Tools
	Techniques
	Materials
Supply Chains	Players & Linkages
	Management
	Resilience
Processes	Optimisation (lean, JIT etc)
	Cross-fertilisation of Processes
	Creation of New Processes
Deployment	Installation & Set-up
	Monitoring
	Active Management & Maintenance
Integrated Operations	Inter-operability
	Information Transparency & Exchange
	Decision-making

Figure 14. Defining the key manufacturing challenges.

9.4.2 *Manufacturing process innovation*

Manufacturing process innovation can be grouped into three broad categories as follows:

- Optimisation approaches based on the goal of either optimising resource inputs or focusing on desired outputs such as time-to-market or process flexibility. Most firms are likely to focus on this approach using well-defined methods such as **lean manufacturing**, with an emphasis on resource optimisation, or **just-in-time methods** which focus on optimising the supply chain.
- Firms deploying more innovative technologies may need to create new manufacturing processes using a **cross-fertilisation strategy** based on adapting tried and tested manufacturing approaches from other market spaces. This can enable more cost-effective use of equipment, originally developed for other uses, with modest changes to reflect the new need; for example, adapting products and technologies used in the printing industry to effectively 'print' new solar panels for use in solar arrays; another example is the use of manufacturing processes originally designed for electronic chip manufacturing and assembly to manufacture new structures based on nanomaterials which can be deployed in equipment to enable bedside bioprocessing.
- Firms creating entirely **new manufacturing processes** to take their products to market, a more difficult task given the complexity of simultaneously innovating both the technology and the manufacturing processes required to take it to market. This can be an expensive task fraught with difficulty which sometimes cannot be avoided; a good example of this is a firm trying to develop new plastic electronics technologies *and* the new manufacturing processes required to deploy the technologies, in effect trying to build a new market space in the process. It is important not to underestimate the complexity involved in creating an entirely new market space.

> **You need to be clear about whether manufacturing processes matter for your firm and how they matter.**

Manufacturing optimisation	Lean manufacturing
	Just-in-time
Processes cross-fertilization	Processes adaptation
	Materials re-purposing
Innovation in manufacturing processes	New processes
	New materials

9.4.3 *Integrating design, simulation, manufacturing, deployment and management*

Probably the biggest emerging manufacturing challenge relates to the integration and logistics of design, simulation, manufacturing, deployment and management.

Cloud computing firms provide a good illustration of this challenge. The technologies for secure data processing, storage and distribution are well developed, but the logistics of how products and services based on these technologies are deployed remains a major challenge; for example, the logical and physical rules for how cloud platforms and infrastructures operate, how they interact with customers and the business models which support these offerings.

These logistic challenges are becoming more acute with the proliferation of more granular data, very large volumes of data, very fast response networks and more sophisticated end-user functionality in the hands of customers. Proposed new *'internet of things' or IoT* services highlight this, where the challenge is not in the enabling technologies, but in the logistics of product and service deployment.

Firms in media and entertainment, telecommunications, electronics and hardware and software and computing market spaces face this challenge. The same logistic challenge is fundamental to the design of new products and services enabling gene therapy for patients in the healthcare market space, for example, personalised bedside bioprocessing and treatment.

This integration challenge is now being addressed under the umbrella of a global initiative labelled **Industry 4.0**, which promotes the wider computerisation of design, simulation and manufacturing: the first industrial revolution mobilised the mechanisation of production using water and steam power; the second industrial revolution introduced mass production with the help of electric power, followed by the third digital revolution and the use of electronics and information technologies to further automate production.

9.4.4 Assess your manufacturing priorities

Manufacturing Priorities can change significantly along the commercialisation journey:

- Around Chasm I, early in the journey, when the focus is on building the first prototype product, manufacturing issues are rarely important.
- When crossing Chasm II, where commercial sustainability becomes critical, all the manufacturing components become very important, particularly when the success of a new product depends on new components, processes and supply chains.
- Around Chasm III, processes and components have already been established and so the emphasis shifts to deployment and integrated operations; this is where typically the importance of Industry 4.0, for example, can become very important. Management of supply chains is also very critical at this level of maturity.

Typical Priority Weightings across the Three Chasms

| | | Scoring ranges: 0-10 | | |
		Chasm I	Chasm II	Chasm III
Components	Tools	2	8	1
	Techniques	2	7	1
	Materials	2	7	4
Supply Chains	Players & Linkages	1	7	8
	Management	1	6	9
	Resilience	1	3	9
Processes	Optimisation (lean, JIT etc)	2	7	2
	Cross-fertilisation of Processes	2	8	2
	Creation of New Processes	2	9	1
Deployment	Installation & Set-up	2	5	9
	Monitoring	2	6	9
	Active Management & Maintenance	2	6	9
Integrated Operations	Inter-operability	3	4	8
	Information Transparency & Exchange	3	5	9
	Decision-Making	3	4	8

Assess the importance of these variables based on the maturity of your proposition as illustrated in Figure 15.

		Scoring ranges: 0-10		
	Variable	Relevance Score	Execution Score	Weighted Impact Score (Relevance x Execution)
Components	Tools	2	8	16
	Techniques	5	7	35
	Materials	2	7	14
Supply Chains	Players & Linkages	7	2	14
	Supplier Management	7	2	14
	Resilience	6	2	12
Processes	Optimisation (lean, JIT)	2	2	4
	Cross-fertilisation of Processes	7	6	42
	Creation of New Processes	2	3	6
Deployment	Installation & Set-up	2	5	10
	Monitoring	2	2	4
	Active Management & Maintenance	2	1	2
Integrated Operations	Inter-operability	3	2	6
	Information Transparency & Exchange	3	3	9
	Decision-Making	3	2	6

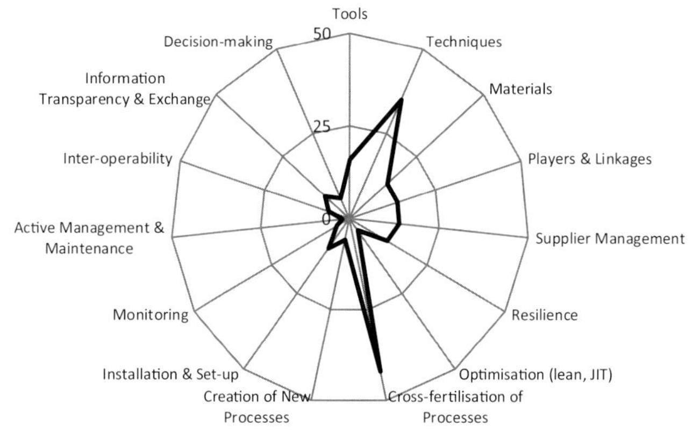

Figure 15. Profiling the importance of variables for your manufacturing & deployment vector.

9.5 Talent, Leadership & Culture

This vector is a critical component of success for all firms but there are two challenges in tackling this head-on:

- Insufficient clarity in understanding the different **components** which make up this critical vector and how these components can impact scale-up.
- Firms need to understand **how** the **relative importance** of these components can change significantly with the maturity of the firm.

The Talent, Leadership & Culture vector can be deconstructed into five key components, as shown in Figure 16, which should not be conflated because they can impact growth in different ways:

Talent: Firms need to understand the core competences of the available human capital including skills and expertise in key technologies, products and markets; distinct from these competencies, firms also need to understand the entrepreneurial orientation of key individuals; and firms also need to understand the hybrid techno-commercial skills which are so critical, especially for commercialising technology-centric ideas.

Teams: In addition to understanding the available talent, firms also need to understand how this talent can be combined into teams, in particular, the roles and processes within a team; in early-stage firms, this distinction between roles and processes may not always be clear. Firms also need to understand team performance management, using psychometric profiling tools and techniques where appropriate.

Building high-performance teams, in particular, requires a clear understanding of team objectives.

Organisational Structures: Firms often confuse the structure of an organisation with teams. Organisational structures usually reflect the maturity of a firm and are concerned with issues of control. Control systems need to operate in tandem with communications systems and processes. A key issue for scale-up businesses is understanding the trade-offs between firm size and structure; as firms grow structures may need to become explicit, but they can have a profound effect on effectiveness which needs to be managed carefully.

Leadership: The historical view of leadership based on the hierarchical leader–follower model may not be the most appropriate model for growth firms. Most business research (based on large mature firms) has emphasized this but the 'flatter' DAC model, based on emphasizing *direction, alignment and commitment*, may be better-suited to many firms. In practice, some firms may operate hybrid leadership models, combining these two approaches.

Culture: The culture of a firm may be the critical success factor, in particular, understanding the power of the narrative or myth which drives the ethos, values and objectives. Building and sustaining the right culture requires an understanding of the real power structures in the firm (which may not be reflected in the organisational structure) and whether they are consistent with the remuneration and rewards policies of the firm. The culture of firms may of course change with maturity, which firms need to be aware of.

Talent	Core Competences
	Entrepreneurial Orientation
	Hybrid Techno-commercial Skills, including 'T-Shaped' Expertise
Teams	Use of Psychometric Profiling Tools and Techniques
	Team Roles & Processes
	Team Performance Management
Organisational Structure & Management	Size vs Structure Tradeoffs
	Control Systems
	Communications
Leadership	Conventional Leader-Follower-Shared Goals Paradigm
	Hybrid Approaches to Leadership
	'Flat' Structures based on the DAC Paradigm
Culture	The Narrative: Stories & Myths
	Power Structures
	Remuneration and Rewards

Figure 16. Talent, leadership & culture — The key variables. Adapted from *Camels, Tigers & Unicorns* [1].

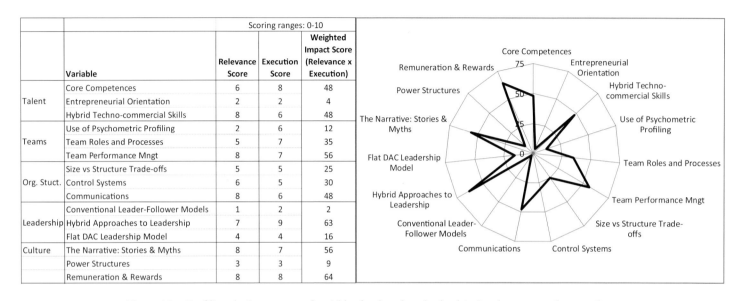

	Scoring ranges: 0-10		
Variable	Relevance Score	Execution Score	Weighted Impact Score (Relevance x Execution)
Talent			
Core Competences	6	8	48
Entrepreneurial Orientation	2	2	4
Hybrid Techno-commercial Skills	8	6	48
Teams			
Use of Psychometric Profiling	2	6	12
Team Roles and Processes	5	7	35
Team Performance Mngt	8	7	56
Org. Stuct.			
Size vs Structure Trade-offs	5	5	25
Control Systems	6	5	30
Communications	8	6	48
Leadership			
Conventional Leader-Follower Models	1	2	2
Hybrid Approaches to Leadership	7	9	63
Flat DAC Leadership Model	4	4	16
Culture			
The Narrative: Stories & Myths	8	7	56
Power Structures	3	3	9
Remuneration & Rewards	8	8	64

Figure 17. Profiling the importance of variables for the talent, leadership & culture vector for your firm.

Firms need to understand how to model the impact of the different variables as shown in Figure 17 above.

Figure 18 shows how the typical relevance of human capital components varies across the Chasms.

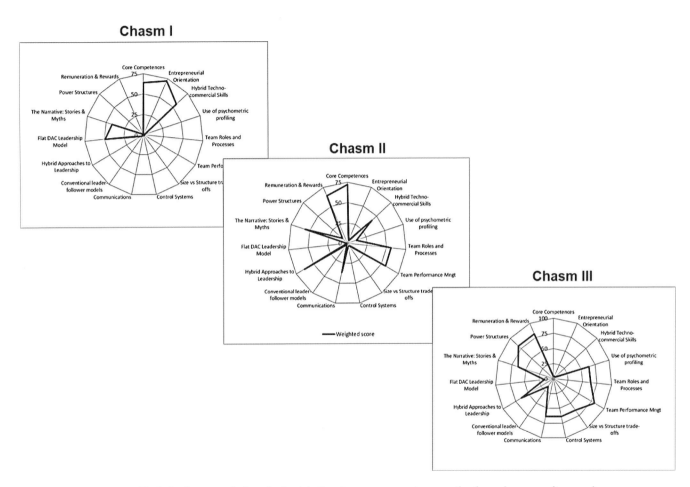

Figure 18. Typical relevance of talent, leadership & culture components across the three chasms, as firms scale-up.

9.5.1 *Talent and teams*

Scaling-up successfully depends on the ability of firms to attract and hold on to the right talent.

Entrepreneurial orientation in the talent pool is critical for growth companies. Cross-functional skills, sometimes described as T-shaped profiles, where individual expertise straddles several disciplines (the top of the 'T') combined with in-depth knowledge of a specific area (the bottom part of the 'T') are also very important. Underpinning this is the need to have the right core competences.

The importance of entrepreneurial orientation is well recognised, as is the importance of networks which support and mentor entrepreneurs. The critical issues, which are hard to quantify, are the motivation, self-awareness, social skills and relationship management capabilities of entrepreneurs, combined with the **ability to synthesise** new ideas, concepts, products and services.

When it comes to assembling effective teams, two key things matter:

- Functional subject matter expertise, as defined by core competences, which clearly depends on the technologies under consideration and the target market spaces.

- Behaviour types, as defined by one of the common behavioural metrics, for example, the *Belbin* [7] approach.

Despite some criticisms and reservations, *Belbin* and other different approaches to team role inventory and analysis are still widely used. Provided it is not used as a psychometric instrument, the 9-role tool with 360° feedback is also a helpful approach to defining roles in most firms.

Typically, teams in high growth firms need to use role models in conjunction with psychometric indicators. The *Myers–Briggs* [8] Type Indicator (MBTI) is the most commonly used psychometric indicator, based on four cognitive functions: thinking, feeling, sensation and intuition. Each function displays one of two polar orientations (extraversion or introversion), giving a total of eight dominant functions. The MBTI based on these eight hypothetical functions continues to be used, despite many reservations, because it is a simple tool which can provide useful behavioural insights.

9.5.2 *Leadership*

The success of most firms depends critically on leadership philosophy and management structures. The conventional approach to leadership of all firms is based on the **tripod of leaders, followers and their shared goals**.

As leadership becomes more peer-based and collaborative, there is recognition that this approach, with its strong emphasis on leaders and followers, can impose limitations on growth.

Drath [9] has proposed a new leadership ontology, commonly referred to as DAC, in which the essential entities are three leadership **outcomes**:

- Direction: Widespread agreement in a 'collective' or group sense on the overall goals, aims and mission of the firm.
- Alignment: The organisation and coordination of knowledge and work in the team working collectively.
- Commitment: The willingness of members of this collective to subsume their own interests and benefit within the direction and alignment agreed by the collective.

The DAC approach to leadership in inherently collaborative and may hold the key to successful scale-up. Most firms need to be more collaborative when they first start but may gradually move to a more explicit leader–follower model as they expand. The leadership model may also reflect the nature of the prevailing market space. In many technology-intensive market spaces, for example, in engineering and telecommunications, the conventional leader–follower–shared goals leadership paradigm is still dominant. The 'flatter' DAC-based leadership paradigm is strong in media and entertainment, software and computational tools and educational markets, where **hybrid approaches** are widespread. Hybrid approaches are also more prevalent in newer market spaces based on biotechnology, and in energy and lighting and financial services, compared to the heavy engineering-based markets.

> **Firms need to identify the 'best' leadership model for their level of maturity in their market space.**

9.5.3 *Organisational structure*

Greiner's work [10] provided some of the early basis for understanding the structure and dynamics of firms as they grow, but the insights were based on analysing the growth of relatively well-established firms with more than 50 employees. Discussion about organisational structures mostly assumes that all firms, as they grow, develop *M-form divisional* structures based on distinct product groups, and that *integrated U-form* structures based on functional lines gradually atrophy as firms grow (for a detailed discussion of this, see *Camels, Tigers & Unicorns* [1]).

This broad view has been challenged by some high-growth firms, who argue that a functional approach supports faster growth.

The links between size and organisational structure do change with the effective size of the firm, as shown in Figure 19. The key metrics firms need to look at are:

- Management Focus, in terms of the commercial objective of the firm
- Organisation Structure, in particular the processes, roles and relationships between them

- Management Style
- Control Systems, which reflect the need to manage resources and outputs
- Management Reward emphasis, which looks at how non-salary-based rewards are prioritised.

The size of a firm as it grows can be described using 10 categories: the single entrepreneur; *ad hoc* teams; early teams, (which are the first formal teams to emerge from *ad hoc* structures); launch teams focused on getting the first product or service into the hands of a charter customer; high-performance teams focused on the effective delivery of new products and services; integrated teams, organised to deliver the firm's overall commercial objectives; U-form teams, which reflect unitary organisation of the firm; M-form teams, which are organised into distinct divisions each responsible for a particular product or service, or product and service families; and H-form teams, which reflect a hybrid of U-form and M-form organisation.

Scale-up firms need to understand the impact of changes in organisational structure and take decisions consistent with their maturity.

	Single Entrepreneur	Founding Group	Ad-hoc Team	Early Team	Launch Team	High-performance Team	Integrated Team	U-form Team	M-form Team	H-form Team
Management Focus	The Idea	First Prototype	Developing Prototype	First 'Charter' Customer	Commercially Viable Product	Develop Commercial Product	Prepare for Full Launch	Major Commercial Launch	Develop Markets	Maximise Revenue
Organisational Structure		Informal Relationships	Formal Responsibilities	Process vs Role Mapping	Formal Organisational Map	Streamlined Organisation	Functional Responsibilities	Functional Structure	Divisional Structure	Matrix Structure
Management Style	Highly Personal	Collaborative-Combative	Collaborative	Focused on Results	Focused on Results	Performance Focus	Firm Focus	Directive	Delegative	Delegative
Control System				Resource Allocation	Cost Management	Performance Management	Market Results	Market Results	Reporting & Profit Centres	Goal Setting & Monitoring
Management Reward Emphasis	Ownership	Shared Ownership	Shares + Early Options	Structured Options	Structured Options	Performance Incentives	Group Bonuses	Personal Bonuses	Profit Sharing + Stock Options	Profit Sharing + Stock Options

Figure 19. Leadership and management priorities change as firms grow: understand where you are in this continuum.

9.5.4 Why culture matters?

There is a general awareness of the importance of culture in scale-up firms, but the precise relationship between culture and the performance of the firm is not always clear. There is widespread agreement that the culture in a firm impacts strongly on the behaviour of members of the firm, but less clarity on the relationship between rewards and behaviour. So why does this matter? Better understanding of the links between culture, behaviours and rewards has the potential to significantly improve the chances of success.

Culture is a three-dimensional construct: the content of *norms*, for example, teamwork and integrity; how forcefully these are held by organisational members, the *intensity*; and how widely members agree about the norms within the organisation, the *consensus*. Strong cultures can boost performance, especially in dynamic environments. Figure 20 shows how to build a culture map for your firm.

Firms can use culture maps to understand what shapes the performance of firms:

- **Stories and myths**, which constitute the 'internal narrative' of the firm.
- **Power structures** in the firm which determine who makes decisions and how these decisions are made.
- **Remuneration and rewards**, the way in which individuals are rewarded for their contribution with financial rewards and overall recognition.
- **Control systems** which are used to manage the firm.
- **Communications** inside and outside the firm can contribute both positively and negatively to the overall culture of the firm.
- **Organisational structure** can determine the formal and informal relationships between employees of the firm and impact the culture strongly.

Culture Web Variable	Scoring ranges: 0-10		
	Relevance Score	Execution Score	Weighted Impact Score (Relevance x Execution)
Stories & Myths	9	6	54
Remuneration & Rewards	7	7	49
Power Structures	5	9	45
Control Systems	7	8	56
Communication	9	9	81
Organisational Structures	7	7	49

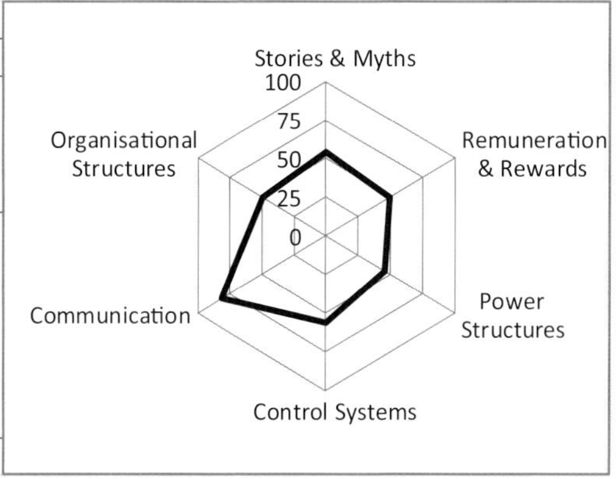

You need to build your culture map as it is now, define what you would like it to be, and then address the gap

Most firms find there is a gap between the rhetoric and the reality, but the culture map is a powerful tool for tackling this

Figure 20. Building a culture map for your firm.

9.6 Funding and Investment

9.6.1 *Understanding funding sources*

The heavy concentration of wealth in private hands, ideological biases against state funding and the preference for corporate investment based on short-term criteria, tends to highlight the importance of private funding: in reality, most funding and investment is driven by a **mix of public and private sources**.

Public and private funding can be provided in different forms, as illustrated in Figure 21:

Grants, where the funds are provided outright, with no financial returns expected, although there may be other targets set, such as generation of intellectual property, the level of technology readiness, or the number of new jobs created as a result of the funding.

Loans, where the funds provided need to be returned at some point; the cost of servicing these loans and the security required can vary, with interest rates for borrowing the money ranging from zero to rates linked to the cost of borrowing in commercial markets.

Payments contingent on the provision of specific products and services, for example, some firms can raise funds by providing specific services linked to their offerings.

Equity funding, where the investment is provided in return for ownership of part of the firm; this ownership can be structured using different financial instruments, usually shares in the firm, with attached conditions spelt out in the term sheet.

Firms can raise funding from a wide range of sources, depending on the constraints and conditions.

Funding Sources	Characteristics
Personal Savings	Personal savings and borrowing by founder or founding team
Friends & Family	Usually small amounts of funding from close friends and family on generous terms; generally for equity or loans on soft terms
Crowd-funding	Funding based on relatively small sums from a large body of individual investors, usually for equity
State Agencies	Funding provided by civic, regional and national institutions and bodies, as grants or loans, less commonly as equity
Angels	Investment from individuals, usual high net-worths, where the angel commonly has knowledge of the market space or is in local eco-system
Seed Funds	Formally constituted investment funds, usually for small, early stage investment, as equity (sometimes as convertible loans)
Incubators	Formally constituted investment and advisory companies, who provide funding for equity stakes, usually at early stages of growth
Accelerators	Formally constituted investment and advisory companies, who provide funding for equity stakes, usually when firm has been established
Venture Capital	Formally constituted and regulated investment vehicle with money from Venture Partners, managed by professional investment managers; usually equity, sometimes convertible loans
Private Equity	Funds with more fire-power than Venture Capital, usually with greater financial structuring expertise; usually invest for equity, but may also combine with debt finance for larger amounts required for rapid expansion
Public Markets	Public markets open to firms once they have listed on appropriate stock exchange, enabling their equity to be bought and sold under well-defined rules; investors can be individuals, organisations or firms who trade in listed stocks and shares
Corporates	Larger firms, who may want access to new products & services, new markets or financial returns on their investment , usually invest for equity but may pay for joint development of new things
Banks	Typically lending institutions, who provide structured loan funding against 'secured' assets; may sometimes make investments for equity
Customers	Customers who use and pay for the firm's products and services, thereby providing funding to run and grow the firm; usually the cheapest from of finance

Figure 21.   Sources of funding. Adapted from *Camels, Tigers & Unicorns* [1].

9.6.2 *Deciding on the most appropriate form of funding*

Funding choices depend on **how far** you have travelled along the commercialisation journey, as shown in Figure 22. The most appropriate forms of funding depend on understanding this and the resulting trade-offs between risk and reward. Firms need to understand the inherent characteristics of different types of funding and *separate the rhetoric from the reality*.

Personal savings and support from families and friends of entrepreneurs need little explanation. Crowd funding refers to a large group of investors, the *crowd*, each providing relatively small amounts of money, usually as equity funding. State agencies, at local, national and international levels, play a significant role in funding, usually in the form of grants and loans, and sometimes equity. State funding can be critical for propositions which require the creation of new infrastructure. Angels are typically high net-worth individuals who provide equity funding and commercial expertise to firms. Seed funds operate in the same space and often consist of a group of angels, constituted as an investment vehicle. Incubators and Accelerators are 'intervention' agencies who provide a range of services to early-stage firms, usually investment of money and resources in return for equity. Venture capital (VC) and private equity consists of formally constituted and structured investment vehicles, run by professional managers who handle equity investment of funds provided by wealthy individuals, firms and other organisations; Public markets are usually only used by firms to raise expansion capital, where they typically sell a part of the firm to public investors to generate cash to fund growth plans. Banks, of course, are familiar as sources of loan finance. Customer funding, where 'early' customers support the development of new products and services, is a critical source of funding that is often overlooked.

Typically, VC funds look to invest in firms where small investments can generate huge returns, in the process usually avoiding market spaces with high capital needs. What this means in practice is that despite the popular rhetoric, most firms are unlikely to attract VC investment to fund their growth.

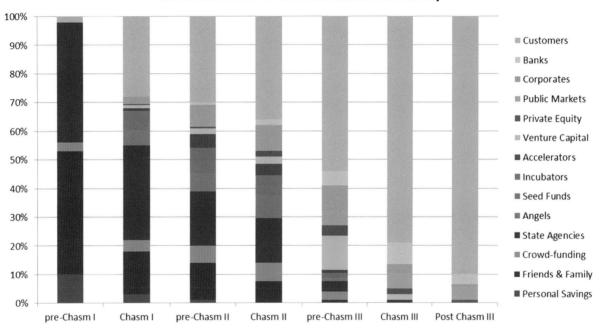

Figure 22.   How funding sources change with maturity. Adapted from *Camels, Tigers & Unicorns* [1].

9.6.3 *Customer revenues as the funding source*

Customer revenues represent the cheapest form of funding for a firm because the firm does not have to give up equity in return for the money. There are also no borrowing costs associated with the funding, as there would be if loans were involved. Customer funding can play a critical role in the funding of early stage technology firms.

Bootstrapping can be used to fund start-ups, where an entrepreneur starts a firm with little or no capital but uses operating revenues to fund growth. Post start-up, customer funding can also provide dialogues with customers which can help shape new products and services. Firms can raise customer revenues in several ways, as shown in Figure 23:

- **Pay-in-advance models**, based, for example, on giving the 'charter customer' early or privileged access to new or enhanced functionality.
- **License revenues** can be a significant source of customer revenues, where the firm can charge upfront, as a commitment or enabling fee, for a percentage of the total license fee payable for products and services.
- **Matchmaker models**, based on payments made to facilitate dialogues or interactions between the charter customer, partners, suppliers and customers.
- **Subscription models:** Most customers are comfortable with paying monthly or annual subscriptions in advance for services yet to be rendered, or to build out infrastructure or capability, in order to provide the service.
- **Upfront subscription revenues** typically include access fees, payment for provision of different types of functionality, or the delivery of content or related services.
- **Scarcity models** include upfront payments to secure access to scarce resources or discounted access.
- **Sponsorship** can be used by firms as a way of generating early revenues, which can help with the costs of developing new products and services; this type of funding can also be used to support marketing costs.

Component	NRE	Licenses		Royalties	Leasing	Outright Sale		Commission	Matchmaker	Transactions	Subscriptions		Proxies	
		Perpetual	Time-bound			Core	Consumables				Time-metered	Value-metered	Advertising	Sponsorship
Services									√	√	√	√	√	√
Products	√			√		√	√	√		√				
Meta-Content				√		√							√	√
Content				√		√		√			√	√	√	√
Apps, Tools & Processes	√	√	√	√							√	√	√	√
Technology Platforms	√	√	√		√	√					√	√		√
Application Technologies	√	√	√	√										
Base Technologies	√	√	√	√		√								

Figure 23. How firms can use funding from customers.

9.6.4 *Equity funding & company valuation*

The valuation of a firm can be critical when it comes raising equity funding.

The *valuation* of a firm plays a critical role in equity-based funding: a higher valuation means the firm needs to give up a smaller percentage of the firm's equity in return for an investment. This can have a significant bearing on the management and control of the firm and the value accruing to the other shareholders on 'exit' when the firm lists on the public markets or is acquired by another firm.

But the valuation of early-stage firms is far from an exact science.

When firms list on public markets, there are criteria based on experience which can be used to value firms on the basis of revenues, profits and market-specific growth metrics. For earlier stage companies which may have little or no revenues, or where the growth trajectory is still subject to uncertainty, valuation of the firm can be a challenge.

For these firms, valuation, like beauty, can be in the 'eyes of the beholder', with the valuation based on whether the person doing the valuation is buying or selling!

Some of the approaches used include sophisticated financial models based on the idea of net present value (NPV) and discounted cash flows. Ultimately, any valuation can be reduced to an aggregation of many different components, and the relative importance of these different components can vary with the maturity of the firm.

> **You can use a simple framework to create a defensible valuation for a firm, as shown in Figure 24.**

Main Contribution to Valuation	Stage of Maturity			
	Pre-Chasm I	Pre-Chasm II	Pre-Chasm III	Post-Chasm III
The value of underlying intellectual property				
Technology	■	■	■	
Process		■	■	
Brand			■	■
The overall packaging and positioning of this IP in the market space			■	■
Product or Service Mix				
Portfolio				■
Differentiation			■	■
The underlying business model and its resilience			■	■
General Metrics				
Size of Market			■	■
Market Structure				■
Market Share				■
Quality of Management Team				
Leadership		■	■	■
Core Competences	■	■	■	■
Usual Metrics of financial performance (revenues, profitability)				
Revenues			■	■
Profit (EBIT, EBITDA etc)				■
Perceptions of future prospects	■	■	■	■

Figure 24. Typical sources of value underpinning firm valuations. Adapted from *Camels, Tigers & Unicorns* [1].

Chapter 10

Intervention Shaping: *Composite* Vectors

The external vectors enable us to characterise the external environment which can shape the features of a product. The internal vectors describe the variables we can shape when designing and building a product. Launching any new product involves making judgements on the trade-offs between external and internal vectors: the composite vectors describe these trade-offs. Figure 1 provides an overview of the composite vectors.

Commercialisation Strategy:

The commercialisation strategy vector articulates the qualitative trade-offs any firm makes between the external vectors describing the external environment and the internal vectors which define the specific interventions designed and executed by the firm.

Firms can, and often do, make different judgements on the priorities, based on the views of management. This strategic diversity can be the source of competitive advantage.

Business Model(s):

Business models reflect the quantitative calculations arising from the qualitative strategic judgements. Firms may typically experiment with several business models before selecting a model to implement. The research we conducted for *Camels, Tigers & Unicorns* [1] also revealed that different business models typically undergo multiple iterations until a firm finds the right formula. It is not un-common for firms to take 5–6 iterations before they find a model that works, a situation unfortunately lost on some private equity and venture capital funds.

```
┌─────────────────────────────────────────────────────────────────────┐
│ Commercialisation Strategy                                            │
│                                                                       │
│ Qualitative Approach based on Strategic Mapping Tool                  │
│ Quantitative approach based on Relevance & Execution Scores           │
└─────────────────────────────────────────────────────────────────────┘

┌─────────────────────────────────────────────────────────────────────┐
│ Business Model                                                        │
│                                                                       │
│ Qualitative Approach based on defining business model architecture and│
│ components                                                            │
│ Quantitative approach based on building detailed spreadsheet model    │
│ covering revenues, costs, funding and cash flow                       │
└─────────────────────────────────────────────────────────────────────┘
```

Figure 1.   Overview of the composite vectors.

10.1 Commercialisation Strategy

10.1.1 *Approaches to strategy formulation*

There are many approaches and tools for tackling strategy formulation, development, and testing — the usefulness of these tools depends on their practical relevance, granularity, and accuracy. The value of any approach depends on how the challenge is framed, and whether it provides insights at a broad industry level or at the level of an individual firm.

There are seven broad approaches to framing strategy, as shown in Figure 2:

- Provision of general insights at an industry level
- Firm-level insights
- Positioning-based 'external' approaches drawing on the work of *Porter* [4] and others
- Competence-based models drawing on the resources of the firm, the most well-known being *Prahalad and Hamel's work* on core competences [11]
- Organisational models, in particular *Teece's work* [12] on dynamic capabilities
- Game theory-based approaches
- Integrated dynamic approaches, for example, *Burgelman's work* [13], *Johnson's approach* [14] based on the economics of strategic diversity, and the vector-based approach described in *Camels, Tigers & Unicorns* [1].

Our dynamic approach to **Commercialisation Strategy** addresses the main problems with existing approaches: it allows the relative importance of external and internal vectors to be handled in an integrated way, it provides the level of granularity and detail to develop firm-level commercialisation strategy; it enables the approach to be applied consistently to the firm at different points on its commercialisation journey; and it can be used to model and assess the impact of significant market, technology and operational innovations, even for mature firms.

Strategic Approaches	Strategic Imperatives			
	Influences	Attributes	Processes	Drivers
Industry Insight Models	PESTEL	Strategy Chessboard (Kearney)	Consolidation Endgame Curve	Gartner Hype Cycle
	3C's			
Firm-specific Insight Models		SWOT		
		ANSOFF Matrix		
		BCG Matrix		
		GE-McKinsey Matrix		
Positioning-based Models		Generic Strategies (Porter)		The 5 Forces + Firm-centric value chains (Porter)
		Technology-based Disruption (Christensen)		
		Stars Framework		
		Blue Ocean Strategy		
Competence-based Models		Innovative Landscape Map	Experience Curve (Henderson)	Core Competences (Prahalad & Hamel)
		Gartner Magic Quadrant		
Organisational Models		New Power Model (HBR)	Dynamic Capabilities (Teece et al)	
Game-theory based Approaches		Gaming Approaches (Nalebuff & Dixit)	Options Theory	
Integrated Dynamic Approaches		Strategy Dynamics (Burgelman & Grove)		Economics of Strategic Diversity (Johnson)
				Commercialisation Strategy (Phadke et al)

Figure 2. Comparing different approaches to strategy — Commercialisation strategy approach in context. Adapted from *Camels, Tigers & Unicorns* [1].

10.1.2 *Applying the vector-based approach to strategy development*

Figure 3 summarises the vectors used to define commercialisation strategy. Figure 4 shows how to apply the approach to commercialisation strategy.

Type of Vector	Vector
External	Market Spaces
	Proposition Framing & Competitive Environment
	Customer Definition
	Distribution, Marketing & Sales
Internal	IP Management
	Manufacturing & Assembly
	Product & Service Definition & Synthesis
	Technology Development & Deployment
	Talent, Leadership & Culture
	Funding & Investment
Composite	Commercialisation Strategy
	Business Models

Figure 3.   Summary of the vectors used to define commercialisation strategy.

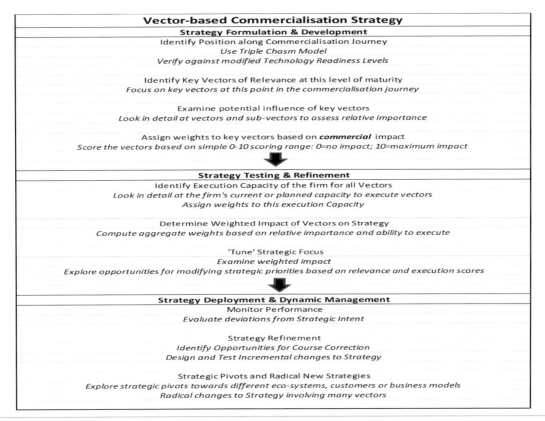

Vector-based Commercialisation Strategy

Strategy Formulation & Development

Identify Position along Commercialisation Journey
Use Triple Chasm Model
Verify against modified Technology Readiness Levels

Identify Key Vectors of Relevance at this level of maturity
Focus on key vectors at this point in the commercialisation journey

Examine potential influence of key vectors
Look in detail at vectors and sub-vectors to assess relative importance

Assign weights to key vectors based on ***commercial*** impact
Score the vectors based on simple 0-10 scoring range: 0=no impact; 10=maximum impact

Strategy Testing & Refinement

Identify Execution Capacity of the firm for all Vectors
Look in detail at the firm's current or planned capacity to execute vectors
Assign weights to this execution Capacity

Determine Weighted Impact of Vectors on Strategy
Compute aggregate weights based on relative importance and ability to execute

'Tune' Strategic Focus
Examine weighted impact
Explore opportunities for modifying strategic priorities based on relevance and execution scores

Strategy Deployment & Dynamic Management

Monitor Performance
Evaluate deviations from Strategic Intent

Strategy Refinement
Identify Opportunities for Course Correction
Design and Test Incremental changes to Strategy

Strategic Pivots and Radical New Strategies
Explore strategic pivots towards different eco-systems, customers or business models
Radical changes to Strategy involving many vectors

The vector-based approach to strategy depends on a three-step process, which allows firms to articulate their key priorities and assess trade-offs

Figure 4. How to apply the commercialisation strategy approach. Adapted from *Camels, Tigers & Unicorns* [1].

10.1.3 *Changing strategic priorities as you grow*

Most approaches to strategy development tend to focus on larger, more mature, firms: the bigger challenge of the strategic priorities of firms as they grow gets less attention.

Strategic clarity is just as important, if not critical, at the earlier stages of growth, especially given the shortage of resources typically affecting these firms early in their lives. The vector-based dynamic model enables firms to understand changes in strategic priorities along the commercialisation journey, as they cross Chasms I, II and III, as illustrated in Figure 5.

There are three different scenarios where this can be critical:

- Firms operating in relatively stable environments, where the approach can support small **incremental changes** in the different vectors to 'fine-tune' performance.

- Significant changes in market spaces, where the overall shape of the market space is dramatically altered by changes in technology or regulation, for example. This may result in the need to target different customers and use new distribution channels, which requires a major **strategic 'pivot'**, affecting several vectors including technology, product synthesis and business models.

- **Disruption** in technology, business models and distribution channels can significantly impact many vectors driving overall commercialisation strategy. This kind of radical transformation does not happen often, but requires a broader strategic response based on understanding the new sources of competition and new product opportunities.

> The dynamic vector approach enables ongoing tuning of commercial strategy: your strategy needs to reflect your level of maturity.

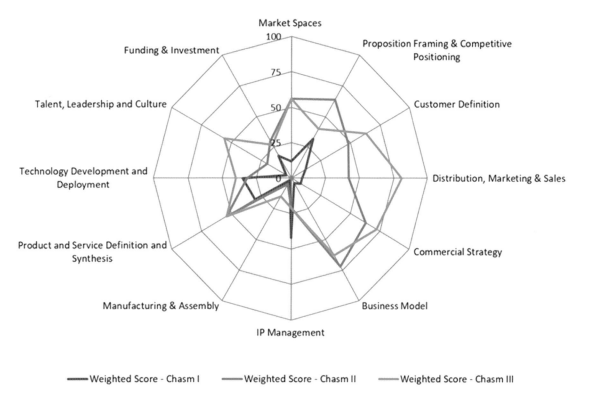

Market Spaces

Funding & Investment

Proposition Framing & Competitive Positioning

Talent, Leadership and Culture

Customer Definition

Technology Development and Deployment

Distribution, Marketing & Sales

Product and Service Definition and Synthesis

Commercial Strategy

Manufacturing & Assembly

Business Model

IP Management

—— Weighted Score - Chasm I   —— Weighted Score - Chasm II   —— Weighted Score - Chasm III

Figure 5. Example showing changes in strategic priorities across the three chasms.

10.2 Business Models

10.2.1 *Defining business models*

At the most basic level, a business model can be defined as **'how the firm plans to make money'**.

A better description of a business model is that proposed by *Teece* [12] who wrote that **'a business model articulates the logic and provides data and other evidence that demonstrates how a business creates and delivers value to customers**. It also **outlines the architecture of revenues, costs and profits associated with the business enterprise'**.

Many firms equate business models with spreadsheets which make explicit the assumptions and components for a firm and compute the relationships between these variables. Spreadsheets, however, are only part of business models and provide the basis for making explicit and testing the key elements of a business plan: the customer value proposition, the profit formula, key resources, and key processes.

The key objective of a business model is to link the 'narrative' for a firm to the actual numbers for the different components of the model. We treat the business model as a unique vector consisting of the following components, as shown in Figure 6:

- The Narrative and Assumptions
- Revenues, Costs, Margins & Cash Flow
- Revenue and Cost Allocation Logic
- Intellectual Property and other assets, such as Property and Licenses
- Funding (including investment)
- Scenarios and Sensitivity Analysis.

You need to explicitly address all these business model components.

Business Model Vector Deconstructed	
Overall Narrative	Target Marketspace
	Target Customers
	Proposition
Assumptions	Narrative-based drivers, logic
	Customer Numbers
	Pricing
Revenues	Primary
	Secondary eg Advertising
	Distribution-Adjusted
Costs	Technologies, Materials
	People
	Third Parties eg premises, legal, acct services
Revenue & Cost Allocation Logic	Parametric Dependencies
	Time-based variation
Margins	Product and Service basis
	Time Basis
Cash Flow	Leading and Lagging Criteria
	Time-based variation
Intellectual Property	Registered Rights
	Un-Registered Rights
	'Open' Rights
Other Assets	'Hard' Assets
	'Soft' Assets
Funding	Customer Revenues
	Debt
	Equity
	Gap Analysis
Scenarios	Alternative Narratives
	Scenario Generation
	Modelling
Sensitivity Analysis	Base Case
	Pessimistic scenarios
	Optimistic scenarios

Figure 6. Business model components. Adapted from *Camels, Tigers & Unicorns* [1].

10.2.2 *Potential revenue sources*

Business model narratives are shaped strongly by the way in which revenues are generated. There is a wide range of ways in which firms can generate revenues, as shown in Figure 7:

- **Non-recurring engineering (NRE)** revenues which enable a customer to develop and deploy the product or service they are buying.
- **Royalties** are payments made for the use of a component, either standalone or integrated with other components, typically on the basis of the volume of usage.
- **Leasing** follows the usual rules, where the customer is allowed to lease and use a product for a fixed period of time, during which ownership remains with the supplier.
- **Outright sale** of a technology, content or product follows the usual rules for the sale and transfer of ownership; where products require consumables to function, there are opportunities for different business models.

- **Transaction revenues** have become more relevant as payment technologies enable smaller transactions to be carried out effectively —for example, charging for after-sales support.
- **Matchmaker revenues** apply where services are provided which typically involve connecting buyers and sellers; these can be charged as fixed fees or as a percentage of the revenues resulting from the matchmaking activity.
- **Subscription revenues** have become very important over the last decade, 'metered' by either value or time. Development of digital technologies and infrastructures has dramatically increased the scope for this.
- **Proxy methods** of revenue generation, where advertisers or sponsors effectively subsidise the consumption of products and services, have grown dramatically over the last decade.

> Developing sustainable business models for new products and services is difficult: firms may go through 5–6 *iterations* before they establish a sustainable business model.

Component	NRE	Licenses		Royalties	Leasing	Outright Sale		Commission	Matchmaker	Transactions	Subscriptions		Proxies	
		Perpetual	Time-bound			Core	Consumables				Time-metered	Value-metered	Advertising	Sponsorship
Services									√	√	√	√	√	√
Products	√				√	√	√	√		√				
Meta-Content				√		√							√	√
Content				√		√		√			√	√	√	√
Apps, Tools & Processes	√	√	√	√							√	√		√
Technology Platforms	√	√	√		√	√					√	√		√
Application Technologies	√	√	√	√										
Base Technologies	√	√	√	√		√								

Example: focus based on subscription-based revenues for the provision of content and application tools

Figure 7. Potential revenue sources — Defining your focus.

10.2.3 *Typical financial metrics*

Business model components can provide a comprehensive basis for defining the key metrics which firms need to track on a regular basis. All firms need to focus on the same key metrics:

- **Sales revenue** which is defined as the income from customer purchases of products and services. Typically, sales data may be correlated to advertising campaigns, price changes, seasonal forces, competitive actions and other costs of sales.
- **Overhead costs** are fixed costs that are not dependent on the level of products or services produced by the firm, such as salaries or rents being paid per month.
- **Variable costs** are expenses that change in proportion to the activity of a firm. Fixed costs and variable costs make up the two components of the total cost. These include the 'cost of goods sold' and other items that increase with each sale.
- **Customer loyalty** is about attracting the right customer, getting them to buy, buy often, buy in higher quantities and bring in even more customers. There are three ways of measuring this: customer surveys, direct feedback at purchase and purchase analysis.
- **Cost of customer acquisition** is a measure of the total cost associated with acquiring a new customer, including all aspects of marketing and sales. Customer acquisition cost is calculated by dividing total acquisition expenses by total new customers over a given period.
- **Gross margin** calculated as total sales revenue minus the cost of goods sold, divided by the total sales revenue, expressed as a percentage. Tracking margins is critical for growing companies, since increased volumes should improve efficiency.
- **Profit** is not simply the difference between the costs of the product or service and the price being charged for it. The calculation must include the fixed and variable costs of operation, including such rent or mortgage payments, utilities, insurance and taxes.
- **Cash flow**, which tracks the actual cash in the firm on a regular basis; as we have observed earlier, this can differ from the profit or loss figure and impact the amount of capital required in a firm.

All firms need to ensure that they monitor these key metrics regularly, but the advent of new **service-based business models** has driven the need for firms to focus on some new metrics more relevant to managing the delivery of continuous services.

Additional Metrics for Subscription-based Services	
Committed Monthly Recurring Revenue (CMRR)	CMRR is the combined value of the recurring subscription revenue on a monthly basis plus signed contracts currently committed and going into 'production', minus any 'churn'. the recurring subscription revenue on a monthly basis plus signed contracts currently committed and going into 'production', minus any 'churn'.
CMRR Pipeline (CPipe)	CMRR Pipeline (CPipe) is the sales pipeline for future subscription revenues not yet confirmed.
Churn	Churn is typically measured as the % of customers who cancel their subscriptions; customers who renew subscriptions at the end of the committed period determine the renewal rate.
Customer Acquisition Cost (CAC)	subscriptions; customers who renew subscriptions at the end of the committed period determine the renewal rate.
Customer Life Time Value (CLTV)	CLTV is the net present value of the recurring profit streams of a specific customer less the acquisition cost.

Chapter 11

The Commercialisation Monitor

11.1 Building an Integrated View

The commercialisation monitor provides a structured way of describing the current status of a single product concept, proposition or firm, based on analysing maturity along the commercialisation journey and detailed assessment of the meso-economic vectors. The idea behind the commercialisation monitor is to provide a snapshot view of the situation at a particular point in time.

The monitor summarises the following components:

- The vision driving the commercialisation journey is shown in the **top left corner of the monitor**, as a textual description.
- The maturity of the proposition or firm is shown in the **top right corner**, based on the mTRl/CRL level and position relative to the three chasms, as discussed **in Section 4.2**. This position can be confirmed using values of C/C-max as discussed in **Section 8.3**.
- The external vectors are defined on the **right-hand side** of the monitor:
  - the market space and market space-centric value chain are based on the approach described in **Section 8.1**, including an estimate of T-max.
  - proposition framing is summarised based on the approach described in **Section 8.2**.
  - customer definition and estimation of C-max is based on the application of **Section 8.3**.
  - distribution marketing & sales is summarised using the m7Ps approach covered in **Section 8.4**.

- The internal vectors are defined on the **left-hand side** of the monitor:
  - technology, where applicable, is characterised using the approach in **Section 9.1**.
  - intellectual property is summarised using the approach described in **Section 9.2**.
  - the approach to product and service synthesis is based on the options described in **Section 9.3**.
  - manufacturing and deployment are summarised based on the approach defined in **Section 9.4**.
  - the funding and investment parameters are defined based on the treatment in **Section 9.5**.
  - talent, leadership and culture is outlined using the approaches defined in **Section 9.6**.
- The **centre of the monitor** shows the status of the two composite vectors:
  - The polar plot of the relative importance of the vectors summarises the commercialisation strategy, as discussed in **Section 10.1**.
  - The variables underneath this plot summarise the status of the key elements of the business model, as discussed in **Section 10.2**.

Figures 1 and 2 show two commercialisation monitors: a blank monitor and an example of a completed monitor.

THE COMMERCIALISATION MONITOR

The Vision		Chasm Locator				I			II			III

mTRL CRL	0	1	2	3	4	5	6	7	8	9

Contingent Technology Deployment

Base Tech	App. Tech	Platform	Apps & Tools	Product	Service

Intellectual Property Management

Def.Key Comp.	Def. Prior.	Protect. in Place

Product & Service Synthesis

User-centred	Tech-driven	Imped. Matchin	Creat. Synth.	9-layer model	Service Wrap.

Manufacturing, Assembly & Deployment

Def. Chall.	Integ. Deploy.	Innov. Req

Funding & Investment

Pref.	Fund.Quant.	Valuation

Talent, Leadership & Culture

Over. Prior.	Talent	Team	Org struct.	Leadership	Culture

Commercialisation Strategy

Current Vector Strength

Defined Strategic Goal?

Strategic Gap Clarity?

Business Model

Defined Narrative

Explicit Architecture

Components Defined

Business Model Metrics

Revenues & Costs

Cash Flow Projections

Market Space

	Value Chain

Local	Nationa	Global	T-max		Mths

Proposition Framing

Propos. Defn.	Comp.	Reg.	Diff.	Partners & Suppliers

Source of Differentiation

Single Component   Overall Chain   Re-framing Chain

Customer Definition

Business	Govt.	Consumer	Knowledge Workers

Max Accessible No of Customers   **Cmax**

Distribution Marketing & Sales

Defined Go to Market Priorities

Defined Channel Strategy   Overall m7Ps

Product	Pos.	Pricing	Place	Prom.	Pro	Partn.

Figure 1. Blank commercialisation monitor.

THE COMMERCIALISATION MONITOR　　　　　　　　　　　　　　　　　　　　　　　　　　　　　　　　　**ME 1**

The Vision	Provision of image-based content and services to SME's and digital media entrepreneurs based on a new low cost business model

Chasm Locator					I			II			III
mTRL CRL	0	1	2	3	4	5	6	7	8	9	

Technology Dev & Contingent Deployment

Base Tech	App. Tech	Platform	Apps & Tools	Product	Service
		√			

Intellectual Property Management

Def.Key Comp.	Def. Prior.	Protect. in Place
√	√	

Product & Service Synthesis

User-centred	Tech-driven	Imped. Matchin	Creat. Synth.	9-layer model	Service Wrap.
			√		

Manufacturing & Deployment

Def. Chall.	Integ. Deploy.	Innov. Req

Funding & Investment

Pref.	Fund.Quant.	Valuation
Private	£3m	£10m

Talent, Leadership & Culture

Over. Prior.	Talent	Team	Org struct.	Leadership	Culture
√	√				

Commercialisation Strategy

Current Vector Strength

(radar/spider chart with axes: Market Space, Proposition Framing & Competitive Positioning, Customer Definition, Distribution, Marketing & Sales, Business Model, Commercialisation Strategy, IP Management, Manufacturing & Deployment, Product and Service Definition and Synthesis, Technology Development and Contingent Deployment, Talent, Leadership and Culture, Funding & Investment — Weighted score)

Defined Strategic Goal?	√
Strategic Gap Clarity?	

Business Model

Defined Narrative	√
Explicit Architecture	
Components Defined	√
Business Model Metrics	
Revenues & Costs	
Cash Flow Projections	

Market Space

Media & Entertainment	Value Chain	√

Local	National	Global		
	√		T-max	60 Mths

Proposition Framing

Propos. Defn.	Comp.	Reg.	Diff.	Partners & Suppliers
√	√	√	√	

Source of Differentiation

Single Component	Overall Chain	Re-framing Chair
	√	

Customer Definition

Business	Govt.	Consumer	Knowledge Workers
√			√

Max Accessible No of Customers	Cmax	1 milion SMEs

Distribution Marketing & Sales

Defined Go to Market Priorities	√
Defined Channel Strategy		Overall m7Ps

Product	Pos.	Pricing	Place	Prom.	Proc.	Partn.
√						

Figure 2. Example of completed commercialisation monitor.

Chapter 12

Tackling Multi-Product Firms

Tackling multi-product firms is based on the following approach:

- Apply the single-product firm approach to **each product** in the firm's portfolio.
- Each of these products is likely to exhibit different levels of maturity.
- Aggregate the impact of the different products in order to build an integrated picture of the overall impact on the firm.
- This aggregated impact needs to cover the different external, internal and composite vectors.
- Firms need to understand the impact of integrating the products on the overall strategic direction and execution capacity of the firm.
- We group these impacts into two broad variables:
  ○ The overall **strategic impact**, based on aggregating all the vectors.
  ○ The **financial impact**, using the usual financial measures for the performance of a firm.

There are broadly three types of multi-product firms, as shown in Figure 1:

- Firms with multiple products targeted at the *same customers in the same market space*.
- Firms where multiple products are targeted at the *same market space but at different customer groups*.
- Firms where multiple products are targeted at *different customers and different market spaces*.

Firms need to understand the differences between them when applying the vector-based approach to firm profiling.

	Vectors	Sub-Vectors	Single-Product Firms	Multiple-Product Firms		
				Same Customers & Same Market Space	Same Market but Different customers	Different Markets and Different Customers
Overall Commercial Summary						
		Commercialisation Monitor for each Product	√	√	√	√
		Maturity Assessment for each Product	√	√	√	√
		Product Portfolio Map	X	√	√	√
External Vectors	**Market Spaces**					
		Define Single Market Space	√	√	√	
		Define Multiple Market Spaces				√
	Proposition Framing, Competition & Regulation					
		Frame Single Proposition	√			
		Frame Multiple Propositions	√	√	√	√
	Customer Definition					
		Define Single Customer	√	√		
		Define Multiple Customers	√		√	√
		Size Aggregate Market	√	√	√	√
	Distribution, Marketing & Sales					
		Define m7Ps for single product	√			
		Define m7Ps for mutiple products		√	√	√
		Build Aggregate View of m7Ps		√	√	√
Composite Vectors	**Commercialisation Strategy**					
		Single Strategy	√			
		Multiple Strategies			?	?
		Integrated Strategy		√	?	?
	Business Model Development					
		Single Business Model	√	?	?	
		Multiple Business Models		?	?	√
Internal Vectors	**Technology Development & Contingent Deployment**					
		Single Approach to Deployment	√			
		Multiple Deployment Approaches		√	√	√
	IP Management					
		Narrow focus on IP Management				
		Integrated Approach to IP Management	√	√	√	√
	Product & Service Definition and Synthesis					
		Single Product Focus	√			
		Multiple Product Focus		√	√	√
		Family of Products Approach		√	√	√
	Manufacturing & Deployment					
		Single Product Focus	√			
		Integrated Approach		√	√	√
		Multiple Approaches			?	?
	Talent, Leadership & Culture					
		Firm Level Approach	√	√	√	√
	Funding & Investment					
		Firm Level Approach	√	√	√	√

Figure 1. Applying the vector-based approach to multi-product firms.

12.1 Aggregating Product Families

Firms with multiple products targeted at the same customers in the same market space:

The vectors and the commercialisation trajectory for each product are treated just as they would for a single-product firm. The maturity of the firm should reflect the aggregate maturity of the individual products. Firms can be rejuvenated by the launch of new products as older products become more mature. The products may be delivered using different business models. Distribution, marketing and sales tactics may need to be different for each product. Firms exhibiting this behaviour can be found across all market spaces: consumer electronics firms provide a very good example, where firms can develop and sell a range of electronic hardware and software products and services, often providing different functionalities under a single brand, to the same group of consumers. Figure 2 illustrates aggregated monitors for three such products.

Firms where multiple products are targeted at the same market space but at different customer groups:

Multi-product firms which target *different types of customers*, but still within the *same market space*, need to address all the factors described already, which relate to multiple products aimed at the same customers. For example, medical firms may provide products and services to consumers, patients and clinicians, all very different types of customers, but all in the same healthcare market space. These multi-product firms need to understand the different customers for the different products,

the synergies between them and the implications for the addressable market. Dealing with different customers in the same market space often requires a clear understanding of the relative positioning of the different products and services across the value chain and how they can impact different business models. These firms also need to deal with the challenges of organisational structure, management and leadership resulting from the broader focus: this may require significant attention to how the firm is structured to address the market opportunity effectively. It also means that remuneration incentives need to reflect the overall commercial objectives.

Firms where multiple products are targeted at different customers and different market spaces:

These firms need to address all the challenges discussed above but also need to understand the different market spaces in which they operate and the relevant value chains in these market spaces. As opposed to a single-product firm which is typically dealing with a single-value chain, these firms need to master different market spaces, which in turn may influence business models and go-to-market strategies. The organisational, management and leadership challenges in these firms can be quite daunting because the cultures of the different market spaces may require very different ways of managing talent, teams and motivation. Firms may need to address the trade-offs between 'unified' and 'distributed' organisational structures which reflect the reliability, pace and agility needed in different market spaces.

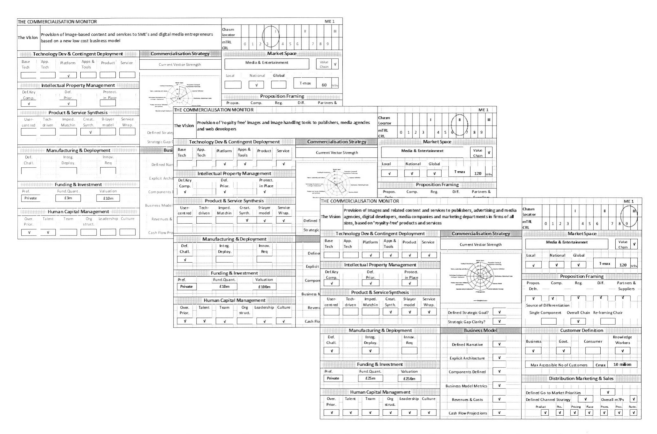

Figure 2. Aggregated commercialisation monitors for three different products provided by the same firm.

12.2 Product Portfolio Mapping

Product portfolio mapping is based on mapping the commercial impact vs the financial impact, based on normalised values. Figure 3 illustrates the strategic and financial impact variables typically used for portfolio analysis.

The **strategic impact** is based on the following approach:

- Assign a relative weighting at the firm level, for each of the 20 **impact variables** defined here, grouped in line with the main vectors.
- These impact variables have been chosen to reflect the research insights discussed previously in *Camels, Tigers & Unicorns* [1].
- As a starting point, the relevance of these vectors is normally set at the same level, which means that all these impact variables matter equally for all products for the firm; in some cases, firms may choose to bias the impact of some of these impact variables, relative to others, for the firm as a whole.
- Estimate the performance of each impact variable for a specific product.
- Compute the weighted relevance of each variable for a chosen product.
- Aggregate these values to compute the single value which describes the commercial impact of this product on the firm.
- Normalise the commercial impact score based on the total potential scores, so that the impact of different products can be compared.

The **Financial Impact** is based on a similar approach, with the following key differences:

- The five recommended financial impact variables for each product are defined as follows:
  - Revenue potential
  - Margin, usually based on earnings before interest and tax (EBIT)
  - Investment required to create the product
  - Time to payback for the product
  - Ease of access to investment.
- As for the strategic impact variables, the relevance of each financial impact variable is usually set at the same level.
- However, based on the firm's priorities, these weightings may be altered; some firms may decide that revenue potential is much more important than the margin, or some firms may favour products which need lower investment, or some firms may add other variables.
- The effective performance, weighted performance, aggregate impact and normalisation are treated in the same way as for strategic impact assessment. Figures 4 and 5 show an example calculation for a typical product portfolio.

Vectors	Strategic Impact Variables
Market Spaces	Market Potential (low to high)
	Entry Barriers (high to low)
	Characteristic Time, Tmax (long to short)
Proposition Framing, Competition & Regulation	Value Chain Impact (narrow to broad)
	Competitive Intensity (High to Low)
	Regulatory Constraints (High to Low)
Customer Definition	Max. No. Customers, Cmax (low to high)
	Total Market Size (low to high)
Distribution, Marketing & Sales	Distribution Network Maturity (low to high)
	Cost of Marketing & Sales (high to low)
	Channel Complexity (High to Low)
Commercialisation Strategy	Strategic Clarity (low to high)
Business Model Development	Bus Model Innov. Reqd (High to low)
	Business Model Complexity (High to Low)
Intelllectual Property Management	IP Strength (low to high)
Manufacturing & Deployment	Manufacturing Complexity (High to Low)
	Supply Chain Complexity (High to Low)
Product Synthesis & Definition	Product Complexity (High to Low)
Technology Development & Deployment	Tech Deploy. Complexity (High to Low)
Talent, Leadership & Culture	Access to Core Comp. (low to high)
	Financial Impact Variables
Funding & Investment	Revenue Potential (low to high)
	Margin, EBIT (low to high)
	Investment Required (high to low)
	Time to Payback (long vs short)
	Access to Investment (low to high)

Figure 3. Mapping strategic and financial impact against vectors for portfolio analysis.

Product Portfolio Analysis

	Scoring Logic (0-10)	Relevance Weighting	Product 1		Product 2		Product 3		Product 4		Product 5	
			Estimated Perf.	Weighted Perf.	Estimated Perf.	Weighted Perf.	Estimated Perf.	Weighted Perf.	Estimated Perf.	Weighted Perf.	Estimated Perf.	Weighted Perf.
Strategic Impact												
Market Spaces	Market Potential (low to high)	1	5	5	8	8	8	8	8	8	8	8
	Entry Barriers (high to low)	1	2	2	5	5	5	5	5	5	5	7
	Characteristic Time, Tmax (long to short)	1	7	7	5	5	5	5	5	5	5	7
Proposition Framing, Competition & Regulation	Value Chain Impact (narrow to broad)	1	3	3	7	7	7	7	7	7	7	7
	Competitive Intensity (High to Low)	1	2	2	8	8	8	2	8	8	8	8
	Regulatory Constraints (High to Low)	1	7	7	7	7	7	2	7	7	7	7
Customer Definition	Max. No. Customers, Cmax (low to high)	1	5	5	7	7	7	7	7	7	7	7
	Total Market Size (low to high)	1	6	6	7	7	7	7	7	7	7	7
Distribution, Marketing & Sales	Distribution Network Maturity (low to hi)	1	8	8	8	8	8	8	8	8	8	8
	Cost of Marketing & Sales (high to low)	1	3	3	7	7	7	7	7	7	7	7
	Channel Complexity (High to Low)	1	2	2	2	2	2	2	2	2	2	6
Commercialisation Strategy	Strategic Clarity (low to high)	1	5	5	8	8	8	8	8	8	8	8
Business Model Development	Bus Model Innov. Reqd (High to low)	1	6	6	6	6	6	6	6	3	6	6
	Business Model Complexity (High to Low)	1	3	3	7	7	7	7	9	9	7	7
IP Management	IP Strength (low to high)	1	3	3	6	6	8	8	6	6	6	6
Manufacturing & Deployment	Manufacturing Complexity (High to Low)	1	7	7	7	7	7	7	7	7	7	7
	Supply Chain Complexity (High to Low)	1	3	3	6	6	6	6	6	6	8	8
Product Definition and Synthesis	Product Complexity (High to Low)	1	5	5	8	8	7	7	7	3	7	7
Technology Dev. & Contingent Deployment	Tech Deploy. Complexity (High to Low)	1	4	4	5	5	5	5	5	5	5	8
Human Capital:Talent, Leadership & Culture	Access to Core Comp. (low to high)	1	4	4	6	6	6	6	6	6	6	6
Total Impact Score				90		130		120		124		142
Normalised Impact Score				0.45		0.65		0.60		0.62		0.71
Financial Impact												
Funding & Investment	Revenue Potential (low to high)	1	8	8	6	6	5	5	5	5	5	5
	Margin, EBIT (low to high)	1	8	8	6	6	6	6	6	6	1	1
	Investment Required (high to low)	1	7	7	2	2	5	5	7	7	1	1
	Time to Payback (long vs short)	1	8	8	6	6	6	6	6	6	2	2
	Access to Investment (low to high)	1	7	7	7	7	7	7	7	7	3	3
Total Impact Score				38		27		29		31		12
Normalised Impact Score				0.76		0.54		0.58		0.62		0.24

Figure 4. Example of a typical product portfolio calculation for a firm with five products.

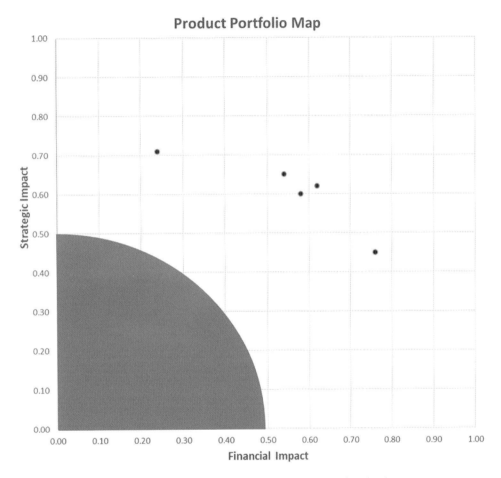

Figure 5. Typical product portfolio map at the firm level.

Part III

Learnings from Case Studies

Chapter 13

Key Learnings from Case Studies

13.1 General Learning from All the Case Studies

Figure 1 provides an overview of the case studies discussed in this section. Users of this manual can draw the following general conclusions from the case studies presented in Chapters 14–17:

- Innovators, entrepreneurs and firms need to have a firm grasp on the **relative maturity** of their propositions because this will affect their priorities at any point in their commercialisation journeys.
- Understanding your **market space** is a critical factor in positioning and differentiating your proposition.
- The relative **importance of the different vectors** can change significantly as firms cross Chasms I, II and III.
- In some situation, firms may need to **re-cross the earlier chasms** if market conditions require significant adjustment to business goals.
- For virtually all firms, the key to commercial success lies in **successfully crossing Chasm II**.

13.2 Specific Insights from the Case Studies

- Innovators and entrepreneurs working on the early stages of growth, in research labs or nascent firms, should look in particular at the case studies described in Sections 14.1, 14.2, 14.4, 15.1, 15.4 and 16.2.
- Firms operating around Chasm I should look in particular at Chapters 14–16.
- Firm operating around Chasm II should look in particular at Chapters 15 and 16.
- Firms operating around Chasm III should look in particular at Chapter 16.
- Firms with multiple products in their portfolio should address the following, based on their market and customer focus
  - Same market space and customers: Section 17.1
  - Same market space but different customers: Section 17.2
  - Different market spaces and customers: Section 17.3.
- Non-technology firms should look at Sections 14.4, 15.4 and 16.3.
- Firms need to understand the differences between technology products and technology enabled products (for example, the differences between the case studies in Section 16.1).

Market Space		Aerospace Engineering	Computing & Electronics	Oil & Gas Engineering	Bio-Pharma	Automotive Engineering	Energy & Lighting	Medical Diagnostics	Healthcare Services	Media & Entertain.	Financial Services	Agri-food	Fashion & Retail	Food & Drink	Social Provision
		Technology Products & Services							**Technology-enabled Products & Services**				**Non-Technology Products & Services**		
Product or Service Proposition		Design & Simulation Tools	Computing architectures & platforms	Corrosion monitoring	Drug-discovery Engine	Satellite-based Navigation	Electronic Lighting & Controls	Genetic profiling products	Low-cost lower body metrology	Low-cost imagery & tools	AI-supported insurance services	Agri-cereals tracking & tracability	Women's Fashion Clothing	New Energy Drink	Social Housing
Maturity of proposition or firm	Early Stage	Section 14.1	Section 16.2	Section 15.1					Section 14.2					Section 14.4	Section 15.4
	Around Chasm I	Section 14.1	Section 16.2	Section 15.1	Section 15.2				Section 14.2	Section 16.1	Section 15.3	Section 14.3	Section 16.3	Section 14.4	Section 15.4
	Around Chasm II		Section 16.2	Section 15.1	Section 15.2					Section 16.1	Section 15.3		Section 16.3		
	Around Chasm III		Section 16.2							Section 16.1			Section 16.3		
Portfolio Mngt	Same market & customers							Section 17.1							
	Same market but different customers					Section 17.2									
	Different markets & customers						Section 17.3								

Figure 1. Overview of case study coverage.

Chapter 14

Focus on Early Stage Growth

14.1 Engineering Design and Simulation Tools

14.1.1 *Crossing Chasm I*

Opportunity: The idea for this firm arose from a technology project which created a new **parallel computing platform** capable of solving multi-physics problems at a significantly lower cost than before. The founders identified the opportunity to apply this platform to provide engineering design and simulation tools for engineering SMEs unable to afford the expensive current approaches.

Vision: To provide state-of-the-art engineering and design simulation tools to engineering SMEs globally based on accessing shared resources on a subscription basis.

Approach: Integrate the high-performance computing platform with 3rd party design and simulation tools, proprietary optimisation methods, advanced data entry and visualisation tools and a new workflow engine to provide a service accessible to users via the web.

Trajectory: The starting point for this journey was to understand the key technical, commercial and financial issues in delivering the vision. The first challenge was to convert this conceptual idea into a *prototype* product and service offering — a classical Chasm I challenge. The key to crossing this chasm was to match the technology capability versus the perceived customer need, and to frame and create the proposition which satisfied these needs. The next challenge was to optimise the platform functionality based on the potential revenue and cost envelopes. The final challenge was to identify and implement the solution with the first proto-customer. The end point of this part of the journey was a working service which could then be deployed with the first charter customers.

Insights & Observations

External vectors: The commercialisation monitor emphasizes the critical importance of focusing on the proposition framing and customer definition vectors at this point in the maturity of the firm; it is too early to worry about distribution channels at this point beyond envisaging a broad approach based on embracing the web.

Internal vectors: The critical internal vectors at this point in the journey are synthesizing the product and service based and making the right choices on selecting and deploying the technology components; it was this analysis which confirmed an approach based on providing a platform rather than a packaged design service.

Composite vectors: The commercialisation strategy vector confirmed this approach; and that it was too early to think about the best business model at this stage. Figures 1, 2, and 3 summarise the key insights from this case study.

THE COMMERCIALISATION MONITOR

The Vision: To provide state-of-the-art engineering and design simulation tools to engineering SMEs globally based on accessing shared resources on a subscription basis.

Chasm Locator: I (circled) | II | III

mTRL CRL: 0 1 2 3 (circled) 4 5 6 7 8 9

Contingent Technology Deployment

Base Tech	App. Tech	Platform	Apps & Tools	Product	Service
		√	√		

Intellectual Property Management

Def.Key Comp.	Def. Prior.	Protect. in Place
√	√	

Product & Service Synthesis

User-centred	Tech-driven	Imped. Matchin	Creat. Synth.	9-layer model	Service Wrap.
		√		√	

Manufacturing, Assembly & Deployment

Def. Chall.	Integ. Deploy.	Innov. Req

Funding & Investment

Pref.	Fund.Quant.	Valuation
Private	£1m	£3m

Talent, Leadership & Culture

Over. Prior.	Talent	Team	Org struct.	Leadership	Culture
	√	√			

Commercialisation Strategy

Vector Focus: Crossing Chasm I

Defined Strategic Goal?	√
Strategic Gap Clarity?	√

Business Model

Defined Narrative	√
Explicit Architecture	
Components Defined	
Business Model Metrics	
Revenues & Costs	
Cash Flow Projections	

Market Space

Engineering		Value Chain	√

Local	Nationa	Global	T-max	120	Mths
		√			

Proposition Framing

Propos. Defn.	Comp.	Reg.	Diff.	Partners & Suppliers
√	√		√	

Source of Differentiation

Single Component	Overall Chain	Re-framing Chain
	√	

Customer Definition

Business	Govt.	Consumer	Knowledge Workers
√			

Max Accessible No of Customers	Cmax	30,000

Distribution Marketing & Sales

Defined Go to Market Priorities	
Defined Channel Strategy	

Overall m7Ps

Product	Pos.	Pricing	Place	Prom.	Pro	Partn.

Figure 1. Engineering design & simulation commercialisation monitor @ Chasm I.

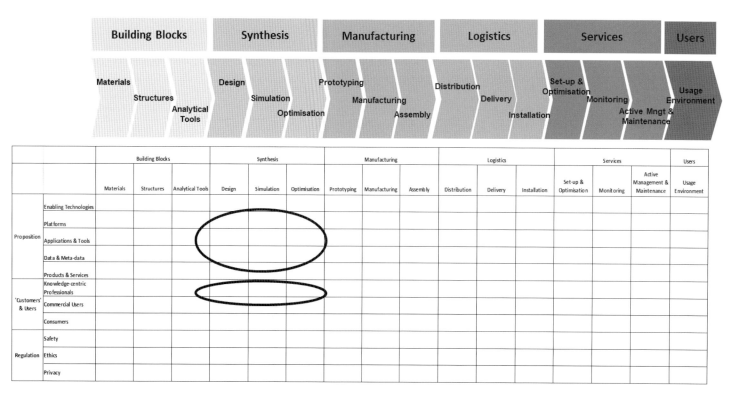

Figure 2.   Proposition framing vs engineering design and manufacturing value chain.

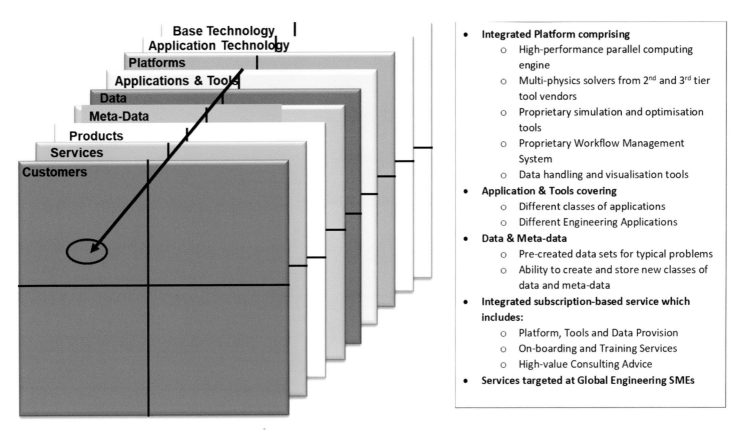

Figure 3. Product decomposition framework — Key elements of the proposition for engineering SMEs.

14.2 Low-Cost Human Lower Body Metrology

14.2.1 *Post-Chasm I*

Opportunity: The firm had developed a low-cost method for human lower body metrology based on the commercial sensor in the Microsoft Kinect Xbox, combined with a data model describing the musculo-skeletal system. The approach did not require patient limb or joint tagging and presented a number of opportunities in the healthcare market space.

Vision: To provide gait and movement metrology, diagnostics and predictive analytics as a service for healthcare providers, med-tech corporates and consultancies.

Approach: Run a broad set of trials with potential users of the system, then use the feedback to identify the best deployment options in terms of functionality and viable business models to enable Chasm II to be addressed.

Trajectory: The starting point for this journey was post-Chasm I, with a prototype installation already in place with the first proto-customer in a rehab clinic. The focus over the next year was on identifying the best commercialisation pathway. The proposition framing activity identified two different areas for deployment: provision of services to clinicians in primary diagnostic healthcare settings; and the provision of packaged products for patients in post-intervention situations such as care in the community. Both (different) opportunities were explored: the second option provides simplified functionality to a large number of potential customers. The service aimed at clinicians, in contrast, depends on a high value-added service underpinned by robust clinical data. The firm has still not crossed Chasm II.

Insights & Observations

External vectors: The need to decide on a single proposition and then develop the right business model resulted in a focus on the Proposition Framing Vector, combined with a new to understand the evolving market space and customer definition. The emerging strategy focused on clinical customers should accelerate the eventual crossing of Chasm II.

Internal vectors: Consistent with the external focus, the two key internal vectors are the detailed product & service synthesis and the technology deployment strategy, which guides the platform architecture.

Composite vectors: Work on the commercialisation strategy and business model has been delayed by the lack of clarity of future direction; the monitor confirms continuing lack of clarity about the strategic goal. Figures 4, 5, and 6 summarise the key insights from this case study.

THE COMMERCIALISATION MONITOR

The Vision: Gait and movement metrology, diagnostics and predictive analytics as a service for healthcare providers, medtech corporates and consultancies

Chasm Locator					I			II		III
mTRL / CRL	0	1	2	3	4	5	6	7	8	9

Contingent Technology Deployment

Base Tech	App. Tech	Platform	Apps & Tools	Product	Service
		√	√		

Intellectual Property Management

Def.Key Comp.	Def. Prior.	Protect. in Place
√	√	√

Product & Service Synthesis

User-centred	Tech-driven	Imped. Matchin	Creat. Synth.	9-layer model	Service Wrap.
			√	√	

Manufacturing, Assembly & Deployment

Def. Chall.	Integ. Deploy.	Innov. Req
√		

Funding & Investment

Pref.	Fund.Quant.	Valuation
Private	£0.5M	£3m

Talent, Leadership & Culture

Over. Prior.	Talent	Team	Org struct.	Leadership	Culture
	√	√		√	

Commercialisation Strategy

Vectors: Post Chasm I challenge

Defined Strategic Goal?	
Strategic Gap Clarity?	

Business Model

Defined Narrative	
Explicit Architecture	
Components Defined	
Business Model Metrics	
Revenues & Costs	
Cash Flow Projections	

Market Space

Healthcare diagnostics & rehabilitation — Value Chain √

Local	Nationa	Global		
		√	T-max	60 Mths

Proposition Framing

Propos. Defn.	Comp.	Reg.	Diff.	Partners & Suppliers
√			√	√

Source of Differentiation

Single Component	Overall Chain	Re-framing Chain
	√	

Customer Definition

Business	Govt.	Consumer	Knowledge Workers
√	√		√

Max Accessible No of Customers	Cmax	5000

Distribution Marketing & Sales

Defined Go to Market Priorities	
Defined Channel Strategy	Overall m7Ps

Product	Pos.	Pricing	Place	Prom.	Prod	Partn.

Figure 4. Human lower-body metrology commercialisation monitor @ Chasm I.

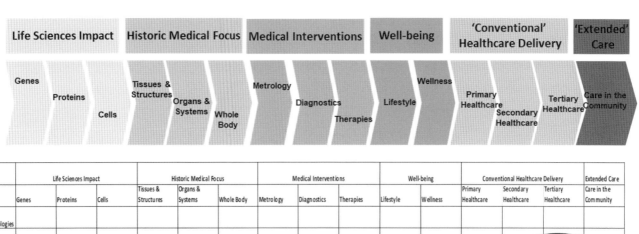

| | | Life Sciences Impact | | | Historic Medical Focus | | | Medical Interventions | | | Well-being | | Conventional Healthcare Delivery | | | Extended Care |
		Genes	Proteins	Cells	Tissues & Structures	Organs & Systems	Whole Body	Metrology	Diagnostics	Therapies	Lifestyle	Wellness	Primary Healthcare	Secondary Healthcare	Tertiary Healthcare	Care in the Community
Technology	Enabling Technologies															
	Devices & Platforms															
	Data & Meta-data															
'Customers' & Users	Consumers															
	Knowledge-centric Professionals															
	Businesses															
Regulation	Safety															
	Ethics															
	Privacy															

Figure 5.   Human lower-body metrology — Market space positioning options.

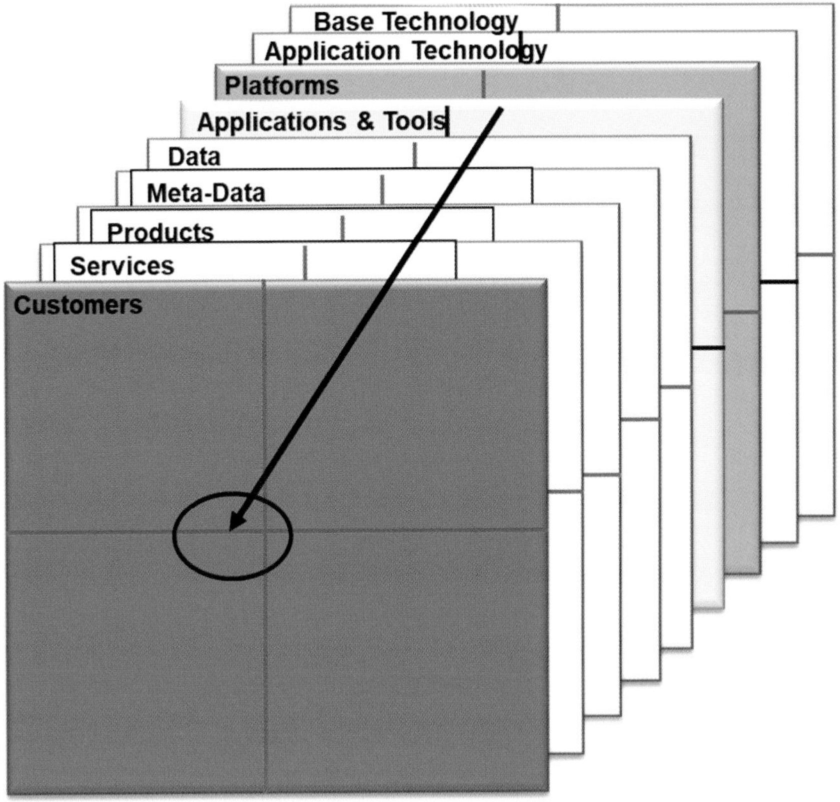

- **Metrology Platform comprising**
  - Kinect Imaging Sensor
  - Human body musculo-skeletal model & data
  - Platform integration software
  - Virtual Reality tools to provide augmented environment
  - Heuristic and knowledge based tools to harness patient cohort data
- **Application & Tools covering**
  - Diagnostic tools to support para-clinicians
  - Clinician support based on anonymised cohort data
- **Integrated subscription-based service targeted at clinicians in primary care settings**
  - Platform + Services
  - On-boarding and Training Services
- **Services targeted at Knowledge-centric customers in clinical settings**

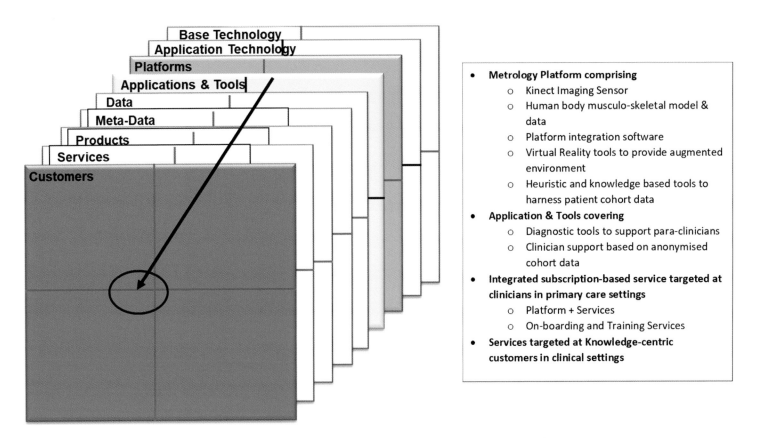

Figure 6. Product decomposition framework — Key elements of the proposition for clinicians.

14.3 Agri-cereals Tracking and Traceability

14.3.1 *Crossing Chasm I*

Opportunity: New sensor technologies, nanosatellite technologies and data processing have created opportunities to monitor products across the entire agri-food value chain, from crop planting to the farm gate to supermarket shelves, enabling enhanced tracking and traceability. This firm recognised the opportunity to offer an integrated data-centric tracking platform for agricultural products.

Vision: Real time tracking of crop growth and key environmental drivers.

Approach: Build prototype data collection, processing and reporting system to demonstrate technical and commercial viability of the approach, including taxonomy and partnerships with sources of data.

Trajectory: The starting point for this journey was to design the data architecture of the platform, identify the data sources, and agree deals with commercial partners. The next stage was to build and demonstrate the viability of the platform, in terms of data provision. The final part of this trajectory was to demonstrate the ability of this platform to provide a continuous monitoring service providing information on the key variables of interest to all the stakeholders identified in the market space map, and prepare the ground for crossing Chasm II.

Insights & Observations

External vectors: Although the basic concept is simple, the key external vectors at this stage of maturity are proposition framing and customer definition, based on an overall understanding of the market space. In particular, the proposition needed to reflect the priorities of different farming communities.

Internal vectors: Successful crossing of Chasm I required significant attention to the technology deployment vector combined with clarity on the product and service synthesis and definition. The technology vector was critical in terms of defining a new meta-data model which allowed the large volume of data to be handled cost-effectively.

Composite vectors: Significant effort went into defining the commercialisation strategy to create a valuable proposition subsequently capable of supporting a robust business model, when crossing Chasm II. Figures 7, 8, and 9 summarise the key insights from this case study.

THE COMMERCIALISATION MONITOR

The Vision | Real time tracking of crop growth and key environmental drivers

Chasm Locator					I		II			III
mTRL CRL	0	1	2	3	4	5	6	7	8	9

Contingent Technology Deployment

Base Tech	App. Tech	Platform	Apps & Tools	Product	Service
		√	√		

Intellectual Property Management

Def.Key Comp.	Def. Prior.	Protect. in Place
√		

Product & Service Synthesis

User-centred	Tech-driven	Imped. Matchin	Creat. Synth.	9-layer model	Service Wrap.
√				√	

Manufacturing, Assembly & Deployment

Def. Chall.	Integ. Deploy.	Innov. Req

Funding & Investment

Pref.	Fund.Quant.	Valuation
Private	£1m	£5m

Talent, Leadership & Culture

Over. Prior.	Talent	Team	Org struct.	Leadership	Culture
	√	√			

Commercialisation Strategy

Vector Focus: Crossing Chasm I

Defined Strategic Goal? √

Strategic Gap Clarity?

Business Model

Defined Narrative	√
Explicit Architecture	
Components Defined	
Business Model Metrics	
Revenues & Costs	
Cash Flow Projections	

Market Space

Agri-food	Value Chain	√

Local	Nationa	Global			
		√	T-max	180	Mths

Proposition Framing

Propos. Defn.	Comp.	Reg.	Diff.	Partners & Suppliers
√				√

Source of Differentiation

Single Component	Overall Chain	Re-framing Chain
	√	

Customer Definition

Business	Govt.	Consumer	Knowledge Workers
√			

Max Accessible No of Customers	Cmax	100,000

Distribution Marketing & Sales

Defined Go to Market Priorities

Defined Channel Strategy		Overall m7Ps	

Product	Pos.	Pricing	Place	Prom.	Pro	Partn.

Figure 7. Agri-cereals tracking commercialisation monitor @ Chasm I.

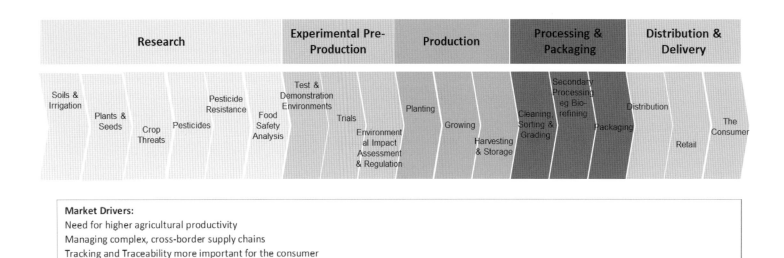

Market Drivers:
Need for higher agricultural productivity
Managing complex, cross-border supply chains
Tracking and Traceability more important for the consumer
Innovation driven by new smaller players is changing industry structure

Technology Drivers
Genetic Technologies can create new strains, improve yields and protect crops
Sensing and monitoring technologies which enable precision farming and integrated production and delivery
Data-centric technologies enable better food tracking, regulation and supply chain integration

Regulatory Drivers
Greater awareness of environmental contamination
Pesticide resistance is a big threat to regulation
Better understanding of market and technology impact driving new regulation

Figure 8. Proposition framing — Real-time cereals data tracking, monitoring & analytics.

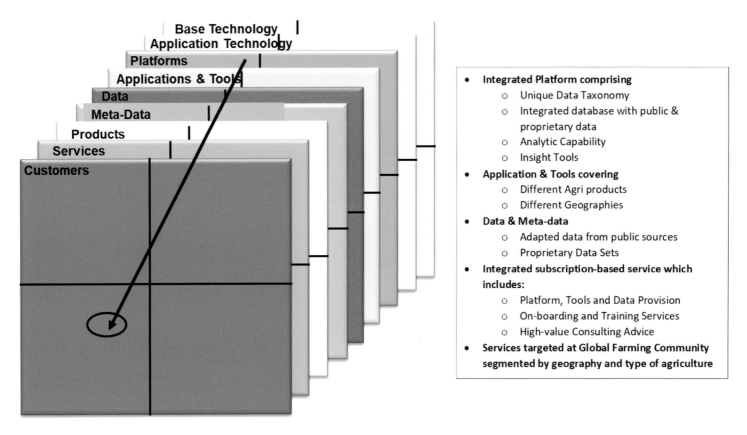

Figure 9. Product decomposition framework — Key elements of the proposition for farmers.

The image contains the following labels and text:

- Base Technology
- Application Technology
- Platforms
- Applications & Tools
- Data
- Meta-Data
- Products
- Services
- Customers

- Integrated Platform comprising
  - Unique Data Taxonomy
  - Integrated database with public & proprietary data
  - Analytic Capability
  - Insight Tools
- Application & Tools covering
  - Different Agri products
  - Different Geographies
- Data & Meta-data
  - Adapted data from public sources
  - Proprietary Data Sets
- Integrated subscription-based service which includes:
  - Platform, Tools and Data Provision
  - On-boarding and Training Services
  - High-value Consulting Advice
- Services targeted at Global Farming Community segmented by geography and type of agriculture

14.4 New Energy Drink

14.4.1 *Crossing Chasm I*

Opportunity: The small team running a health-food restaurant had identified an opportunity to create a new energy drink based on a unique set of ingredients from a number of geographic locations, blended in a specific way, which could be offered to consumers.

Vision: To make and sell a new branded 'natural' energy drink.

Approach: To create and test a number of formulations of this drink with young people in the 18–25 age group to decide on the best formulation and also explore positioning messages.

Trajectory: The starting point for this journey was the acquisition of the key ingredients from suppliers mainly in Latin America, followed by setting up a mixing facility to prototype a number of potential mixtures. This was then followed by user testing with small cohorts of young athletes. The results of this were used to define the desired formulation to create a prototype drink to take forward to the next stage of commercialisation.

Insights & Observations

External vectors: As illustrated by the commercialisation monitor, the key external vectors involved in crossing Chasm I for this product were clearly defining the market space and positioning the product in this market space, which was relatively straight-forward given that the product will be sold through the existing food and drink distribution system. The key focus at this stage was to obtain clarity on the target consumers, based on the test data.

Internal vectors: For this relatively simple product, at this stage of the journey, the key focus is on defining the specific product and its associated attributes.

Composite vectors: At this stage, the focus was on the qualitative trade-offs between the proposition, the customers and specific product formulation; no business model issues were addressed at this point. Figures 10, 11, and 12 summarise the key insights from this case study.

THE COMMERCIALISATION MONITOR

The Vision	New energy drink formulation for active consumers

Chasm Locator							I		II			III
mTRL CRL	0	1	2	3	4	5	6		7	8	9	

Contingent Technology Deployment

Base Tech	App. Tech	Platform	Apps & Tools	Product	Service
				√	

Intellectual Property Management

Def.Key Comp.	Def. Prior.	Protect. in Place
√		

Product & Service Synthesis

User-centred	Tech-driven	Imped. Matchin	Creat. Synth.	9-layer model	Service Wrap.
√					

Manufacturing, Assembly & Deployment

Def. Chall.	Integ. Deploy.	Innov. Req

Funding & Investment

Pref.	Fund.Quant.	Valuation
Private	£0.5m	£1m

Talent, Leadership & Culture

Over. Prior.	Talent	Team	Org struct.	Leadership	Culture
		√			

Commercialisation Strategy

Vector Focus: Crossing Chasm I

Defined Strategic Goal?	√
Strategic Gap Clarity?	

Business Model

Defined Narrative	√
Explicit Architecture	
Components Defined	
Business Model Metrics	
Revenues & Costs	
Cash Flow Projections	

Market Space

Food & Drink	Value Chain	√

Local	Nationa	Global			
		√	T-max	36	Mths

Proposition Framing

Propos. Defn.	Comp.	Reg.	Diff.	Partners & Suppliers
√	√	√	√	

Source of Differentiation

Single Component	Overall Chain	Re-framing Chain
√		

Customer Definition

Business	Govt.	Consumer	Knowledge Workers
		√	

Max Accessible No of Customers	Cmax	10 million

Distribution Marketing & Sales

Defined Go to Market Priorities		√
Defined Channel Strategy		Overall m7Ps	

Product	Pos.	Pricing	Place	Prom.	Pro	Partn.
√	√					

Figure 10. New energy drink commercialisation monitor @ Chasm I.

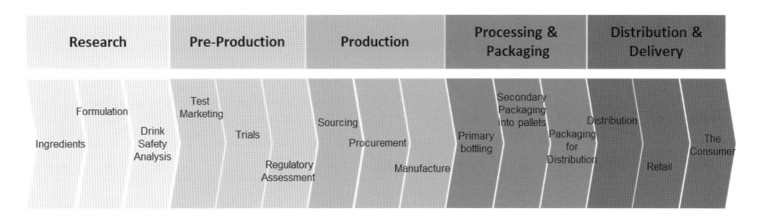

Research | Pre-Production | Production | Processing & Packaging | Distribution & Delivery

Ingredients
Formulation
Drink Safety Analysis
Test Marketing
Trials
Regulatory Assessment
Sourcing
Procurement
Manufacture
Primary bottling
Secondary Packaging into pallets
Packaging for Distribution
Distribution
Retail
The Consumer

Market Drivers:

Using well-established market space for food and drink distribution

Need to demonstrate dietary impact of the new drink

Tracking and Traceability of components may be important for the consumer

Incremental Innovation-so product positioning and branding likely to be critical

Regulatory Constraints

None, all ingredients already approved by the Food and Drink standards agencies

Figure 11. Proposition framing: New energy drink in the food and drink market space.

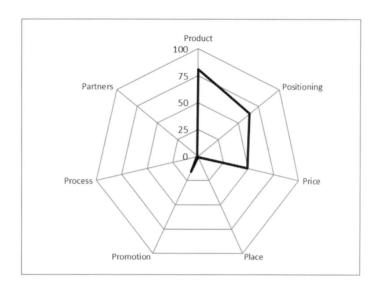

The firm will need to focus on three key factors for a successful launch:

- The Product, including its formulation and packaging
- Positioning the product in a highly competitive market space
- Pricing is likely to be the key to the overall business model

Figure 12. m7Ps profile for new energy drink post-Chasm I.

Chapter 15

From Inception to Sustainable Business Model

15.1 Corrosion Monitoring System for Oil & Gas

15.1.1 *Crossing Chasm I*

Opportunity: Commercial pressures in the oil & gas industry have led to the need to refine crude oil with much higher tar content than before. This in turn has led to serious corrosion problems in pipelines for refineries. This new sensor technology offered the potential to monitor wall thickness over time and hence monitor corrosion activity.

Vision: To create a continuous monitoring system for corrosion measurement for structures in the oil & gas industry.

Approach: To build an integrated network of intelligent sensors, connected using wireless technology, analysing and managing the data to provide diagnostic and maintenance information for refinery operators.

Trajectory: The goal was to build and demonstrate a prototype system, to cross Chasm I on this commercialisation journey. The starting point was to design the overall concept, using the proven sensor technology but focusing on two key areas: linking sensor data to corrosion chemistry and processes in a real environment; and designing the best way to get the data to a central collecting point from multiple sensors. The end point for this part of the journey was the demonstration of a working prototype in a pilot plant located in a refinery.

Insights & Observations

External vectors: The key focus at this stage of the commercialisation journey was on defining the market space precisely, in particular the market-space centric value chain for this type of engineering deployment and then deciding where to precisely locate the proposition. This also required some understanding of the target customer.

Internal vectors: The main focus at this stage was in looking at the technology integration and deployment challenges and understanding trade-offs to define and synthesize the precise product and service proposition.

Composite vectors: The commercialisation strategy at this stage was focused on the importance of the market-facing vectors and technology and product development, and ensuring there was sufficient funding to build and deploy the first prototype. Figures 1, 2, and 3 summarise the key insights from this case study.

THE COMMERCIALISATION MONITOR

The Vision	To create a continuous monitoring system for corrosion measurement for structures in the Oil & Gas Industry

Chasm Locator: I, II, III

mTRL CRL: 0 1 2 3 (circled) 4 5 6 7 8 9

Contingent Technology Deployment

Base Tech	App. Tech	Platform	Apps & Tools	Product	Service
	√		√	√	

Intellectual Property Management

Def.Key Comp.	Def. Prior.	Protect. in Place
√		

Product & Service Synthesis

User-centred	Tech-driven	Imped. Matchin	Creat. Synth.	9-layer model	Service Wrap.
		√		√	

Manufacturing, Assembly & Deployment

Def. Chall.	Integ. Deploy.	Innov. Req

Funding & Investment

Pref.	Fund.Quant.	Valuation
Private	£1m	£7.5m

Talent, Leadership & Culture

Over. Prior.	Talent	Team	Org struct.	Leadership	Culture
	√	√			

Commercialisation Strategy

Vector Focus: Crossing Chasm I

Defined Strategic Goal? √

Strategic Gap Clarity? √

Business Model

Defined Narrative	
Explicit Architecture	
Components Defined	
Business Model Metrics	
Revenues & Costs	
Cash Flow Projections	

Market Space

Oil & Gas	Value Chain	√

Local	Nationa	Global	T-max	100	Mths
		√			

Proposition Framing

Propos. Defn.	Comp.	Reg.	Diff.	Partners & Suppliers
√				√

Source of Differentiation

Single Component	Overall Chain	Re-framing Chain
√		

Customer Definition

Business	Govt.	Consumer	Knowledge Workers
√			

Max Accessible No of Customers	Cmax	500

Distribution Marketing & Sales

Defined Go to Market Priorities

Defined Channel Strategy ___ Overall m7Ps ___

Product	Pos.	Pricing	Place	Prom.	Pro(	Partn.

Figure 1. Corrosion monitoring — Commercialisation monitor @ Chasm I.

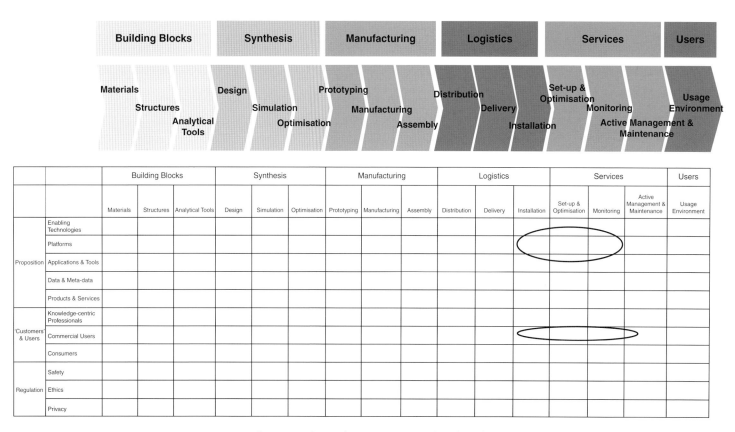

Figure 2. Proposition framing vs the market-space centric value chain for engineering market.

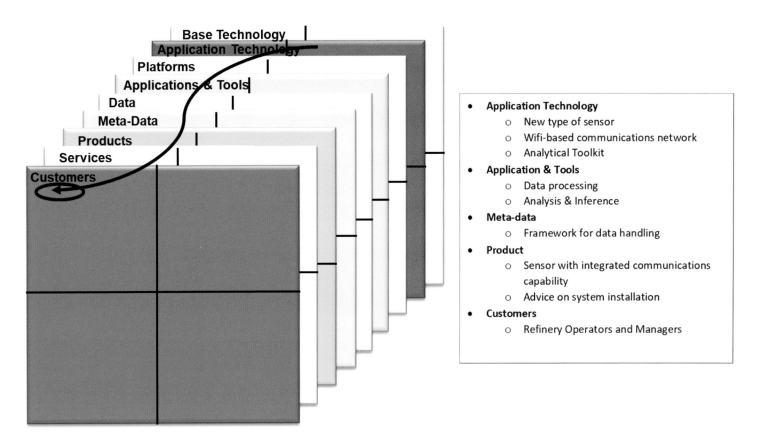

Figure 3. Product decomposition framework — Key elements of the proposition.

15.1.2 *Crossing Chasm II*

Opportunity: Success in crossing Chasm I led to a re-appraisal of the opportunity: this concluded that there was a bigger potential market based on corrosion monitoring in both upstream and downstream environments, provided the product could be re-packaged and a resilient business model demonstrated.

Vision: To provide a continuous corrosion monitoring system for upstream and downstream applications in the oil & gas industry.

Approach: The firm decided to widen the target market based on the market opportunity, add integrated data insight services desired by customers and to experiment with business model options.

Trajectory: At the start of this phase of growth, the firm had demonstrated a viable product in the market space as the commercialisation vector plot around Chasm I demonstrated. Crossing Chasm II depended on addressing a much wider set of vectors, as shown in the Chasm II crossing vector plot. The focus here shifted towards understanding customers better, fine tuning the product and understanding pricing issues. The firm experimented with several different business models before finally adopting a model which consisted of the following components: outright sales of the wave-guided-based sensors; service fees for assessing needs and designing the optimum deployment; subscription-based software tools for monitoring results from the sensors to enable preventive maintenance.

Insights & Observations

External vectors: The importance of the market space vector gave way to increasing importance of customer definition, with the distribution vector starting to become important.

Internal vectors: The human capital vector was clearly very important in crossing chasm, with the need for additional funding and product refinement also contributing to success. IP issues were not critical in this transformation.

Composite vectors: Commercialisation strategy and business model were critical in crossing Chasm II successfully.

*The most obvious pattern was the **importance of all vectors** in crossing Chasm II, compared to Chasm I.* Figures 4, 5, and 6 summarise the key insights from this case study.

THE COMMERCIALISATION MONITOR

The Vision | To provide a continuous corrosion monitoring system for upstream and downstream applications in the Oil & Gas Industry

Chasm Locator					I				II			III

mTRL / CRL	0	1	2	3		4	5	6	7	8	9

Contingent Technology Deployment

Base Tech	App. Tech	Platform	Apps & Tools	Product	Service
	√		√	√	√

Intellectual Property Management

Def.Key Comp.	Def. Prior.	Protect. in Place
√	√	√

Product & Service Synthesis

User-centred	Tech-driven	Imped. Matchin	Creat. Synth.	9-layer model	Service Wrap.
			√	√	√

Manufacturing, Assembly & Deployment

Def. Chall.	Integ. Deploy.	Innov. Req
√	√	

Funding & Investment

Pref.	Fund.Quant.	Valuation
Private	£2m	£20m

Talent, Leadership & Culture

Over. Prior.	Talent	Team	Org struct.	Leadership	Culture
√	√	√		√	

Commercialisation Strategy

Vector Focus: Crossing Chasm II

Defined Strategic Goal?	√
Strategic Gap Clarity?	√

Business Model

Defined Narrative	√
Explicit Architecture	√
Components Defined	√
Business Model Metrics	
Revenues & Costs	√
Cash Flow Projections	√

Market Space

Oil & Gas	Value Chain	√

Local	Nationa	Global		
		√	T-max	120 Mths

Proposition Framing

Propos. Defn.	Comp.	Reg.	Diff.	Partners & Suppliers
√	√		√	√

Source of Differentiation

Single Component	Overall Chain	Re-framing Chain
√		

Customer Definition

Business	Govt.	Consumer	Knowledge Workers
√			

Max Accessible No of Customers	Cmax	2,000

Distribution Marketing & Sales

Defined Go to Market Priorities		√
Defined Channel Strategy	√	Overall m7Ps	√

Product	Pos.	Pricing	Place	Prom.	Pro	Partn.
√	√	√	√		√	√

Figure 4. Corrosion monitoring — Commercialisation monitor @ Chasm II.

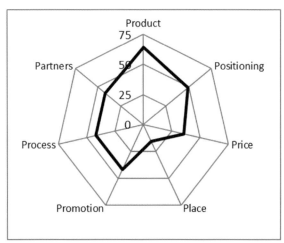

Observations	
Product	Stable Product with focus on sensor sale & Installation
Positioning	Positioning based on reducing refinery outage times
Price	Good early pricing-price elasticity not yet clear
Place	Direct delivery and installation at refinery sites
Promotion	Early days, based on 'strategic' customer sign-up
Process	Sales proces established but needs scale-up
Partners	Early partners across market value chain in place

Figure 5.   Coverage of the m7Ps.

Roles	Chief Executive	Chief Architect	VP Service Deployment	Chief Scientist	VP Services	VP Sales	Hd of Mktg	Chairman	Board	Freq
People	A1	A2	A3	A4	A5	A6	A7	A8		
Key Processes										
Commercial										
Overall Strategy	●	o	o	o	o	o	o	o	◊	Q
Competitive Positioning	◊, ●			o	o	o	o	o		Q
Business Model	◊, ●		o	o	o	o	o	o	R	Q
Key Customers	◊, ●	o	o	o	o	o	o			M
Key Contracts & Agreements	◊, ●		o	o	o	o				M
Strategic Partnerships	◊, ●	o	o	o	o	o	o	o		M
Key Supplier Relationships	◊, ●	o	o	o	o	o	o	o		M
Legal										
IP Protection & Management	◊, ●	o	o	o	o	o	o		R	Q
Software Licensing	◊, ●	o	o	o	o	o	o		R	Q
Compliance	◊, ●		o	o	o				R	Q
Service Delivery Implications	◊	o	o	o	●	o	o	o		M
Finance										
Business Model	◊, ●	o	o	o	o	o	o	o	R	Q
Procurement Mngt.	●	o	n	o	o	o	o	o		M
MIS	◊, ●	o	o	o	o	o	o	o		M
Procedures, Reporting & Controls	◊, ●	o	o	o	o	o	o	o		M
Cash Flow Management	◊, ●	o	o	o	o	o	o	o	R	M
Human Resources										
HR Terms & Conditions	◊	o	o	o	o	o	o	o	R	Q
Recruitment	●	o	o	o	o	o	o	◊		M
Personnel Mngt	◊, ●	o	o	o	o	o	o			M
Technology & Service Development										
Overall Architecture:Design & Maintenance	o	●	o	◊	o	o	o			Q
Core Service Functions(Design & Build)	o	◊, ●	o	o	o	o	o			M
Customer Experience(Design, Build and Enhance)	o	◊, ●	o	o	o	o	o			M
Customer and Usage Tracking Tools(D,B, E)	o	◊, ●	o	o	o	o	o			M
Service Monitoring & Mngt Tools(D,B,E)	o	◊, ●	o	o	o	o	o			M
Additional Functional Capability(D,B, E)	o	◊, ●	o	o	o	o	o			M

Key					
Process Owner	●				
Process Contributor	o			Quarterly Review	Q
Decision Maker	◊			Monthly Review	M
Ratification	R				

Figure 6. Talent & leadership unpacked — Roles vs processes for small but flexible team.

15.2 Drug Discovery Platform

15.2.1 *Crossing Chasm I*

Opportunity: Advances in research created an opportunity to create a new drug discovery platform to speed up the creation of new therapies in oncology and cardiology. The pharma industry needs to identify promising new compounds, to accelerate their development and to guide their progress through testing and clinical trials.

Vision: Build a new drug discovery platform for oncology targets.

Approach: To integrate the scientific approach developed into a platform which enables a systematic approach to be applied to charactering and identifying potential compounds.

Trajectory: The starting point of this journey was the science and application technologies created by the founding team in their previous academic setting. Crossing Chasm I required the scientific insights to be converted into a systematic and repeatable approach, which includes capturing a large amount of data and devising a meta-data schema to hold and access these insights in a coherent way. The end point of this part of the journey was to build and test a prototype platform, which could be used to raise the funding required to build a production platform and tools.

Insights & Observations

External vectors: The critical external vector at this point in the commercialisation process was framing the proposition in the context of the bio-pharma market-space centric value chain. The other external vectors mattered little at this point in the commercialisation journey.

Internal vectors: The internal vectors were more critical at this point, with the focus on technology development and deployment, synthesizing the product and service, and managing the intellectual property developed by the scientific team.

Composite vectors: For this bio-pharma firm, the commercialisation strategy and business model were not priorities at this stage of commercialisation. Figures 7, 8, and 9 summarise the key insights from this case study.

THE COMMERCIALISATION MONITOR

The Vision	Build a new Drug Discovery Platform for Oncology Targets

Chasm Locator					I			II		III
mTRL CRL	0	1	2	3	4	5	6	7	8	9

Contingent Technology Deployment

Base Tech	App. Tech	Platform	Apps & Tools	Product	Service
	√	√	√		√

Intellectual Property Management

Def.Key Comp.	Def. Prior.	Protect. in Place
√	√	

Product & Service Synthesis

User-centred	Tech-driven	Imped. Matchin	Creat. Synth.	9-layer model	Service Wrap.
	√		√	√	

Manufacturing, Assembly & Deployment

Def. Chall.	Integ. Deploy.	Innov. Req

Funding & Investment

Pref.	Fund.Quant.	Valuation
Private	£5m	£12m

Talent, Leadership & Culture

Over. Prior.	Talent	Team	Org struct.	Leadership	Culture
	√	√			

Commercialisation Strategy

Vector Profile Crossing Chasm I

Defined Strategic Goal?	√
Strategic Gap Clarity?	

Business Model

Defined Narrative	
Explicit Architecture	
Components Defined	
Business Model Metrics	
Revenues & Costs	
Cash Flow Projections	

Market Space

Global		Value Chain	√

Local	Nationa	Global	T-max	180	Mths
		√			

Proposition Framing

Propos. Defn.	Comp.	Reg.	Diff.	Partners & Suppliers
√				√

Source of Differentiation

Single Component	Overall Chain	Re-framing Chain
	√	

Customer Definition

Business	Govt.	Consumer	Knowledge Workers
			√

Max Accessible No of Customers	Cmax	200

Distribution Marketing & Sales

Defined Go to Market Priorities	

Defined Channel Strategy		Overall m7Ps	

Product	Pos.	Pricing	Place	Prom.	Pro	Partn.

Figure 7. Drug discovery platform — Commercialisation monitor @ Chasm I.

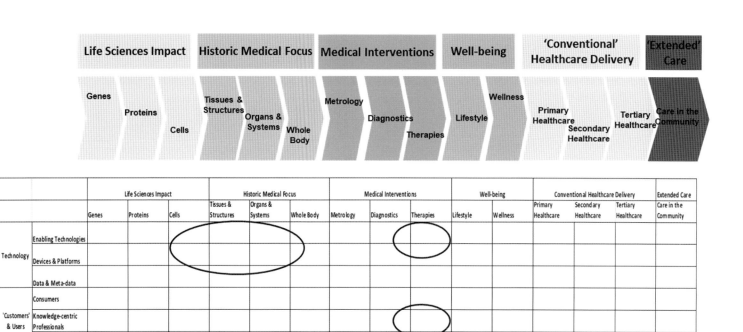

Figure 8.   Proposition framing for drug discovery platform.

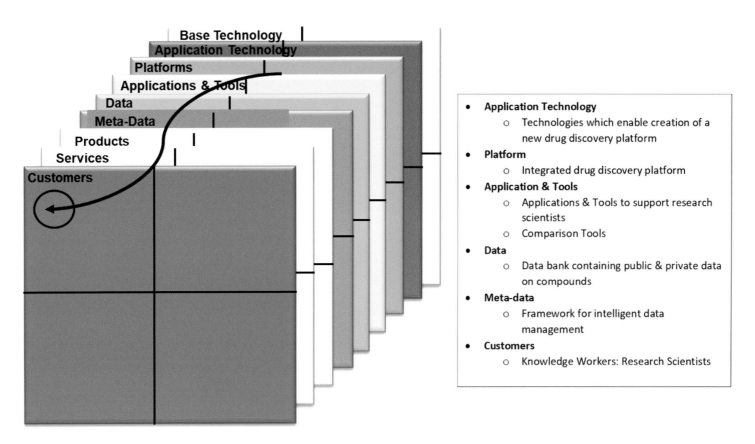

Base Technology
Application Technology
Platforms
Applications & Tools
Data
Meta-Data
Products
Services
Customers

- **Application Technology**
  - Technologies which enable creation of a new drug discovery platform
- **Platform**
  - Integrated drug discovery platform
- **Application & Tools**
  - Applications & Tools to support research scientists
  - Comparison Tools
- **Data**
  - Data bank containing public & private data on compounds
- **Meta-data**
  - Framework for intelligent data management
- **Customers**
  - Knowledge Workers: Research Scientists

Figure 9. Drug discovery platform targeted at corporate R&D labs.

15.2.2 *Crossing Chasm II*

Opportunity: Having successfully demonstrated a prototype drug discovery platform, the challenge facing the firm was to focus on a specific therapeutic area and establish commercial traction.

Vision: Provision of a unique drug discovery platform to small, medium and big pharma companies to accelerate development of new oncology treatments.

Approach: The firm decided to focus on drug discovery for oncology based on the size of the market opportunity and the expertise and experience of the scientific team; and to construct a robust platform with a clear revenue model.

Trajectory: The starting point of this part of the journey was to build a techno-commercial team which enabled the firm to build and test a pre-production platform with a strategic charter customer. This also enabled the commercial issues to be explored, as the firm tested the functionality delivered versus the perception of strategic and financial value for this early proxy corporate customer. This also enabled the firm to confirm that the target customers should be bio-pharma firms, not researchers in academia.

Insights & Observations

External vectors: The key external vector at this point was distribution, marketing & sales, as the firm had to figure out the best way to take the platform to market; in particular, the m7Ps model highlighted the importance of mastering the process and clarifying the role of partners.

Internal vectors: The critical internal vector at this point was understanding and developing the human capital required to deploy this sophisticated proposition and to raise sufficient funding to support go-to-market.

Composite vectors: The commercialisation strategy vector was critical because the firm needed to make some hard techno-commercial choices about the right way to take the product to market. These qualitative insights then had to be translated into a business model where the key was to identify and prioritise the different sources of revenue. Figures 10, 11, and 12 summarise the key insights from this case study.

THE COMMERCIALISATION MONITOR

The Vision	Provision of a unique drug discovery platform to small, medium and big pharma companies to accelerate development of new oncology treatments

Chasm Locator				I			II		III

mTRL CRL	0	1	2	3	4	5	6	7	8	9

Contingent Technology Deployment

Base Tech	App. Tech	Platform	Apps & Tools	Product	Service
	√	√	√	√	√

Intellectual Property Management

Def.Key Comp.	Def. Prior.	Protect. in Place
√	√	√

Product & Service Synthesis

User-centred	Tech-driven	Imped. Matchin	Creat. Synth.	9-layer model	Service Wrap.
			√	√	√

Manufacturing, Assembly & Deployment

Def. Chall.	Integ. Deploy.	Innov. Req
√		

Funding & Investment

Pref.	Fund.Quant.	Valuation
Private	£30m	£100m

Talent, Leadership & Culture

Over. Prior.	Talent	Team	Org struct.	Leadership	Culture
	√	√		√	

Commercialisation Strategy

Vector Focus crossing Chasm II

— Weighted score

Defined Strategic Goal?	√
Strategic Gap Clarity?	√

Business Model

Defined Narrative	√
Explicit Architecture	√
Components Defined	√
Business Model Metrics	
Revenues & Costs	√
Cash Flow Projections	√

Market Space

	Value Chain	√

Local	Nationa	Global		
		√	T-max	120	Mths

Proposition Framing

Propos. Defn.	Comp.	Reg.	Diff.	Partners & Suppliers
√		√		√

Source of Differentiation

Single Component	Overall Chain	Re-framing Chain
	√	

Customer Definition

Business	Govt.	Consumer	Knowledge Workers
√			

Max Accessible No of Customers	Cmax	3000

Distribution Marketing & Sales

Defined Go to Market Priorities	√
Defined Channel Strategy	√	Overall m7Ps	√

Product	Pos.	Pricing	Place	Prom.	Pro	Partn.

Figure 10. Drug discovery platform — Commercialisation monitor @ Chasm II.

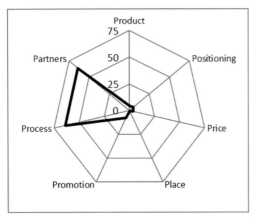

Observations	
Product	Proven engine for oncology dd
Positioning	Not critical given small specialist audience
Price	May be important later?
Place	Not an issue-development at specialist site
Promotion	Promotion to small specialist audience
Process	Need to master clinical trials-centric process
Partners	Big Pharma partnerships critical for go-to-market

Figure 11. The distribution challenge at Chasm II.

Component	NRE	Licenses		Royalties	Leasing	Outright Sale		Commission	Matchmaker	Transactions	Subscriptions		Proxies	
		Perpetual	Time-bound			Core	Consumables				Time-metered	Value-metered	Advertising	Sponsorship
Services														
Products	√													
Meta-Content				√										
Content				√										
Apps, Tools & Processes	√	√	√	√										
Technology Platforms	√	√	√	√	√									
Application Technologies	√	√	√	√										
Base Technologies		√	√	√										

Potential Revenue Sources for Business Model

Figure 12.   Input to business model development.

15.3 Financial Services-Insurance

15.3.1 *Chasm I*

Opportunity: The insurance industry has long struggled with the cost and time it takes to reliably process claims from customers. The goal here was to speed up processing times with improved fidelity using new software and hardware-based technologies.

Vision: To use artificial intelligence and robotic technologies to speed up the handling of insurance claims.

Approach: This fintech firm adopted a twin-pronged approach: building a detailed understanding of the market space-centric value chain for the insurance industry and exploring where and how new technologies could impact on this value chain. Based on this insight, the firm created a prototype application and service to demonstrate the value of this kind of intervention.

Trajectory: The starting point for this journey was to understand the market space-centric value chain for the insurance in detail, making explicit all the activities associated with the business as a whole, in order to understand the precise opportunity for technology enabled innovation. The potential contribution from technologies was then compared against this to define a new proposition. Crossing Chasm I

involved building and testing a prototype based on the conceptual idea: the prototype was successfully deployed with the proto-customer which provided the basis for further discussions on how to commercialise this in practice.

Insights & Observations

External vectors: Three external vectors drive the crossing of Chasm I: the consumer insurance market space, the customer vector and the vector which defines the proposition and its positioning; the customer definition vector makes explicit that the customers for this proposition are insurance companies, not consumers.

Internal vectors: There are three key internal vectors: technology development and deployment, the intellectual property associated with AI and robotics technologies, and the synthesis of the product or service proposition.

Composite vectors: Commercialisation strategy and business models are not important at this point in the journey. Figures 13, 14, and 15 summarise the key insights from this case study.

THE COMMERCIALISATION MONITOR

The Vision — To use Artificial Intelligence and Robotic Technologies to speed up the handling of insurance claims

Chasm Locator					I		II			III

mTRL CRL	0	1	2	3	4	5	6	7	8	9

Contingent Technology Deployment

Base Tech	App. Tech	Platform	Apps & Tools	Product	Service
	√		√		√

Intellectual Property Management

Def.Key Comp.	Def. Prior.	Protect. in Place
√	√	

Product & Service Synthesis

User-centred	Tech-driven	Imped. Matchin	Creat. Synth.	9-layer model	Service Wrap.
	√			√	

Manufacturing, Assembly & Deployment

Def. Chall.	Integ. Deploy.	Innov. Req

Funding & Investment

Pref.	Fund.Quant.	Valuation
Private	£1m	£5.0m

Talent, Leadership & Culture

Over. Prior.	Talent	Team	Org struct.	Leadership	Culture
	√				

Commercialisation Strategy

Vector Focus: Crossing Chasm I

Defined Strategic Goal?	√
Strategic Gap Clarity?	

Business Model

Defined Narrative	
Explicit Architecture	
Components Defined	
Business Model Metrics	
Revenues & Costs	
Cash Flow Projections	

Market Space

Financial Services-Insurance

Value Chain	√

Local	Nationa	Global
	√	

T-max	40	Mths

Proposition Framing

Propos. Defn.	Comp.	Reg.	Diff.	Partners & Suppliers
√				√

Source of Differentiation

Single Component	Overall Chain	Re-framing Chain
√		

Customer Definition

Business	Govt.	Consumer	Knowledge Workers
√			

Max Accessible No of Customers	Cmax	50

Distribution Marketing & Sales

Defined Go to Market Priorities	
Defined Channel Strategy	

Overall m7Ps

Product	Pos.	Pricing	Place	Prom.	Pro	Partn.

Figure 13. Consumer insurance AI — Commercialisation monitor @ Chasm I.

Figure 14. Proposition framing vs the market space-centric value chain for consumer insurance.

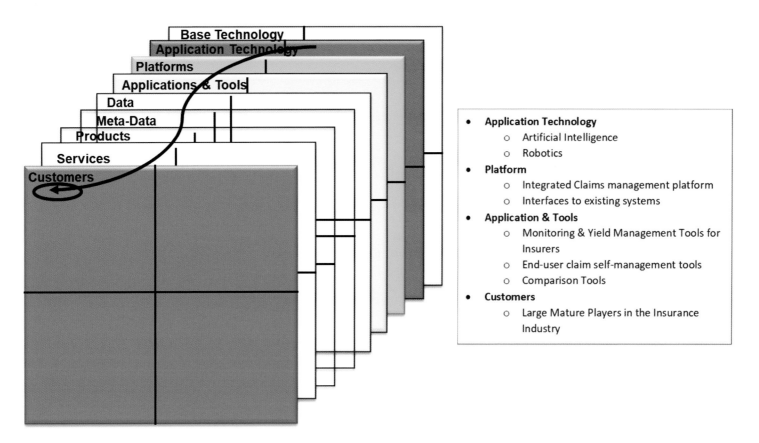

Base Technology
Application Technology
Platforms
Applications & Tools
Data
Meta-Data
Products
Services
Customers

- **Application Technology**
  - o Artificial Intelligence
  - o Robotics
- **Platform**
  - o Integrated Claims management platform
  - o Interfaces to existing systems
- **Application & Tools**
  - o Monitoring & Yield Management Tools for Insurers
  - o End-user claim self-management tools
  - o Comparison Tools
- **Customers**
  - o Large Mature Players in the Insurance Industry

Figure 15.   Claims handling platform and tools for insurance industry.

15.3.2 Chasm II

Opportunity: Having crossed Chasm I successfully, the firm needed to focus on the wider range of vectors which hold the key to developing a commercially viable and sustainable proposition.

Vision: To provide AI & robotics based support to transform speed of claims management for insurance companies serving the consumer market.

Approach: The firm focused on the turning of the prototype service into an integrated platform with applications and tools tailored for use by the professional teams in the insurance company customer. This involved understanding the trade-off between technology functionality and usability.

Trajectory: The journey to cross Chasm II involved a wide range of vectors, with the trajectory largely shaped by the available human and financial capital, where the pace was largely driven by commercial pressures from charter customers looking for competitive advantage.

Insights & Observations

External vectors: There were three key external vectors: re-framing the proposition to accommodate the wider demands from charter customers for more integrated functionality; understanding customers more precisely, and more specifically understanding the user to customer ratio, N-ucr; and focusing on the m7Ps profile.

Internal vectors: The key internal vectors were those concerned with rapid deployment: human and financial capital; the funding came mainly from charter customers in the form of NRE (hence no equity hit) but the human capital priorities needed significant attention; the manufacturing & deployment was also critical at this point as the firm had to figure out to deploy the service in the field.

Composite vectors: The commercialisation strategy and business model vectors were critical: crossing Chasm II successfully depended on figuring out a sustainable business model, which required several iterations with the charter customers. Figures 16, 17, and 18 summarise the key insights from this case study.

THE COMMERCIALISATION MONITOR

The Vision	To provide AI & Robotics based support to transform speed of claims management for insurance companies serving the consumer market

Chasm Locator				I			II		III

mTRL CRL	0	1	2	3		4	5	6	7	8	9

Contingent Technology Deployment

Base Tech	App. Tech	Platform	Apps & Tools	Product	Service
	√	√	√		√

Intellectual Property Management

Def.Key Comp.	Def. Prior.	Protect. in Place
√	√	√

Product & Service Synthesis

User-centred	Tech-driven	Imped. Matchin	Creat. Synth.	9-layer model	Service Wrap.
	√			√	√

Manufacturing, Assembly & Deployment

Def. Chall.	Integ. Deploy.	Innov. Req
√	√	

Funding & Investment

Pref.	Fund.Quant.	Valuation
Private	£3m	£20m

Talent, Leadership & Culture

Over. Prior.	Talent	Team	Org struct.	Leadership	Culture
√	√	√		√	

Commercialisation Strategy

Vector Focus: Crossing Chasm II

Defined Strategic Goal?	√
Strategic Gap Clarity?	√

Business Model

Defined Narrative	√
Explicit Architecture	√
Components Defined	√
Business Model Metrics	
Revenues & Costs	√
Cash Flow Projections	√

Market Space

Financial Services-Insurance	Value Chain	√

Local	Nationa	Global		
		√	T-max	60	Mths

Proposition Framing

Propos. Defn.	Comp.	Reg.	Diff.	Partners & Suppliers
√	√		√	√

Source of Differentiation

Single Component	Overall Chain	Re-framing Chain
√		

Customer Definition

Business	Govt.	Consumer	Knowledge Workers
√			

Max Accessible No of Customers	Cmax	2,000

Distribution Marketing & Sales

Defined Go to Market Priorities		√
Defined Channel Strategy		Overall m7Ps	√

Product	Pos.	Pricing	Place	Prom.	Pro	Partn.
√		√	√		√	√

Figure 16. Consumer insurance AI — Commercialisation monitor @ Chasm II.

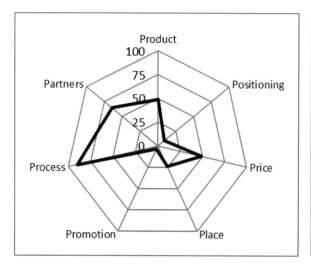

Process:
Crossing Chasm II critically depended on the processes involved in claims processing
Product:
The product and service definition depended strongly on understanding the relationship between users and processes
Partners:
Effective distribution depended on understanding the role of partners, so it could be baked into the product proposition to support the business model
Price: The pricing discussions with customers, including the different revenue components, were critical in formulating a sustainable business model

Figure 17. m7Ps profile at Chasm II for proposition focused on large insurance players.

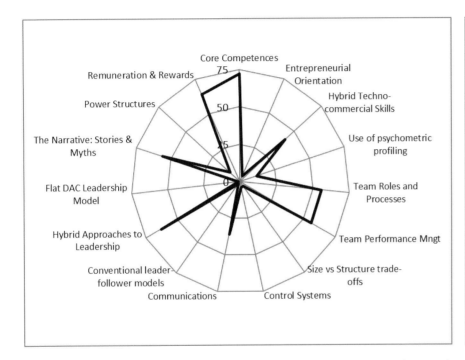

The radar chart axes (clockwise from top):
Core Competences, Entrepreneurial Orientation, Hybrid Techno-commercial Skills, Use of psychometric profiling, Team Roles and Processes, Team Performance Mngt, Size vs Structure trade-offs, Control Systems, Communications, Conventional leader-follower models, Hybrid Approaches to Leadership, Flat DAC Leadership Model, The Narrative: Stories & Myths, Power Structures, Remuneration & Rewards.

Scale markings: 0, 25, 50, 75

The Talent, Leadership & Culture Vector was critical in crossing Chasm II

In particular there was a strong focus on core competences (AI & Robotics expertise). hybrid techno-commercial skills), understanding team roles, processes and performance management.

Given the paucity of the deep technical skills required, there was also a strong emphasis on remuneration and rewards, coupled with a strong narrative around AI-enabled transformation

The leadership model depended on a hybrid approach where top management functioned in a more hierarchical style consistent with corporate insurance customers, whilst the teams building and deploying the product were organised in a flat DAC model. Communicating the reasoning behind this to the whole team was critical

Figure 18. Talent, leadership & culture at Chasm II crossing.

15.4 Assisted Social Housing

15.4.1 *Crossing Chasm I*

Opportunity: There is a recurrent national problem in providing adequate social housing for those with special needs, particularly individuals with physical disabilities. There was an opportunity to deliver integrated social provision to meet this challenge.

Vision: To provide an integrated approach to the delivery of a service for assisted social housing.

Approach: The approach adopted was to understand all the components required to deliver this vision and to focus on two key areas: the main areas of weakness and 'joining up' all the components to deliver a seamless experience for tenants.

Trajectory: The starting point of this journey was to identify all the components required to design, build and test a prototype solution for assisted social housing. This focused on designing, building and adapting the first group of houses with the required features and functionality. This was followed by pilot testing with a small group of selected tenants to understand what changes might be required to the basis design. This also enabled early discussions with relevant parties on the issues around allocation of these properties and their active management.

Insights & Observations

External vectors: The critical external vectors at this point in the commercialisation process covered the market space (including understanding the market-specific value chain), framing the proposition and understanding customer needs in detail.

Internal vectors: The product definition and synthesis vector was the key focus at this stage of maturity, in particular, the precise functionality required.

Composite vectors: The commercialisation strategy, reflecting the qualitative trade-offs between the external and internal vectors was the key focus at this point in the journey. Figures 19, 20, and 21 summarise the key insights from this case study.

THE COMMERCIALISATION MONITOR

The Vision | Build assisted social housing

Chasm Locator				I		II		III
mTRL CRL	0	1	2	3	4	5	6	7	8	9

Contingent Technology Deployment

Base Tech	App. Tech	Platform	Apps & Tools	Product	Service

Intellectual Property Management

Def.Key Comp.	Def. Prior.	Protect. in Place

Product & Service Synthesis

User-centred	Tech-driven	Imped. Matchin	Creat. Synth.	9-layer model	Service Wrap.
√					

Manufacturing, Assembly & Deployment

Def. Chall.	Integ. Deploy.	Innov. Req

Funding & Investment

Pref.	Fund.Quant.	Valuation
State	£1m	£5m

Talent, Leadership & Culture

Over. Prior.	Talent	Team	Org struct.	Leadership	Culture
		√			

Commercialisation Strategy

Vector Profile Crossing Chasm I

Defined Strategic Goal?	√
Strategic Gap Clarity?	

Business Model

Defined Narrative	
Explicit Architecture	
Components Defined	
Business Model Metrics	
Revenues & Costs	
Cash Flow Projections	

Market Space

Global		Value Chain	√

Local	Nationa	Global
	√	

T-max	60	Mths

Proposition Framing

Propos. Defn.	Comp.	Reg.	Diff.	Partners & Suppliers
√	√	√		√

Source of Differentiation

Single Component	Overall Chain	Re-framing Chain
	√	

Customer Definition

Business	Govt.	Consumer	Knowledge Workers
		√	

Max Accessible No of Customers	Cmax	2000

Distribution Marketing & Sales

Defined Go to Market Priorities		
Defined Channel Strategy		Overall m7Ps

Product	Pos.	Pricing	Place	Prom.	Pro	Partn.

Figure 19. Assisted social housing commercialisation monitor @ Chasm I.

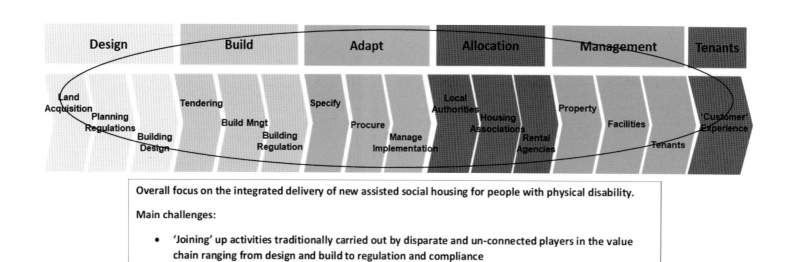

| Design | Build | Adapt | Allocation | Management | Tenants |

Land Acquisition
Planning Regulations
Building Design

Tendering
Build Mngt
Building Regulation

Specify
Procure
Manage Implementation

Local Authorities
Housing Associations
Rental Agencies

Property
Facilities
Tenants

'Customer' Experience

Overall focus on the integrated delivery of new assisted social housing for people with physical disability.

Main challenges:

- 'Joining' up activities traditionally carried out by disparate and un-connected players in the value chain ranging from design and build to regulation and compliance
- Creating an integrated proposition capable of attracting the required funding

Figure 20.   Proposition framing for assisted social housing agency.

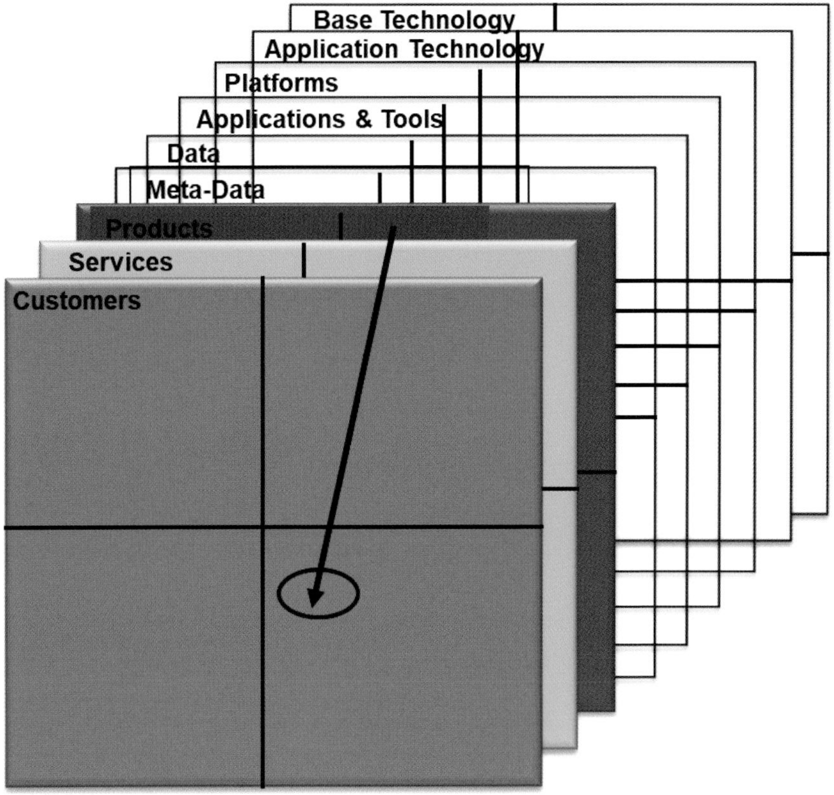
Base Technology
Application Technology
Platforms
Applications & Tools
Data
Meta-Data
Products
Services
Customers

- **Product**
  - New social housing designed for assisted living
  - Built to best regulatory standards
- **Services**
  - Services to enable assisted living
  - Integrated services
- **Customers**
  - Tenants with physical disabilities
  - Tenants re-housed from previous in-adequate accomodation

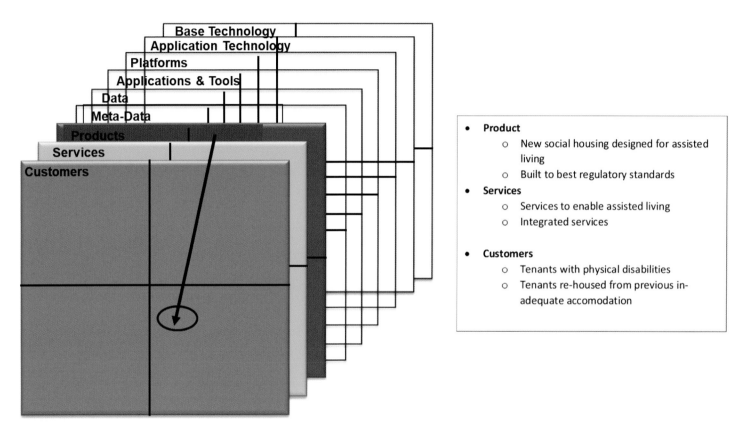

Figure 21. Products and services for assisted social housing.

15.4.2 *Crossing Chasm II*

Opportunity: Having successfully completed a pilot trial based on building a small group of homes specially built and adapted for assisted social living, the challenge now was to scale this up and demonstrate its commercial viability.

Vision: The vision was to create a significant new capacity based on a robust hybrid business model.

Approach: The new assisted living agency focused on scaling up the building programme, assembling a new management team to deliver the integrated proposition and negotiating with funders and stakeholders to create a sustainable business model for the new agency.

Trajectory; The starting point of this part of the journey was the post-Chasm I prototype delivery. The key areas of focus going forward were: 'productionising' the build of new properties, understanding the service delivery challenge, creating a sustainable business model where the revenues and costs could be balanced systematically, and building the new team to deliver the service. The end point of this journey was the successful achievement of these goals, reflected in the crossing of Chasm II.

Insights & Observations

External vectors: The key external vectors included proposition framing and customer definition, but the primary focus was on distribution, marketing and sales, with particular emphasis on the m7Ps priorities to cross Chasm II.

Internal vectors: Apart from the continued focus on the product and service proposition, the focus now was on manufacturing and delivery, funding & investment, and especially the talent, leadership and culture required to deliver the proposition.

Composite vectors: The commercialisation strategy vector reflected the qualitative trade-offs required for successful delivery, but the business model vector was critical to the successful crossing of Chasm II; this required particular attention to the generation of revenues directly from tenants also from those providing proxy funding for tenants. Figures 22, 23, and 24 summarise the key insights from this case study.

THE COMMERCIALISATION MONITOR

The Vision — Deliver and manage assisted social housing for people with physical disabilities

Chasm Locator			I		II		III

mTRL CRL	0	1	2	3		4	5	6	7	8	9

(Chasm Locator circled at II; mTRL/CRL circled around 6–7)

Contingent Technology Deployment

Base Tech	App. Tech	Platform	Apps & Tools	Product	Service

Intellectual Property Management

Def.Key Comp.	Def. Prior.	Protect. in Place

Product & Service Synthesis

User-centred	Tech-driven	Imped. Matchin	Creat. Synth.	9-layer model	Service Wrap.
√				√	√

Manufacturing, Assembly & Deployment

Def. Chall.	Integ. Deploy.	Innov. Req
	√	

Funding & Investment

Pref.	Fund.Quant.	Valuation
State	£30m	£100m

Talent, Leadership & Culture

Over. Prior.	Talent	Team	Org struct.	Leadership	Culture
√		√	√	√	√

Commercialisation Strategy

Vector Focus crossing Chasm II

Defined Strategic Goal?	√
Strategic Gap Clarity?	√

Business Model

Defined Narrative	√
Explicit Architecture	√
Components Defined	√
Business Model Metrics	
Revenues & Costs	√
Cash Flow Projections	√

Market Space

	Value Chain	√

Local	Nationa	Global		
	√		T-max	120 Mths

Proposition Framing

Propos. Defn.	Comp.	Reg.	Diff.	Partners & Suppliers
√	√	√		√

Source of Differentiation

Single Component	Overall Chain	Re-framing Chain
	√	

Customer Definition

Business	Govt.	Consumer	Knowledge Workers
		√	

Max Accessible No of Customers	Cmax	10,000

Distribution Marketing & Sales

Defined Go to Market Priorities	√
Defined Channel Strategy	
Overall m7Ps	√

Product	Pos.	Pricing	Place	Prom.	Pro	Partn.
√	√	√			√	√

Figure 22. Assisted social housing commercialisation monitor @ Chasm II.

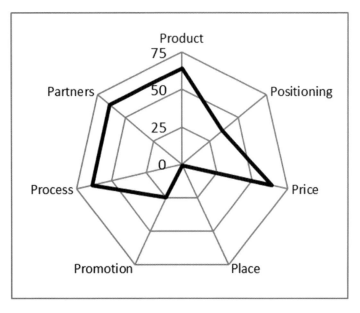

Figure 23. The m7Ps model at Chasm II.

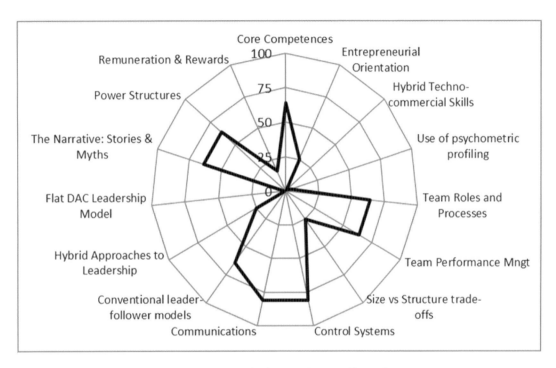

Figure 24. Talent, leadership & culture profile at Chasm II.

Chapter 16

From Inception to Significant Commercial Success

16.1 Provision of Digital Images to the Media Industry

16.1.1 *Crossing Chasm I*

Opportunity: As the volume of web-based content grew dramatically in the late 1990s, the firm recognised the opportunity to provide imagery to media and advertising players building their own websites.

Vision: Provision of image-based content and services to SMEs and digital media entrepreneurs based on a new low-cost business model.

Approach: The approach adopted was to create indexable image databases, to build image banks and allow customers to access and buy content using online tools.

Trajectory: The journey started with the acquisition some image assets; the firm then built a new indexing system and used it to start creating searchable image archives. This included the design of a new taxonomy for image description, the acquisition of image water-marking technology and the construction of an indexed databank of images. The provision of user tools connected to the database completed the construction of a prototype service for testing with a small group of pilot users.

Insights & Observations

External vectors: The key vectors in crossing Chasm I were defining the market space, framing the product and service proposition and defining the target customers.

Internal vectors: Technology development and deployment was a key vector, including integrating image capture, indexing, copyrighting, storing and retrieval into an integrated platform; the other key vector was defining the actual product & service, in terms of functionality, form and features.

Composite vectors: Neither of the two composite vectors, commercialisation strategy and business model, were addressed at this point in the journey. Figures 1, 2, and 3 summarise the key insights from this case study.

THE COMMERCIALISATION MONITOR

ME 1

The Vision	Provision of image-based content and services to SME's and digital media entrepreneurs based on a new low cost business model

Chasm Locator	I	II	III

mTRL CRL	0	1	2	3	4	5	6	7	8	9

Technology Dev & Contingent Deployment

Base Tech	App. Tech	Platform	Apps & Tools	Product	Service
		√			

Intellectual Property Management

Def.Key Comp.	Def. Prior.	Protect. in Place
√	√	

Product & Service Synthesis

User-centred	Tech-driven	Imped. Matchin	Creat. Synth.	9-layer model	Service Wrap.
			√		

Manufacturing & Deployment

Def. Chall.	Integ. Deploy.	Innov. Req

Funding & Investment

Pref.	Fund.Quant.	Valuation
Private	£3m	£10m

Talent, Leadership & Culture

Over. Prior.	Talent	Team	Org struct.	Leadership	Culture
√	√				

Commercialisation Strategy

Current Vector Strength

Market Space
Funding & Investment — Proposition Framing & Competitive Positioning
Talent, Leadership and Culture — Customer Definition
Technology Development and Contingent Deployment — Distribution, Marketing & Sales
Product and Service Definition and Synthesis — Business Model
Manufacturing & Deployment — Commercialisation Strategy
IP Management

— Weighted score

Defined Strategic Goal?	√
Strategic Gap Clarity?	

Business Model

Defined Narrative	√
Explicit Architecture	
Components Defined	√
Business Model Metrics	
Revenues & Costs	
Cash Flow Projections	

Market Space

Media & Entertainment	Value Chain	√

Local	National	Global	T-max	60	Mths
	√				

Proposition Framing

Propos. Defn.	Comp.	Reg.	Diff.	Partners & Suppliers
√	√	√		

Source of Differentiation

Single Component	Overall Chain	Re-framing Chain
	√	

Customer Definition

Business	Govt.	Consumer	Knowledge Workers
√			√

Max Accessible No of Customers	Cmax	1 milion SMEs

Distribution Marketing & Sales

Defined Go to Market Priorities	√
Defined Channel Strategy	
Overall m7Ps	

Product	Pos.	Pricing	Place	Prom.	Proc.	Partn.
√						

Figure 1. Provision of digital imagery commercialisation monitor @ Chasm I.

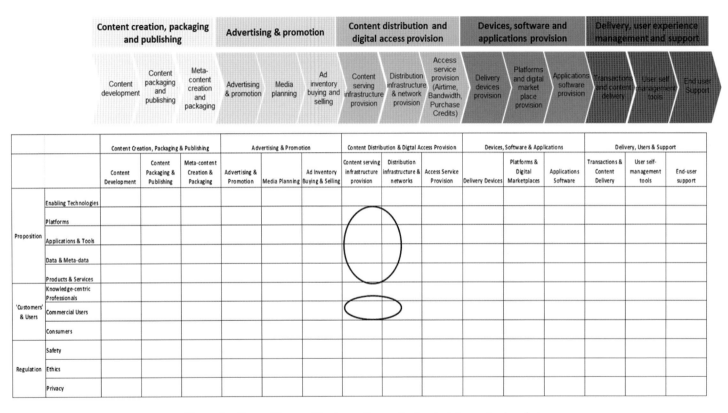

Figure 2. Proposition positioning vs the media & entertainment value chain.

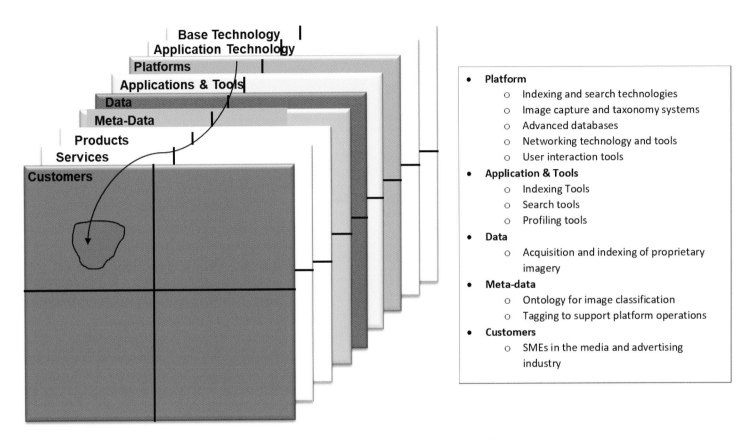

Figure 3. Digital imagery product decomposition @ Chasm I.

- **Platform**
  - Indexing and search technologies
  - Image capture and taxonomy systems
  - Advanced databases
  - Networking technology and tools
  - User interaction tools
- **Application & Tools**
  - Indexing Tools
  - Search tools
  - Profiling tools
- **Data**
  - Acquisition and indexing of proprietary imagery
- **Meta-data**
  - Ontology for image classification
  - Tagging to support platform operations
- **Customers**
  - SMEs in the media and advertising industry

16.1.2 *Crossing Chasm II*

Opportunity: Having demonstrated the prototype, the next task was to build a commercially viable service and demonstrate commercial viability.

Vision: Provision of 'royalty free' images and image handling tools to publishers, media agencies and web developers.

Approach: Build an integrated service platform, test it with charter customers from the key sub-segments in the media and advertising industry, and test it with the first charter customers.

Trajectory: Building on the prototype, the starting point of this journey was to define and build the full-service platform, and then deploy and test with early customer. This involved multiple iterations until the functionality of the platform was stable. The final part of crossing Chasm II was experimenting with different potential business models and performing multiple iterations until the firm alighted on

a model with the desired characteristics of robustness, sustainability and enough margin generation!

Insights & Observations

External vectors: The key priority in crossing Chasm II was to widen and deepen understanding and interaction with customers.

Internal vectors: Managing human talent was very important at this stage but the key focus was on the two composite vectors.

Composite vectors: The key to success lay in defining a clear commercialisation strategy and focusing on execution — but probably the real turning point came in the adoption of a new business model, called **royalty-free** which reversed previous commercial logic based on clearing image rights at the point of sale: instead this new approach was based on pre-clearance or outright ownership of image copyright, so that in effect the images were free of royalty payments, provided the right to use for paid for at the point of transaction. Figures 4, 5, and 6 summarise the key insights from this case study.

THE COMMERCIALISATION MONITOR

ME 1

The Vision	Provision of 'royalty free' images and image handling tools to publishers, media agencies and web developers

Chasm Locator — I, II, III

mTRL CRL — 0 1 2 3 4 5 6 7 8 9

Technology Dev & Contingent Deployment

Base Tech	App. Tech	Platform	Apps & Tools	Product	Service
		√	√		√

Intellectual Property Management

Def. Key Comp.	Def. Prior.	Protect. in Place
√	√	√

Product & Service Synthesis

User-centred	Tech-driven	Imped. Matchin	Creat. Synth.	9-layer model	Service Wrap.
			√	√	√

Manufacturing & Deployment

Def. Chall.	Integ. Deploy.	Innov. Req
√		

Funding & Investment

Pref.	Fund.Quant.	Valuation
Private	£10m	£100m

Talent, Leadership & Culture

Over. Prior.	Talent	Team	Org struct.	Leadership	Culture
√	√	√		√	√

Commercialisation Strategy

Current Vector Strength

Defined Strategic Goal?	√
Strategic Gap Clarity?	√

Business Model

Defined Narrative	√
Explicit Architecture	√
Components Defined	√
Business Model Metrics	√
Revenues & Costs	√
Cash Flow Projections	√

Market Space

Media & Entertainment		Value Chain	√

Local	National	Global	T-max	120	Mths
√	√	√			

Proposition Framing

Propos. Defn.	Comp.	Reg.	Diff.	Partners & Suppliers
√	√	√	√	√

Source of Differentiation

Single Component	Overall Chain	Re-framing Chain
	√	

Customer Definition

Business	Govt.	Consumer	Knowledge Workers
√			√

Max Accessible No of Customers	Cmax	2 milion

Distribution Marketing & Sales

Defined Go to Market Priorities		√
Defined Channel Strategy		Overall m7Ps

Product	Pos.	Pricing	Place	Prom.	Proc.	Partn.
√	√	√	√			

Figure 4. Provision of digital imagery commercialisation monitor @ Chasm II.

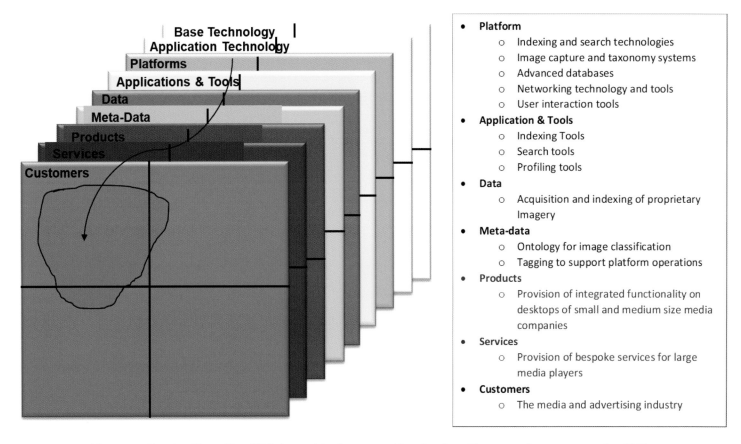

Figure 5. Crossing Chasm II — 'Wider' more joined-up proposition aimed at wider group of customers, not just SMEs.

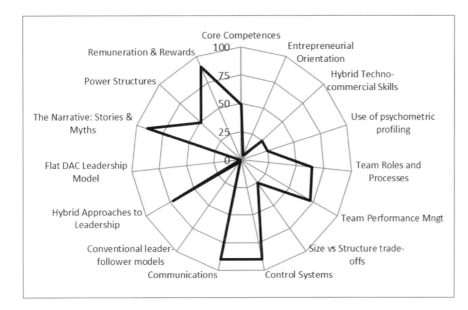

Sustaining rapid growth and maintaining focus required particular attention to three key areas, apart from creating and sustaining the overall raison d'etre:

- Intense and regular communication with the rapidly expanding team to ensure coherence in all customer dealings
- Strong control systems to balance a very free-wheeling and relaxed culture
- Close attention to remuneration and rewards structures to ensure strong motivation of teams

Figure 6. Talent, leadership & culture — The key to crossing Chasm II.

16.1.3 *Crossing Chasm III*

Opportunity: Having demonstrated working product and created a sustainable business with strong charter customers, the opportunity was to scale the firm globally, to widen the customer base and provide a group of services to support the acquisition, use and maximisation of imagery in a very broad range of applications.

Vision: Provision of images and related content and services to publishers, advertising and media agencies, digital developers, media companies and marketing departments in firms of all sizes, based on 'royalty-free' products and services.

Approach: The firm addressed this in three ways: acquisition of firms with significant image assets, integrating these assets into the firm's offering and the provision of more sophisticated service usage tools.

Trajectory: Significant ramping up of revenues to cross Chasm III consisted of three steps:

- Systematic acquisition of a range of companies to provide global coverage, wider sets of imagery and new image manipulation tools.

- Ensuring the provision of all these assets through a single branded access portal.
- Structure marketing and sales programme to ensure an active presence in all key geographies and market segments.

Insights & Observations

External vectors: Apart from the widening of the proposition, the key focus at this stage was on distribution, marketing & sales with the emphasis on pace; the view was to sign up many deals quickly and then fine tune based on experience — classic land-grab approach.

Internal vectors: Attention to the execution team was the most critical internal vector: the land-grab strategy required close attention to having the right talent in the firm and organising it effectively.

Composite vectors: The strategy was well set now, so the focus was on adjustments to the business model to reflect the wider customer base, the wider customer proposition and the emergence of new competitors trying to emulate the firm's approach. Figures 7, 8, and 9 summarise the key insights from this case study.

THE COMMERCIALISATION MONITOR

ME 1

		Chasm Locator			I			II			III
The Vision	Provision of Images and related content and services to publishers, advertising and media agencies, digital developers, media companies and marketing departments in firms of all sizes, based on 'royalty-free' products and services	mTRL CRL	0	1	2	3		4	5	6	7	8	9

Technology Dev & Contingent Deployment

Base Tech	App. Tech	Platform	Apps & Tools	Product	Service
		√	√	√	√

Intellectual Property Management

Def.Key Comp.	Def. Prior.	Protect. in Place
√	√	√

Product & Service Synthesis

User-centred	Tech-driven	Imped. Matchin	Creat. Synth.	9-layer model	Service Wrap.
			√	√	√

Manufacturing & Deployment

Def. Chall.	Integ. Deploy.	Innov. Req
√	√	

Funding & Investment

Pref.	Fund.Quant.	Valuation
Private	£25m	£250m

Talent, Leadership & Culture

Over. Prior.	Talent	Team	Org struct.	Leadership	Culture
√	√	√	√	√	√

Commercialisation Strategy

Current Vector Strength

Defined Strategic Goal?	√
Strategic Gap Clarity?	√

Business Model

Defined Narrative	√
Explicit Architecture	√
Components Defined	√
Business Model Metrics	√
Revenues & Costs	√
Cash Flow Projections	√

Market Space

Media & Entertainment			Value Chain	√

Local	National	Global	T-max	120	Mths
√	√	√			

Proposition Framing

Propos. Defn.	Comp.	Reg.	Diff.	Partners & Suppliers
√	√	√	√	√

Source of Differentiation

Single Component	Overall Chain	Re-framing Chain
	√	

Customer Definition

Business	Govt.	Consumer	Knowledge Workers
√	√		√

Max Accessible No of Customers	Cmax	10 milion

Distribution Marketing & Sales

Defined Go to Market Priorities		√	
Defined Channel Strategy	√	Overall m7Ps	√

Product	Pos.	Pricing	Place	Prom.	Proc.	Partn.
√	√	√	√	√	√	√

Figure 7. Provision of digital imagery commercialisation monitor @ Chasm III.

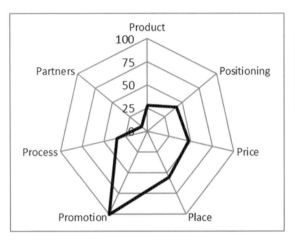

Product: Stable Product Offering

Positioning: Based on fulfilling new digital media needs

Price: Aggressive pricing to drive growth

Place: Online only

Promotion: Big digital marketing push

Process: Sales process streamlined

Partners: Early partners eased out with big own brand push

Figure 8. Focus on new market space needs and distribution models — Wider customer typology to support Chasm III crossing.

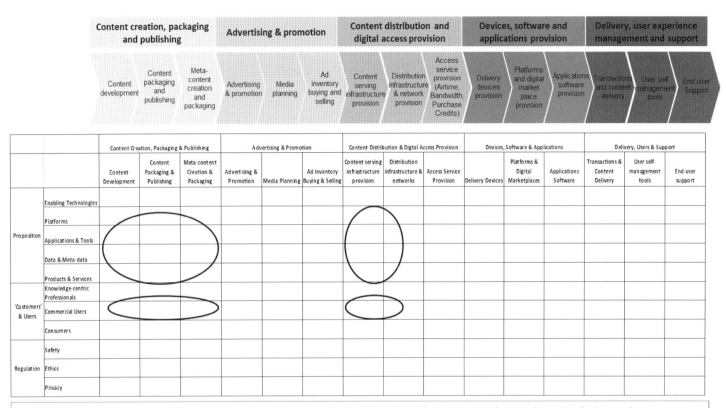

- Acquisition of new related content assets: still and moving imagery, sounds, content packaging & manipulation tools
- Packaging and delivering enhanced services under newly-developed Brand
- Positioning of new integrated brand offer

Figure 9. Widening the proposition.

16.2 Low-Power Computing Architectures, Platforms & Tools

16.2.1 *Crossing Chasm I*

Opportunity: The small team in this start-up firm had developed a new computer architecture which had the potential to create new low-power low-cost processing chips to fire the next generation of growth in both fixed and mobile computing and exploit the emerging commercial opportunity.

Vision: Creation of a low-cost, low-power computing architecture and chipset.

Approach: Small tightly-knit team of analogue and digital designers was assembled and given this challenge to solve.

———————————

Trajectory: The team began working on the conceptual design using experience combined with computational design tools, supported by their intuition. Simple lab prototypes were built to test the working principles, until the team eventually came up with a chip design that could be fabricated. A contract semi-conductor foundry with the right expertise was identified and several versions of the chip were fabricated until the design parameters were met. Having crossed Chasm I successfully, the firm was now ready to explore commercialisation pathways.

———————————

Insights & Observations

External vectors: Understanding the operation of the market-space-centric value chain was critical in shaping the functionality, form and features of this new chip design; The most critical external vector of course was shaping the proposition to meet this requirement.

Internal vectors: The critical internal vector of course was the technology development and deployment vector, supported by the vector which defined the synthesis of the product components; the talent vector was also important, defining the specialised design expertise required.

Composite vectors: Neither the commercialisation strategy or business model vectors were important in crossing Chasm I. Figures 10, 11, and 12 summarise the key insights from this case study.

THE COMMERCIALISATION MONITOR — EH 1

The Vision	Creation of a low-cost, low-power computing architecture and chip-set

Chasm Locator: I, II, III

mTRL / CRL: 0 1 2 ⟨3⟩ 4 5 6 7 8 9

Contingent Technology Deployment

Base Tech	App. Tech	Platform	Apps & Tools	Product	Service
	√				

Intellectual Property Management

Def. Key Comp.	Def. Prior.	Protect. in Place
√		

Product & Service Synthesis

User-centred	Tech-driven	Imped. Matchin	Creat. Synth.	9-layer model	Service Wrap.
	√		√		

Manufacturing & Deployment

Def. Chall.	Integ. Deploy.	Innov. Req

Funding & Investment

Pref. Sour.	Fund. Quant.	Valuation
Private	£3m	£10m

Talent, Leadership & Culture

Over. Prior.	Talent	Team	Org struct.	Leadership	Culture
√	√	√			

Commercialisation Strategy

Vector Profile Chasm I

Defined Strategic Goal?	√
Strategic Gap Clarity?	

Business Model

Defined Narrative	√
Explicit Architecture	
Components Defined	
Business Model Metrics	
Revenues & Costs	
Cash Flow Projections	

Market Space

Electronics & Computing Hardware	Value Chain	√

Local	National	Global	T-max	120	Mths
		√			

Proposition Framing

Propos. Defn.	Comp.	Reg.	Diff.	Partners & Suppliers
√	√		√	

Source of Differentiation:

Single Component	Overall Chain	Re-framing Chain
√		

Customer Definition

Business	Govt.	Consumer	Knowledge Workers
√			

Max Accessible No of Customers	Cmax	700-1000

Distribution Marketing & Sales

Defined Go to Market Priorities	
Defined Channel Strategy	Overall m7Ps

Product	Pos.	Pricing	Place	Prom.	Proc.	Partn.
√						

Figure 10. Low-power computing architectures, tools and chips commercialisation monitor @ Chasm I.

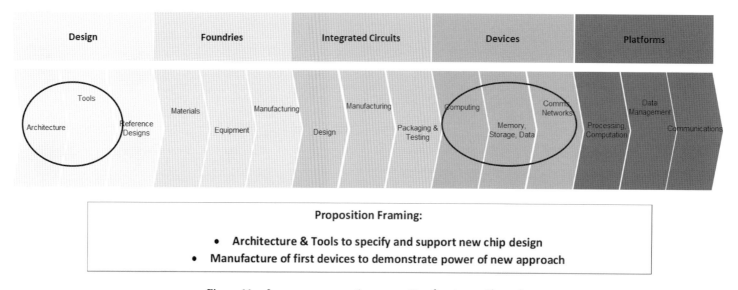

Proposition Framing:

- **Architecture & Tools to specify and support new chip design**
- **Manufacture of first devices to demonstrate power of new approach**

Figure 11. Low-power computing proposition framing at Chasm I.

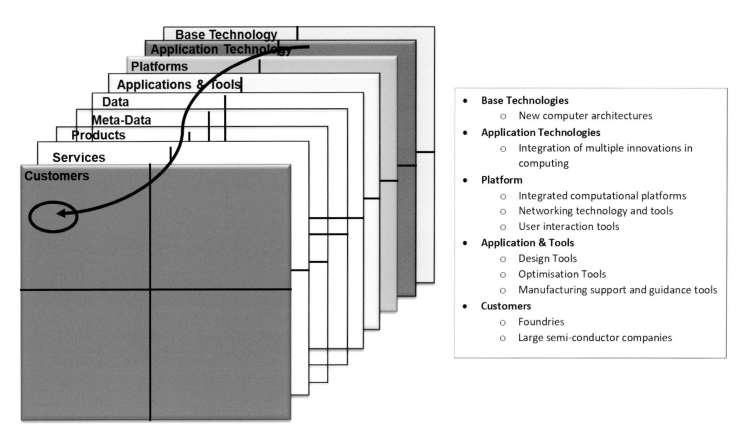

Figure 12. Low-power computing — Product decomposition @ Chasm I.

- **Base Technologies**
    - o New computer architectures
- **Application Technologies**
    - o Integration of multiple innovations in computing
- **Platform**
    - o Integrated computational platforms
    - o Networking technology and tools
    - o User interaction tools
- **Application & Tools**
    - o Design Tools
    - o Optimisation Tools
    - o Manufacturing support and guidance tools
- **Customers**
    - o Foundries
    - o Large semi-conductor companies

16.2.2 Crossing Chasm II

Opportunity: Having crossed Chasm I to successfully demonstrate the concept, the opportunity was to extend this to demonstrate how it could be applied to a wide range of market and application spaces.

Vision: Creation of low-power, low-cost architecture to power next generation of computing platforms.

Approach: The approach adopted was to tackle other parts of the market space-centric value chain to actively demonstrate the power of this approach to next generation processor chips, which required the firm to engage actively in the design of chips, integrated circuits, computing devices and platforms.

Trajectory: This required a very broad approach where different market and application spaces were tackled in parallel; in each case, this required active engagement in the design and manufacture of a wide range of devices, usually in conjunction with partners. This trajectory enabled the firm to experiment with a wide range of potential strategies and business models, leading to the successful crossing of Chasm II.

Insights & Observations

External vectors: All four external vectors were important in crossing Chasm II: understanding the differences in the market space, tuning the core proposition to address the wider application areas, different customer needs and variations in distribution channels for different levels of functional integration.

Internal vectors: All six internal vectors were also critical when crossing Chasm II: human capital, technology and IP remained important given the nature of the proposition, as did the funding vector; but success depended heavily on the synthesis of new products & service coupled with manufacturing and deployment.

Composite vectors: The composite vectors were critical for success, in particular, navigating the different strategic options and making the right business model choices. Figures 13, 14, and 15 summarise the key insights from this case study.

THE COMMERCIALISATION MONITOR

The Vision	Creation of low-power, low cost architecture to power next generation of computing platforms

Chasm Locator					I				II			III
mTRL CRL	0	1	2	3		4	5	6		7	8	9

Contingent Technology Deployment

Base Tech	App. Tech	Platform	Apps & Tools	Product	Service
		√	√		

Intellectual Property Management

Def.Key Comp.	Def. Prior.	Protect. in Place
√	√	√

Product & Service Synthesis

User-centred	Tech-driven	Imped. Matchin	Creat. Synth.	9-layer model	Service Wrap.
	√	√		√	

Manufacturing & Deployment

Def. Chall.	Integ. Deploy.	Innov. Req
√		√

Funding & Investment

Pref. Sour.	Fund.Quant.	Valuation
Private	£20m	£100m

Talent, Leadership & Culture

Over. Prior.	Talent	Team	Org struct.	Leadership	Culture
√	√	√	√	√	

Commercialisation Strategy

Current Vector Strength

Defined Strategic Goal?	√
Strategic Gap Clarity?	√

Business Model

Defined Narrative	√
Explicit Architecture	√
Components Defined	√
Business Model Metrics	
Revenues & Costs	√
Cash Flow Projections	√

Market Space

Electronics & Computing Hardware	Value Chain	√

Local	National	Global	T-max	120	Mths
		√			

Proposition Framing

Propos. Defn.	Comp.	Reg.	Diff.	Partners & Suppliers
√	√		√	√

Source of Differentiation

Single Component	Overall Chain	Re-framing Chain
√		

Customer Definition

Business	Govt.	Consumer	Knowledge Workers
√			√

Max Accessible No of Customers	Cmax	3000

Distribution Marketing & Sales

Defined Go to Market Priorities		√
Defined Channel Strategy	√	Overall m7Ps	

Product	Pos.	Pricing	Place	Prom.	Proc.	Partn.
√	√	√				√

Figure 13. Low-power computing architectures, tools and chips commercialisation monitor @ Chasm II.

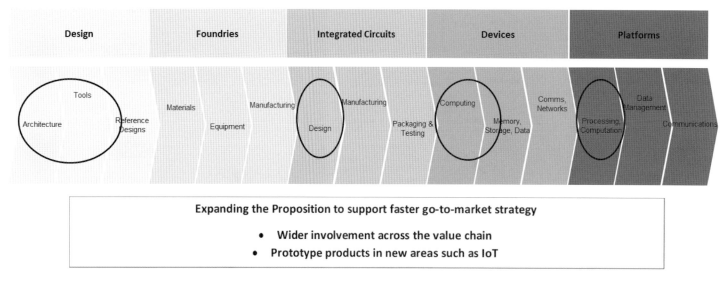

Figure 14.   Low-power computing proposition framing at Chasm II.

Component	NRE	Licenses		Royalties	Leasing	Outright Sale		Commission	Matchmaker	Transactions	Subscriptions		Proxies	
		Perpetual	Time-bound			Core	Consumables				Time-metered	Value-metered	Advertising	Sponsorship
Services														
Products	√													
Meta-Content														
Content														
Apps, Tools & Processes	√	√	√											
Technology Platforms	√	√	√	√	√									
Application Technologies	√	√	√	√										
Base Technologies		√	√	√										

Figure 15. Multiple revenue sources underpinning business model.

16.2.3 *Crossing Chasm III*

Opportunity: Having successfully demonstrated the huge potential of this approach, the opportunity now was to significantly scale the business by becoming a major player in the global electronics and computing market space.

Vision: Licensing of computer architectures, provision of hardware and software design tools and licensing of reference designs for designers and manufacturers to build and sell advanced computing platforms for a wide range of applications in mobile computing and IoT space.

Approach: The strategic approach adopted was to focus on developing, exploiting and managing the strong IP position and partnering with a wider group of players in other parts of the market space-centric value chain.

Trajectory: The starting point was active engagement in enabling a wide range of markets and applications. By a process of re-focusing on the crown jewels and turning partners into customers, and broadening the target customer base, the firm was able to accelerate the crossing of Chasm III without having to invest heavily in the process.

Insights & Observations

External vectors: The market space vector was less important now because the firm had a very good understanding of the future shape of this space arising from the work done when crossing Chasm II; the focus now was re-shaping the proposition, re-setting the dialogues with customers but most importantly focusing on the different distribution challenge.

Internal vectors: The value of the human capital, technology development & deployment and IP management increased significantly due to this new strategic direction; funding was no longer an issue since the firm did an IPO soon after crossing Chasm II.

Composite vectors: The commercialisation strategy was very important in terms of guiding this new direction, but once again, the business model vector held the key to success as the firm's revenue sources were focused on licensing and royalties with some NRE to support new innovation. Figures 16, 17, and 18 summarise the key insights from this case study.

THE COMMERCIALISATION MONITOR

								EH 1

The Vision	Licensing of computer architectures, provision of hardware and software design tools, and licensing of reference designs for designers and manufacturers to build and sell advanced computing platforms for a wide range of applications in mobile computing and IoT space

Chasm Locator: I · II · III (III circled)

mTRL CRL: 0 1 2 3 | 4 5 6 | 7 8 9 (9 circled)

Contingent Technology Deployment

Base Tech	App. Tech	Platform	Apps & Tools	Product	Service
		√	√		

Commercialisation Strategy

Current Vector Strength

— Weighted score

Defined Strategic Goal?	√
Strategic Gap Clarity?	√

Market Space

Electronics & Computing Hardware		Value Chain	√

Local	National	Global
		√

T-max 120 Mths

Intellectual Property Management

Def.Key Comp.	Def. Prior.	Protect. in Place
√	√	√

Product & Service Synthesis

User-centred	Tech-driven	Imped. Matchin	Creat. Synth.	9-layer model	Service Wrap.
	√			√	√

Proposition Framing

Propos. Defn.	Comp.	Reg.	Diff.	Partners & Suppliers
√	√		√	√

Source of Differentiation:

Single Component	Overall Chain	Re-framing Chain
√		

Manufacturing & Deployment

Def. Chall.	Integ. Deploy.	Innov. Req
√	√	

Business Model

Defined Narrative	√
Explicit Architecture	√
Components Defined	√
Business Model Metrics	√
Revenues & Costs	√
Cash Flow Projections	√

Customer Definition

Business	Govt.	Consumer	Knowledge Workers
√			

Max Accessible No of Customers	Cmax	10,000

Funding & Investment

Pref.	Fund.Quant.	Valuation
IPO	£100m	£3000m

Distribution Marketing & Sales

Defined Go to Market Priorities	√
Defined Channel Strategy √	Overall m7Ps √

Product	Pos.	Pricing	Place	Prom.	Proc.	Partn.
√	√	√	√	√	√	√

Talent, Leadership & Culture

Over. Prior.	Talent	Team	Org struct.	Leadership	Culture
√	√	√	√	√	√

Figure 16. Low-power computing architectures, tools and chips commercialisation monitor @ Chasm III.

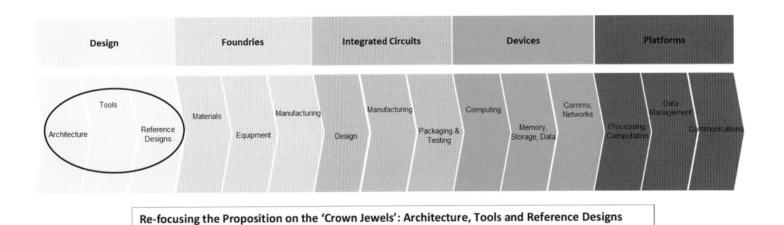

| Design | Foundries | Integrated Circuits | Devices | Platforms |

Architecture | Tools | Reference Designs | Materials | Equipment | Manufacturing | Design | Manufacturing | Packaging & Testing | Computing | Memory, Storage, Data | Comms, Networks | Processing, Computation | Data Management | Communications

Re-focusing the Proposition on the 'Crown Jewels': Architecture, Tools and Reference Designs

Figure 17. The re-focused product proposition to tackle volume markets.

Figure 18. The m7Ps @ Chasm III.

16.3 Womens' Fashion Clothing Retail & E-Commerce

16.3.1 *Crossing Chasm I*

Opportunity: The entrepreneurs who created this firm believed there was an opportunity to create a new line in branded womens' fashion clothing for business wear, to be sold through existing retail channels.

Vision: To create and sell a new range of womens' business fashion clothing.

Approach: The team's approach to this opportunity was to build a new line of clothing, using creative designers and to demonstrate the viability of this idea by selling the products through a single national multi-brand store in a metropolitan area.

Trajectory: The firm started by designing this line of women's fashion ware, having the clothes manufactured in small volumes; they then worked closely with a multi-brand store to launch this limited product range to test consumer responses to the product, it's positioning and it's initial pricing. Positive results confirmed successful crossing of Chasm I.

Insights & Observations

External vectors: The key external vectors on this part of the journey were proposition framing (deciding on the overall profile of the line of clothing) and customer definition (where the focus was on defining the target customer more precisely, in terms of socio-demographics, behavioural attributes and spending capacity).

Internal vectors: The key internal vectors at this stage were clearly product synthesis and shaping, and the talent component of the human capital vector, capturing the design expertise essential to the success of the product; there was also some attention paid to the early profile of go-to-market using the m7Ps model.

Composite vectors: Neither commercialisation strategy nor business models were relevant for the firm at this point in its journey. Figures 19, 20, and 21 summarise the key insights from this case study.

THE COMMERCIALISATION MONITOR

The Vision | To create and sell a new range of womens' business fashion clothing

Chasm Locator				I		II		III

mTRL CRL	0	1	2	3	4	5	6	7	8	9

Contingent Technology Deployment

Base Tech	App. Tech	Platform	Apps & Tools	Product	Service

Intellectual Property Management

Def.Key Comp.	Def. Prior.	Protect. in Place

Product & Service Synthesis

User-centred	Tech-driven	Imped. Matchin	Creat. Synth.	9-layer model	Service Wrap.
			√		

Manufacturing, Assembly & Deployment

Def. Chall.	Integ. Deploy.	Innov. Req
√		

Funding & Investment

Pref.	Fund.Quant.	Valuation
Private	£100k	£250K

Talent, Leadersip & Culture

Over. Prior.	Talent	Team	Org struct.	Leadership	Culture
	√	√			

Commercialisation Strategy

Vector Profile Crossing Chasm I

Defined Strategic Goal?	
Strategic Gap Clarity?	

Business Model

Defined Narrative	√
Explicit Architecture	
Components Defined	
Business Model Metrics	
Revenues & Costs	
Cash Flow Projections	

Market Space

Retail-clothing	Value Chain	√

Local	Nationa	Global		
	√		T-max	36	Mths

Proposition Framing

Propos. Defn.	Comp.	Reg.	Diff.	Partners & Suppliers
√	√		√	

Source of Differentiation

Single Component	Overall Chain	Re-framing Chain
	√	

Customer Definition

Business	Govt.	Consumer	Knowledge Workers
		√	

Max Accessible No of Customers	Cmax	1000

Distribution Marketing & Sales

Defined Go to Market Priorities	
Defined Channel Strategy		Overall m7Ps	

Product	Pos.	Pricing	Place	Prom.	Pro	Partn.

Figure 19. Women's fashion clothing — Commercialisation monitor @ Chasm I.

Product Design, Manufacturing & Procurement	Advertising & Promotion	Product Distribution	Product Retail	Buyer Experience Management and Support

Product Manufacturing

Product Design

Product Procurement & Packaging

Creation of Advertising & promotional material

Media planning & buying

Advertising & Promotion Execution

Distribution Management

Product Warehousing & Storage

Physical Distribution

Physical Retail Outlets

Digital Retail Environments

Customer Delivery

Transaction & Payment Handling

Buyer Experience Management

After-sales Service

Women's Fashion Clothing

- **Design and make the new product range**
- **Test the product in a physical retail outlet (multi-brand retail store in this case)**

Figure 20.   New range of women's clothing — Proposition framing at Chasm I.

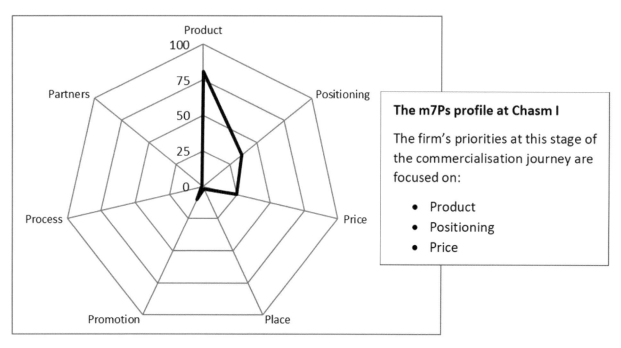

Figure 21. m7Ps profile at Chasm I.

16.3.2 *Crossing Chasm II*

Opportunity: Having successfully demonstrated the viability of the product, the firm's next challenge was to get the new fashion range established in the clothing retail environment.

Vision: To expand coverage of the womens' business fashion range to a wide range of branded retail outlets to create a sustainable business.

Approach: Based on addressing advertising & promotion, distribution and a range of retail environments to establish the new brand of products.

Trajectory: The starting point of this part of the journey was to understand the key issues involved in getting the product into existing physical retail channels. This was followed by developing the new relationships required with branded retailers. Crossing Chasm II depended on establishing a sustainable business model based on realistic pricing, a challenge especially given the notorious practice of heavy discounting by the multiple-brand stores.

Insights & Observations

External vectors: This required serious attention to all four external vectors: market-space clarity, framing the wider proposition in the context of new partners, clarifying customer targets (and understanding the profile of retail stores with these customers), and understanding the broader distribution issues, including marketing and promotion.

Internal vectors: five of the six internal vectors were key to crossing Chasm II: financial and human capital continued to be important but manufacturing, IP management (the brand specifically) and product shaping and enhancement were critical at this stage.

Composite vectors: Commercialisation strategy was critical given the many options open to the firm; and pinning down a sustainable business model, based on understanding pricing, costs, in particular, the impact of distribution and retail costs on the overall margin were critical. This was one of the toughest issues for the firm, given its inability to control heavy price discounting by the retail channels, who were already under pressure from e-commerce players in the market. Figures 22, 23, and 24 summarise the key insights from this case study.

THE COMMERCIALISATION MONITOR

The Vision	To expand coverage of the womens' business fashion range to a wide range of branded retail outlets to create a sustainable business

Chasm Locator				I			II		III
mTRL CRL	0	1	2	3	4	5	6	7	8 9

(Chasm Locator: II circled; mTRL/CRL between 6 and 7 circled)

Contingent Technology Deployment

Base Tech	App. Tech	Platform	Apps & Tools	Product	Service

Intellectual Property Management

Def.Key Comp.	Def. Prior.	Protect. in Place
√	√	√

Product & Service Synthesis

User-centred	Tech-driven	Imped. Matchin	Creat. Synth.	9-layer model	Service Wrap.
			√		

Manufacturing, Assembly & Deployment

Def. Chall.	Integ. Deploy.	Innov. Req
√	√	

Funding & Investment

Pref.	Fund.Quant.	Valuation
Private	£500K	£2m

Talent, Leadership & Culture

Over. Prior.	Talent	Team	Org struct.	Leadership	Culture
√	√	√		√	

Commercialisation Strategy

Vector Profile Crossing Chasm II

Defined Strategic Goal?	√
Strategic Gap Clarity?	

Business Model

Defined Narrative	√
Explicit Architecture	√
Components Defined	√
Business Model Metrics	
Revenues & Costs	
Cash Flow Projections	

Market Space

Fashion Clothing-Retail		Value Chain	√

Local	National	Global		
	√		T-max	60 Mths

Proposition Framing

Propos. Defn.	Comp.	Reg.	Diff.	Partners & Suppliers
√	√		√	√

Source of Differentiation

Single Component	Overall Chain	Re-framing Chain
√		

Customer Definition

Business	Govt.	Consumer	Knowledge Workers
√		√	

Max Accessible No of Customers	Cmax	10,000

Distribution Marketing & Sales

Defined Go to Market Priorities		√	
Defined Channel Strategy	√	Overall m7Ps	√

Product	Pos.	Pricing	Place	Prom.	Pro	Partn.
√	√	√	√		–	√

Figure 22. Women's fashion clothing — Commercialisation monitor @ Chasm II.

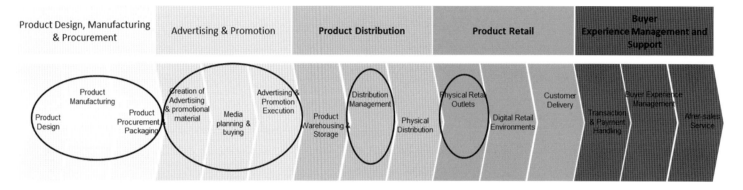

The wider proposition required to use third party distribution and retail channels:

- Resources and Costs required to address advertising & promotion for the new clothing brand
- Setting up product distribution arrangements linked to manufacturing locations
- Understanding and managing relationships with physical retail outlets

Figure 23. Women's fashion clothing — Proposition re-positioning to cross Chasm II.

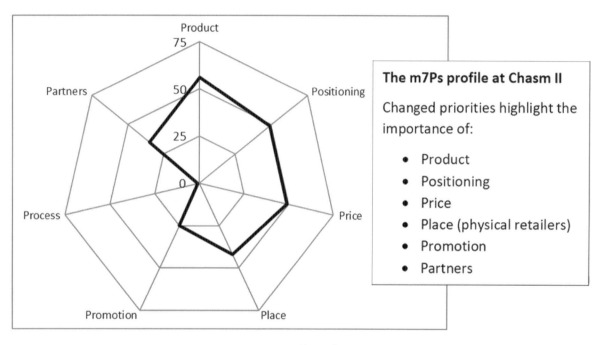

Figure 24. m7Ps profile at Chasm II crossing.

16.3.3 *Chasm III*

Opportunity: The successful crossing of Chasm II, albeit with tight product margins, served to highlight the opportunity to sell the product directly to customers using a branded electronic channel.

Vision: To create a range of branded womens' fashion clothing sold directly over the web to customers.

Approach: Reaching out to customers directly required an approach based on building a branded e-channel which handled marketing, sales and fulfilment management and phasing out the deals with physical retail outlets.

―――――――――――――

Trajectory: The journey across Chasm III depended on building an online electronic marketplace to showcase, market and sell the new range of women's business fashion clothing directly to customers. Once the new e-marketplace had been built, the firm needed to transition across to the new environment where it could control pricing and promotion more effectively. The success of this approach was reflected in crossing Chasm III and generating significant increases in sales volumes, revenues and margins.

Insights & Observations

External vectors: Given the major switch to electronic distribution, all the external vectors came back into play: understanding the changing marketspace, re-shaping the proposition to manage customer returns, better targeting of customers, and implementing highly pro-active distribution, marketing and sales techniques, using digital technology.

Internal vectors: Human and financial capital were again important, given the change in direction; building an online brand added more importance to IP management, and the product and deployment vectors had to keep pace with e-distribution. But the biggest challenge was in building the new e-commerce platform, moving the firm from the category of a non-technology company to a technology-enabled company.

Composite vectors: The commercialisation vector was critical as the firm had to make strategic judgements about building vs buying vs renting an e-commerce platform and the impact of this on time to market in particular; and linked to these qualitative judgements was the business model vector which provided quantitative inputs into these decisions. Figures 25, 26, and 27 summarise the key insights from this case study.

THE COMMERCIALISATION MONITOR

The Vision: To create a range of branded womens' fashion clothing sold directly over the web to customers

Chasm Locator						I			II			III
mTRL CRL	0	1	2	3		4	5	6		7	8	9

(Chasm III circled)

Contingent Technology Deployment

Base Tech	App. Tech	Platform	Apps & Tools	Product	Service
		√			√

Intellectual Property Management

Def.Key Comp.	Def. Prior.	Protect. in Place
√	√	√

Product & Service Synthesis

User-centred	Tech-driven	Imped. Matchin	Creat. Synth.	9-layer model	Service Wrap.
			√	√	√

Manufacturing, Assembly & Deployment

Def. Chall.	Integ. Deploy.	Innov. Req
√	√	√

Funding & Investment

Pref.	Fund.Quant.	Valuation
Private	£2.5m	£10m

Talent, Leadership & Culture

Over. Prior.	Talent	Team	Org struct.	Leadership	Culture
√	√	√	√	√	√

Commercialisation Strategy

Vector Profile Crossing Chasm III

Defined Strategic Goal?	√
Strategic Gap Clarity?	√

Business Model

Defined Narrative	√
Explicit Architecture	√
Components Defined	√
Business Model Metrics	√
Revenues & Costs	√
Cash Flow Projections	√

Market Space

Fashion Clothing hybrid retail & e-commerce	Value Chain	√

Local	Nationa	Global		
		√	T-max	96 Mths

Proposition Framing

Propos. Defn.	Comp.	Reg.	Diff.	Partners & Suppliers
√	√		√	√

Source of Differentiation

Single Component	Overall Chain	Re-framing Chain
√		

Customer Definition

Business	Govt.	Consumer	Knowledge Workers
		√	

Max Accessible No of Customers	Cmax	500,000

Distribution Marketing & Sales

Defined Go to Market Priorities	√

Defined Channel Strategy	√	Overall m7Ps	√

Product	Pos.	Pricing	Place	Prom.	Pro	Partn.
√	√	√	√	√	√	√

Figure 25. Women's fashion clothing — Commercialisation monitor @ Chasm III.

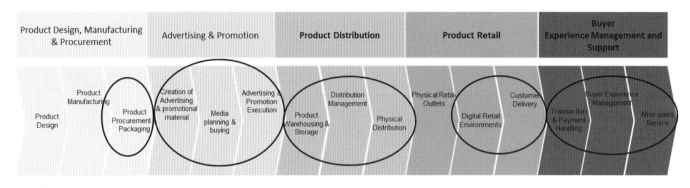

Product Design, Manufacturing & Procurement | Advertising & Promotion | Product Distribution | Product Retail | Buyer Experience Management and Support

Product Design
Product Manufacturing
Product Procurement & Packaging
Creation of Advertising & promotional material
Media planning & buying
Advertising & Promotion Execution
Product Warehousing & Storage
Distribution Management
Physical Distribution
Physical Retail Outlets
Digital Retail Environments
Customer Delivery
Transaction & Payment Handling
Buyer Experience Management
After-sales Service

The revised direct-to-customer product and service proposition

Required e-platform functionality
- Cover the wider range of activities of the firm
- *Integrate* these activities to provide a seamless customer experience
- Enable more effective management of the firm.

Figure 26.   Broader re-positioning driven by the need to embrace e-commerce-based delivery.

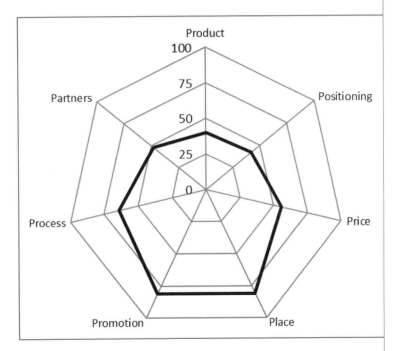

The m7Ps profile at Chasm III

Changed priorities highlight the impact of moving to direct sales to customer based on firm-branded e-commerce platform.

The balance shifted from Product, Partners and Positioning to

- **Process** (critical for the functioning of the *whole firm* now)
- **Promotion** (using wider range of digital channels)
- **Place** (now the web)
- **Price** (for example, the opportunity for dynamic pricing)

Figure 27. m7Ps profile crossing Chasm III.

Chapter 17

Scaling with Multiple Products

17.1 Multiple Products Targeted at the *Same* Customers in the *Same* Market Space

Overview

This firm focused on the provision of medical diagnostic products targeted at the same customers in the same market space.

The customers for all its products were clinicians and para-clinicians (knowledge-intensive workers) in the extended healthcare market space.

The functionality, form and features of the products were different: there were some variations in approaches to go-to-market and business models

Approach:

The firm adopted a structured approach based on:

- Building a clear view of the healthcare delivery market space
- Understanding where its family of products was positioned in this value chain
- Characterising customers, in terms of how its different products were bought and used
- Defining the Product portfolio in terms:
  - o Maturity
  - o Product decomposition (to identify common elements)
  - o Aggregate Commercialisation Monitors
- Building a Product Portfolio Map to shape priorities

Vectors	Sub-Vectors	Single-Product Firms	Multiple-Product Firms		
			Same Customers & Same Market Space	Same Market but Different customers	Different Markets and Different Customers
Overall Commercial Summary					
	Commercialisation Monitor for each Product	√	√	√	√
	Maturity Assessment for each Product	√	√	√	√
	Product Portfolio Map	X	√	√	√
External Vectors	Market Spaces				
	Define Single Market Space	√	√	√	
	Define Multiple Market Spaces				√
	Proposition Framing, Competition & Regulation				
	Frame Single Proposition	√			
	Frame Multiple Propositions	√	√	√	√
	Customer Definition				
	Define Single Customer	√	√		
	Define Multiple Customers	√		√	√
	Size Aggregate Market	√	√	√	√
	Distribution, Marketing & Sales				
	Define m7Ps for single product	√			
	Define m7Ps for multiple products		√	√	√
	Build Aggregate View of m7Ps		√	√	√
Composite Vectors	Commercialisation Strategy				
	Single Strategy	√			
	Multiple Strategies			?	?
	Integrated Strategy		√	?	?
	Business Model Development				
	Single Business Model	√	?	?	
	Multiple Business Models		?	?	√
Internal Vectors	Technology Development & Contingent Deployment				
	Single Approach to Deployment	√			
	Multiple Deployment Approaches		√	√	√
	IP Management				
	Narrow focus on IP Management				
	Integrated Approach to IP Management	√	√	√	√
	Product & Service Definition and Synthesis				
	Single Product Focus	√			
	Multiple Product Focus		√	√	√
	Family of Products Approach		√	√	√
	Manufacturing & Deployment				
	Single Product Focus	√			
	Integrated Approach		√	√	√
	Multiple Approaches			?	?
	Talent, Leadership & Culture				
	Firm Level Approach	√	√	√	√
	Funding & Investment				
	Firm level Approach	√	√	√	√

Figures 1, 2, and 3 summarise the key insights from this case study.

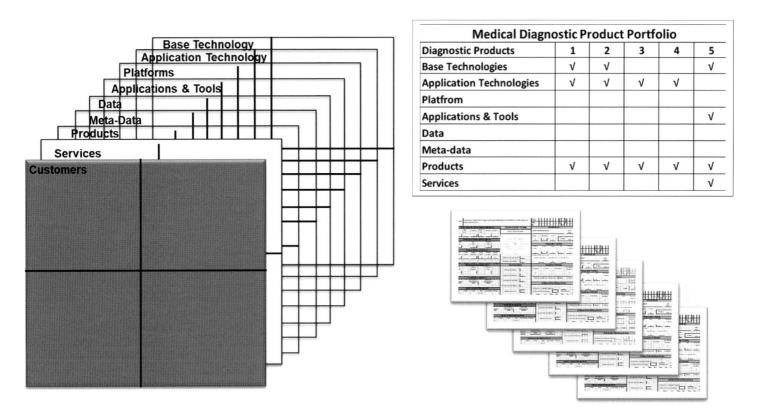

Medical Diagnostic Product Portfolio					
Diagnostic Products	1	2	3	4	5
Base Technologies	√	√			√
Application Technologies	√	√	√	√	
Platfrom					
Applications & Tools					√
Data					
Meta-data					
Products	√	√	√	√	√
Services					√

Figure 1. Portfolio of medical diagnostic products aimed at the same customers in the healthcare market space.

Customers

The target customers for all the products were medically trained clinicians working mainly in primary and secondary health care

The decisions about product procurement were typically made by senior clinicians who were also the users of the products (purchasing decisions were sometimes supported by commercial managers in these environments)

Typical ratio of Users to Customers, N-ucr =7-10

Products with different maturity

The oldest product in the firm's portfolio had already crossed Chasm III

Two other products with major commercial potential were around Chasm II, one having already developed a viable commercial model and early traction

One other product was in prototype form

The final product in the portfolio was still at the stage of conceptual development

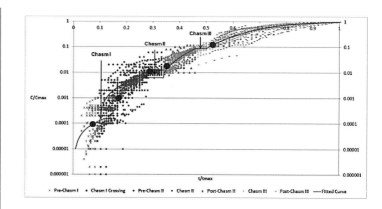

Figure 2.   Customer focus and product portfolio.

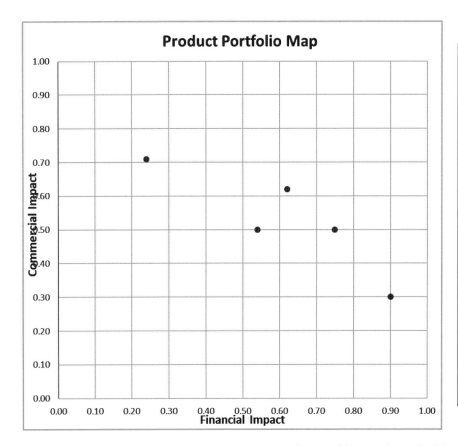

Product Portfolio Map

Overview of Product Portfolio

The five products in the portfolio made different contributions to the overall performance of the firm

- The most mature product had the biggest financial impact on the firm
- The product still at conceptual stage was judged to have the largest commercial potential but the lowest financial impact at this stage of its development
- The product which had just crossed Chasm II had more financial impact (but the same commercial impact) as the product yet to prove its business model
- The product which had just crossed Chasm I was deemed to have similar financial impact, but much greater commercial impact given the potential to integrate it with other clinical systems

Figure 3. Product portfolio map for medical diagnostic products.

17.2 Multiple Products Targeted at *Different* Customers in the *Same* Market Space

Overview

This firm provided a range of **Satellite Navigation** products to 3 different types of customers in the Transport & Logistics Market Space. All the products relied on the same fundamental building blocks, including the routing engine and integration of geo-data and mapping, with different levels of additional technology and packaging

Approach

The firm adopted a phased approach based on:

- Building all the components of the whole solution
- Delivering the first product to the corporate fleet management market
- Then building a family of consumer products
- Creating OEM products to tackle the inevitable flatting in direct consumer sales
- The portfolio based on 3 product families was characterised in terms
  - o Maturity
  - o Product decomposition (to identify common elements)
  - o Aggregate Commercialisation Monitors
- Building a Product Portfolio Map to demonstrate overall priorities

Vectors	Sub-Vectors		Single-Product Firms	Same Customers & Same Market Space	Multiple Product Firms	
					Same Market but Different customers	Different Markets and Different Customers
Overall Commercial Summary		Commercialisation Monitor for each Product	√	√	√	√
		Maturity Assessment for each Product	√	√	√	√
		Product Portfolio Map	X	√	√	√
External Vectors	Market Spaces	Define Single Market Space	√	√	√	
		Define Multiple Market Spaces				√
	Proposition Framing, Competition & Regulation	Frame Single Proposition	√			
		Frame Multiple Propositions		√	√	√
	Customer Definition	Define Single Customer	√	√		
		Define Multiple Customers	√		√	√
		Size Aggregate Market	√	√	√	√
	Distribution, Marketing & Sales	Define m7Ps for single product	√			
		Define m7Ps for mutiple products		√	√	
		Build Aggregate View of m7Ps		√	√	
Composite Vectors	Commercialisation Strategy	Single Strategy	√			
		Multiple Strategies			?	?
		Integrated Strategy		√	?	?
	Business Model Development	Single Business Model	√	?	?	
		Multiple Business Models		?	?	√
Internal Vectors	Technology Development & Contingent Deployment	Single Approach to Deployment	√			
		Multiple Deployment Approaches		√	√	√
	IP Management	Narrow focus on IP Management				
		Integrated Approach to IP Management	√	√	√	√
	Product & Service Definition and Synthesis	Single Product Focus	√			
		Multiple Product Focus		√	√	√
		Family of Products Approach		√	√	√
	Manufacturing & Deployment	Single Product Focus	√			
		Integrated Approach		√	√	√
		Multiple Approaches			?	?
	Talent, Leadership & Culture	Firm Level Approach	√	√		√
	Funding & Investment	Firm Level Approach	√	√	√	√

Figures 4, 5, and 6 summarise the key insights from this case study.

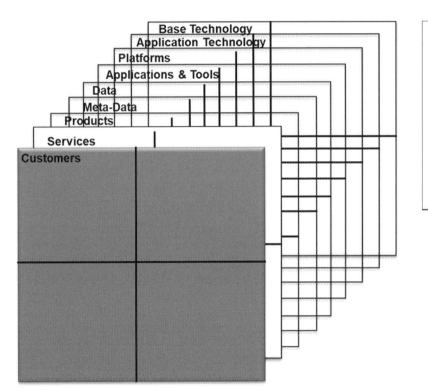

Sat-nav Product Families			
Product Family	Fleet Mngt	Consumer Product	OEM
Base Technologies	√	√	√
Application Technologies	√	√	√
Platfrom	√		
Applications & Tools	√		
Data	√		
Meta-data	√		√
Products		√	
Services	√		

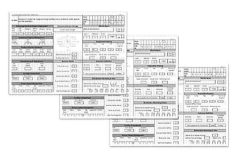

Figure 4. Portfolio of sat-nav products aimed at different customers in the same market space.

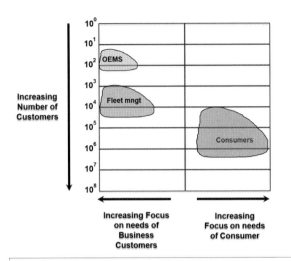

Customers

The 3 product families were targeted at three quite different sets of customers:

- The integrated navigation and logistics system was targeted at Fleet Management Companies who run very large fleets of cars, buses and trucks
- The integrated low cost in-car sat nav products were targeted at consumers
- The OEM offering was targeted at automobile and truck manufacturers

Products with different maturity

The firms approach was based on first deploying a highly integrated system for fleet management, where NRE-based revenues enabled a viable business model to be developed faster (shown post-Chasm III)

This was followed by the development of a branded family of consumer products (all very similar with slightly different packaging (now post Chasm II)

This culminated in the provision of OEM products to automobile and truck manufacturers to integrate into new production vehicles (shown in the process of crossing Chasm II, including establishing a new business model)

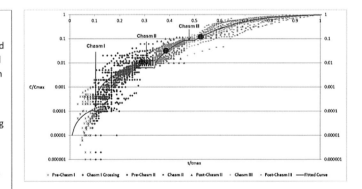

Figure 5. Customer focus and product portfolio maturity.

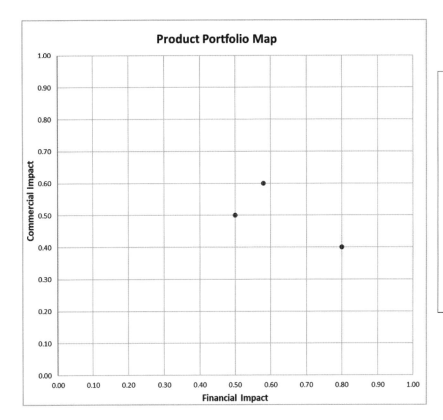

Overview of Product Portfolio

The early products targeted at fleet managers delivered the lowest financial impact but provided good early commercial impact in a number of ways, including establishing the overall viability of the approach

The consumer product had the biggest financial impact, given the very large sales volumes

The final OEM product provided lower financial impact but had significant commercial impact in terms of a long-term sustainable business model, thus helping to protect the firm against the expected entry of new low cost players, and the gradual erosion of margins

Figure 6. Portfolio of sat-nav products.

17.3 Multiple Products Targeted at *Different* Customers in *Different* Market Spaces

Overview

This firm provided electronic lighting and controls to different customers in three different market spaces:

- Smart Lighting Engines to the automotive market space
- Integrated Energy & Lighting Solutions for Industrial Markets
- Provision of products to the consumer lighting market

Approach

The firm adopted 3-pronged approach based on:

- Building the fundamental based and application technologies to target all 3 markets in parallel
- Targeting the industrial controls and lighting market first given the opportunity to generate early revenues
- Then developing automotive lighting engines, where OEM suppliers could move faster than consumer channels
- Finally targeting the huge global market for smart consumer lighting products
- The portfolio based on 3 product families was characterised in terms
  - o Maturity
  - o Product decomposition (to identify common elements)
  - o Aggregate Commercialisation Monitors
- Building a Product Portfolio Map to clarify overall priorities

Vectors	Sub-Vectors	Single-Product Firms	Multiple-Product Firms		
			Same Customers & Same Market Space	Same Market but Different customers	Different Markets and Different Customers
Overall Commercial Summary	Commercialisation Monitor for each Product	√	√	√	√
	Maturity Assessment for each Product	√	√	√	√
	Product Portfolio Map	x	√	√	√
External Vectors — Market Spaces	Define Single Market Space	√	√	√	
	Define Multiple Market Spaces				√
Proposition Framing, Competition & Regulation	Frame Single Proposition	√			
	Frame Multiple Propositions	√	√	√	√
Customer Definition	Define Single Customer	√	√		
	Define Multiple Customers	√		√	√
	Size Aggregate Market	√	√	√	√
Distribution, Marketing & Sales	Define m7Ps for single product	√			
	Define m7Ps for multiple products		√	√	√
	Build Aggregate View of m7Ps		√	√	√
Composite Vectors — Commercialisation Strategy	Single Strategy	√			
	Multiple Strategies			?	?
	Integrated Strategy		√	?	?
Business Model Development	Single Business Model	√	?	?	
	Multiple Business Models		?	?	?
Internal Vectors — Technology Development & Contingent Deployment	Single Approach to Deployment	√			
	Multiple Deployment Approaches		√	√	√
IP Management	Narrow focus on IP Management				
	Integrated Approach to IP Management	√	√	√	√
Product & Service Definition and Synthesis	Single Product Focus	√			
	Multiple Product Approach		√	√	√
	Family of Products Approach		√	√	√
Manufacturing & Deployment	Single Product Focus	√			
	Integrated Approach		√	√	√
	Multiple Approaches			?	?
Talent, Leadership & Culture	Firm level Approach	√	√	√	√
Funding & Investment	Firm level Approach	√	√	√	√

Figures 7, 8, and 9 summarise the key insights from this case study.

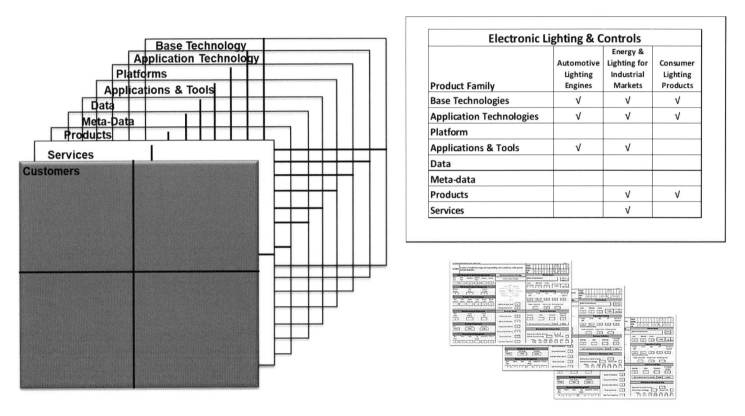

Electronic Lighting & Controls			
Product Family	Automotive Lighting Engines	Energy & Lighting for Industrial Markets	Consumer Lighting Products
Base Technologies	√	√	√
Application Technologies	√	√	√
Platform			
Applications & Tools	√	√	
Data			
Meta-data			
Products		√	√
Services		√	

Figure 7. Portfolio of electronic lighting & control products aimed at different customers in different market spaces.

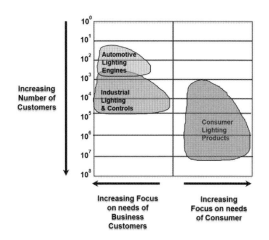

Customers

There were 3 different customers in three different target market spaces

- Companies across the value chain in the industrial lighting and controls market
- OEMs in the automotive market space looking for innovative lighting solutions to incorporate into new vehicle designs
- Consumers of lighting products who need to be reached via a wide range of distribution and retail partners and customers

Products with different maturity

The industrial products were the most mature in the product portfolio, having crossed Chasm II

The OEM products for the Auto industry were in the process of crossing Chasm II, still refining revenue and business models

The consumer lighting products had been demonstrated, successfully crossing Chasm I, but needed significant further development to enable commercial deployment

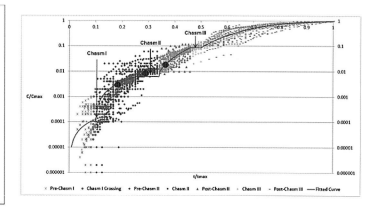

Figure 8. Customers and product portfolio maturity.

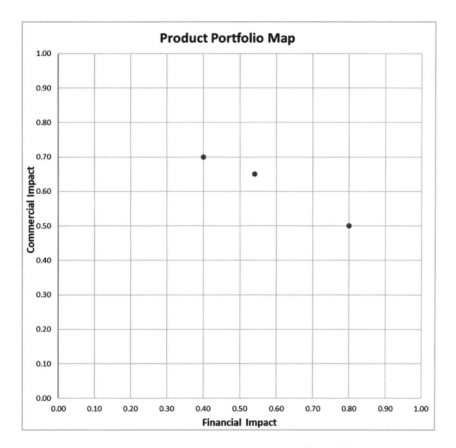

Figure 9. Portfolio of electronic lighting and control products.

Overview of Product Portfolio

The early family of industrial lighting products had the loweest financial impact, but it had the highest commercial impact, given its ability to demonstrate the potential of this new lighting technology and to create a brand

The OEM lighting engines for the automotive supply chain provided better financial impact, given the higher revenues and better margins, with slightly lower commercial impact.

The consumer lighting products had lower overall commercial impact, but significant financial impact given the size of the global lighting market

Part IV

Tackling *Your* Scale-up Challenge

Chapter 18

Scaling Your Proposition

18.1 The Approach

Figure 1 summarises our overall approach to dealing with single product firms vs multi-product firms. You need to distinguish between single-product firms and multi-product firms.

Is your proposition based on developing a single product?

Or

Are you developing a proposition based on a family of products?

In both cases, your core analysis depends on a detailed assessment of *each* product based on understanding:

- The current maturity and the next chasm on the journey
- The current vector profile
- The next chasm which needs to be crossed and the target maturity
- The target vector profile
- The vector gap and the execution plan to tackle this gap.

For a single-product firm, the single-product analysis provides the complete basis for understanding and shaping your commercialisation journey.

For multi-product firms, the key steps are:

- Understand your current product portfolio based on multiple products
- Applying the single-product analysis to each of the products in your portfolio
- Defining your target product portfolio based on strategic vs financial impact
- Build an aggregate execution plan to achieve the target portfolio.

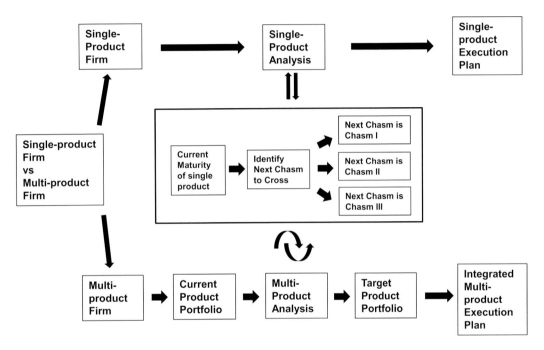

Figure 1. The approach.

18.2 Methodology for Single-product Firms

Figure 2 shows the overall methodology for single product firms, consisting of the following steps.

- Articulate your vision
- Define your proposition
- What is your product or service proposition?
- Who are your target customers?
- How does your proposition fit into the market space?
- What difference will your proposition make?
- Understand the shape and timing of your firm's overall commercialisation journey
- How long will the journey take?
- How big is the opportunity?

- Assess the maturity of your proposition and position along the journey
- How far along are you on the journey?
- What is your next challenge?
- Is it successfully building a prototype?
- Is it validating your proposition and business model?
- Is it ramping up to get more customers for a commercially viable proposition?
- Prioritise the 'levers' or commercialisation vectors important for you to overcome the next challenge
- Create an execution plan to do this.

Figures 3, 4, 5, 6, 7, 8, 9, 10, 11, 12, 13, 14, 15, 16 and 17 illustrate the typical process of crossing Chasms I, II and III.

Single-product Firms						
	Current Product Profile	**'Target' Product Profile**	**The Gap (Target vs Current)**	**Execution Priorities to tackle the Gap**	**Execution Plan**	**The Ultimate Goal**
Vision	Define current vision	Define revised vision				The Big Vision?
Maturity Assessment	Assess your current status	Target maturity after next chasm crossing				Describe future trajectory
External Vectors	Assess current status of vectors	Define target vector profiles	Vector Gaps	Define Tasks based on Vectors		
Internal Vectors	Assess current status of vectors	Define target vector profiles	Vector Gaps	Define Tasks based on Vectors		
Composite Vectors	Assess current status of vectors	Define target vector profiles	Vector Gaps	Define Tasks based on Vectors		
Strategic Vector Profile	Current Strategic Vector Profile	Target Strategic Profile	Define the Vector gap	Define Tasks based on Vectors	Create Plan at the level of Vectors and sub-vectors	Define Final Profile
Commercialisation Monitor	Define current CM	Define target CM after next chasm crossing				

Figure 2. Methodology for single-product firms.

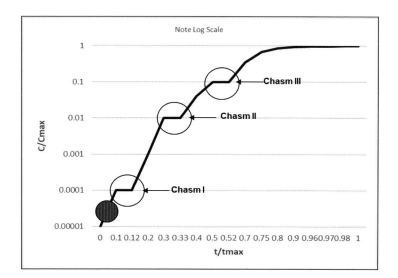

Crossing Chasm I:

Typical Starting Point
- **Strong academic and/or research lab focus**
- **Low technology readiness with mTRL/CRL≈ 0-1**
- **Potential for deployment in wide range of market spaces**
- **Product or service concept may not be clear**
- **Poor understanding of target customers**
- **Early insights into contingent technology deployment**
- **Initial observations on potential commercialisation strategy**

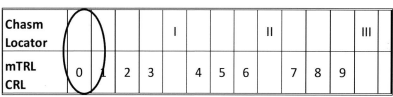

Chasm Locator				I			II			III	
mTRL CRL	0 1	2	3		4	5	6		7	8	9

Figure 3. Crossing Chasm I — The starting point.

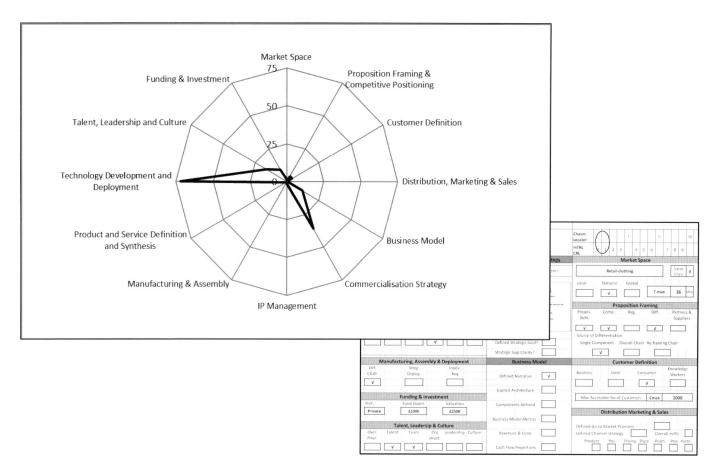

Figure 4. Vector plot and commercialisation monitor at starting point for Chasm I.

Crossing Chasm I:
Typical End Point
- Initial view on potential market space(s)
- Initial Proposition Framing, Positioning and competition
- Some understanding of the first 'charter' customer
- Initial definition of product or service concept
- Technology readiness increased to mTRL/CRL≈ 4
- First formulation of potential commercialisation strategy
- Initial views on potential business models

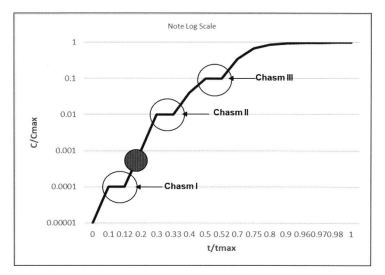

Chasm Locator					I			II			III	
mTRL CRL	0	1	2	3		4	5	6		7	8	9

Figure 5. Crossing Chasm I — The target end-point.

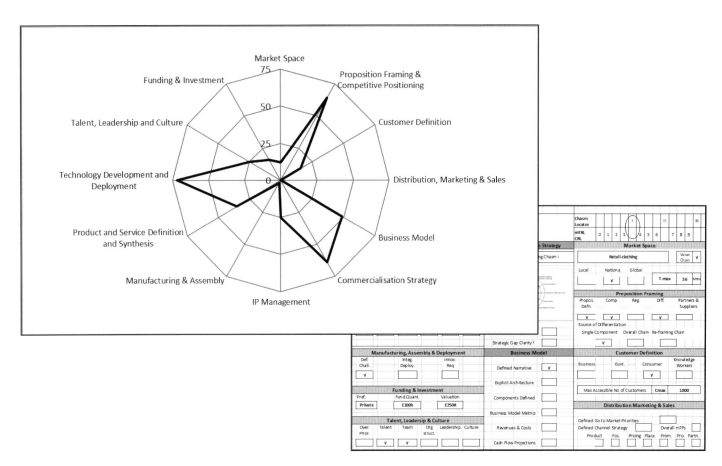

Figure 6. Target vector plot and commercialisation monitor after crossing Chasm I.

18.2.1 *Crossing Chasm I — Some observations*

Many propositions enabled by science and technology innovation typically start with very low mTRL or CRL values.

The early commercialisation journeys for these propositions are usually focused on:

- Increasing the technology readiness to enable a product or service concept to be articulated
- Converting the concept into a prototype which can demonstrate the proposition.

The Execution Plan for crossing Chasm I typically focuses on:

- Technology development and contingent technology deployment
- Early views on the market space and initial proposition framing
- Understanding and starting the process of managing key intellectual property
- Anticipating the mix of human talent critical for future success
- Ensuring there is adequate funding to create a prototype proposition.

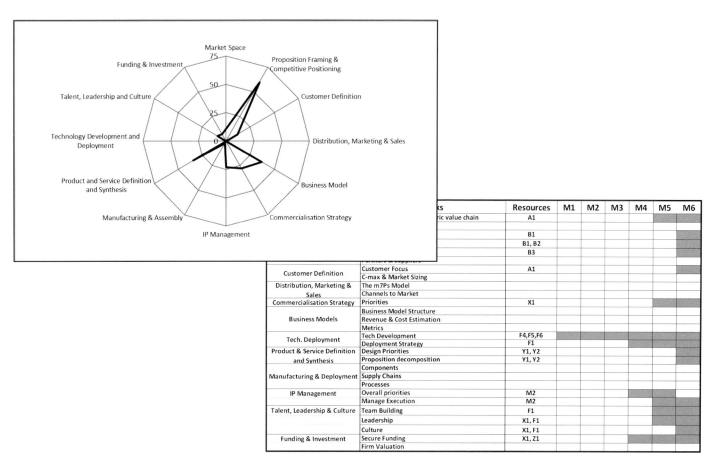

	...ks	Resources	M1	M2	M3	M4	M5	M6
	...ric value chain	A1					▓	▓
		B1						▓
		B1, B2						▓
		B3						▓
	Partners & Suppliers							
Customer Definition	Customer Focus	A1						▓
	C-max & Market Sizing							
Distribution, Marketing & Sales	The m7Ps Model							
	Channels to Market							
Commercialisation Strategy	Priorities	X1						
Business Models	Business Model Structure							
	Revenue & Cost Estimation							
	Metrics							
Tech. Deployment	Tech Development	F4,F5,F6	▓	▓	▓	▓		
	Deployment Strategy	F1			▓	▓		
Product & Service Definition and Synthesis	Design Priorities	Y1, Y2						
	Proposition decomposition	Y1, Y2						
Manufacturing & Deployment	Components							
	Supply Chains							
	Processes							
IP Management	Overall priorities	M2				▓	▓	
	Manage Execution	M2						▓
Talent, Leadership & Culture	Team Building	F1					▓	▓
	Leadership	X1, F1						▓
	Culture	X1, F1						▓
Funding & Investment	Secure Funding	X1, Z1				▓		
	Firm Valuation							

Figure 7. Crossing Chasm I — Gap analysis and execution plan.

Crossing Chasm II:
Typical Starting Point
- **Well-developed technology with mTRL/CRL≈ 4/5**
- **But contingent technology deployment not well-developed**
- **Clear proposition but product still at early stage**
- **Commercialisation strategy well-developed but business model is probably still vague**
- **Sharper customer focus needed to refine product or service functionality**

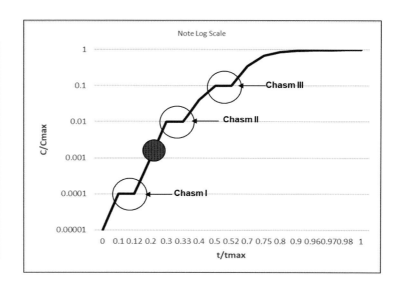

Chasm Locator					I			II				III		
mTRL CRL	0	1	2	3		4	5	6		7	8	9		

Figure 8. Crossing Chasm II — The starting point.

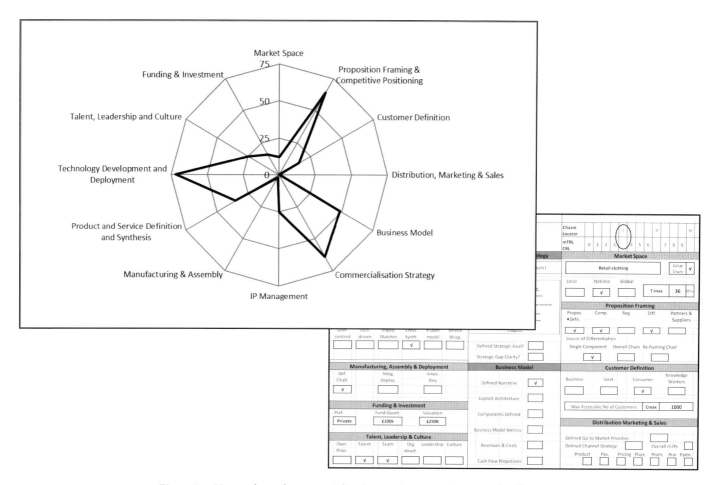

Figure 9. Vector plot and commercialisation monitor at starting point for Chasm II.

Crossing Chasm II:
Typical End Point
- **Clear product or service definition underpinned by sustainable business model**
- **Mature technology with mTRL/CRL≈ 7/8**
- **Clarity on market space and proposition differentiation**
- **Early customers well-established**
- **Leadership and teams to drive future go-to-market in place**
- **Initial plans for distribution, marketing and sales in place**
- **Execution of IP management plans in place**

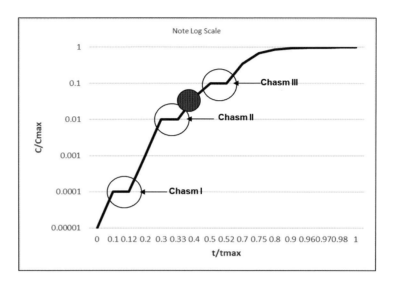

Chasm Locator					I				II				III	
mTRL CRL	0	1	2	3		4	5	6		7	8	9		

Figure 10.   Crossing Chasm II — The target end-point.

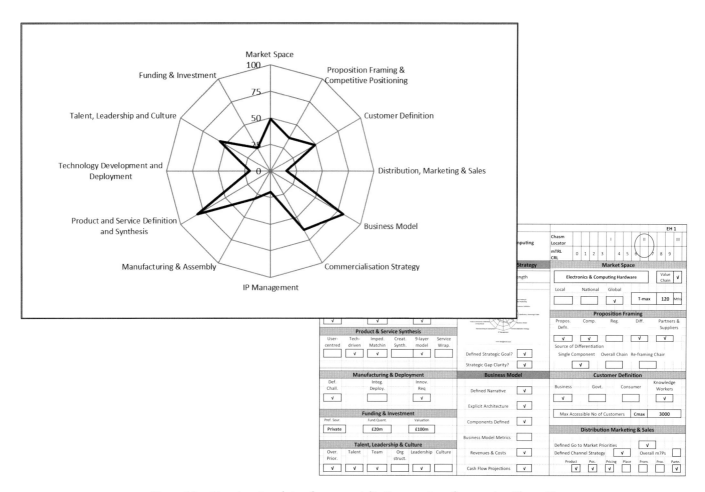

Figure 11. Target vector plot and commercialisation monitor after crossing Chasm II.

18.2.2 *Crossing Chasm II — Some observations*

All 12 vectors are critical when crossing Chasm II.

Effort is still required to increase mTRL/CRL values from 4–5 to 7–8.

Funding & Investment are critical at this point, which can be a challenge, given that the design of a sustainable business model is the output of this activity.

The execution plan reflects the following key priorities:

- Confirm market space focus and competitive proposition framing

- Refine customer definition and messaging

- Understand manufacturing, deployment and distribution priorities

- Develop, test and refine business model narrative, architecture, numbers, and metrics

- Build the team, culture, and leadership

- Confirm the overall commercialisation strategy.

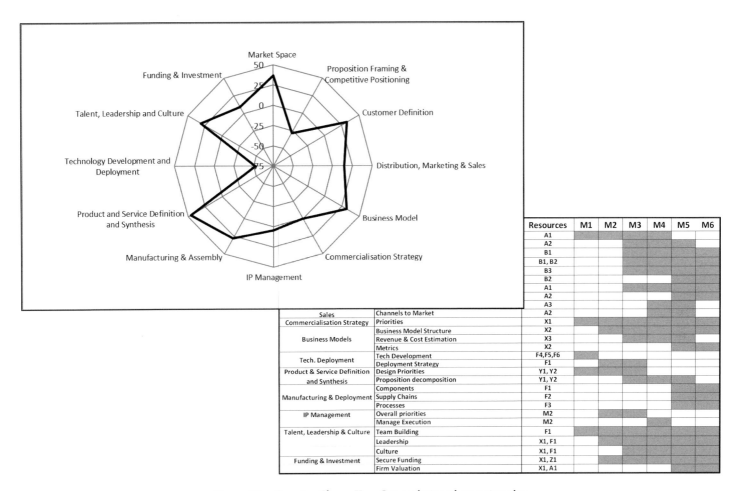

Figure 12. Crossing Chasm II — Gap analysis and execution plan.

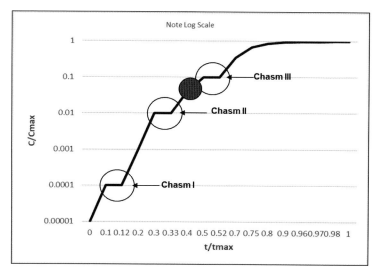

Crossing Chasm III:
Typical Starting Point
- Well developed product and service proposition with a sustainable business model
- Clear commercialisation strategy
- Charter customers in place
- Conventional debt and equity funding now more easily accessible – low commercial risk
- Distribution, marketing & sales activity still relatively unstructured

Chasm Locator				I			II				III	
mTRL CRL	0	1	2	3		4	5	6	7	8	9	

Figure 13. Crossing Chasm III — The starting point.

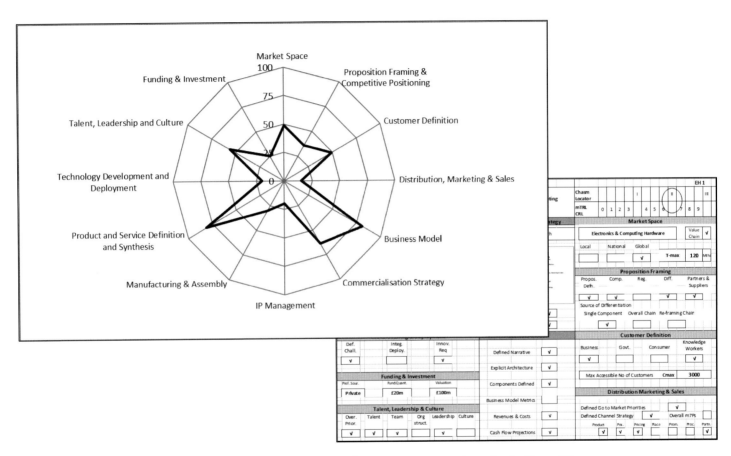

Figure 14. Vector plot and commercialisation monitor at starting point for Chasm III.

Crossing Chasm III:

Typical End Point
- **Clarity on Customers and Channels**
- **Coherent plans for Distribution, Marketing & Sales**
- **Clarity on manufacturing and delivery strategy**
- **Clear commercialisation strategy**
- **Leadership team and structure in place**
- **Understanding new and cross-border market spaces**

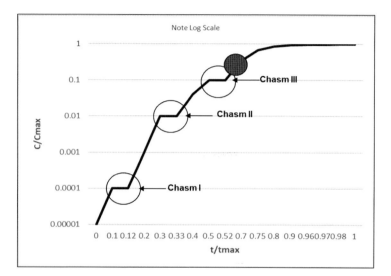

Chasm Locator				I		II			III	
mTRL CRL	0	1	2	3	4	5	6	7	8	9	

Figure 15. Crossing Chasm III — The target end-point.

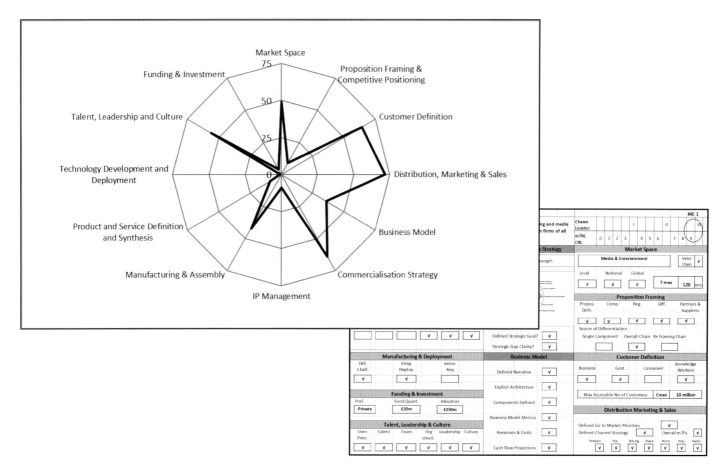

Figure 16. Target vector plot and commercialisation monitor after crossing Chasm III.

18.2.3 *Crossing Chasm III — Key issues*

Number of critical vectors smaller than for Chasm II (4 or 5 not 12).

Focus now is on establishing the capacity of the firm to scale customer numbers and revenues.

The key priorities for the execution plan are:

- Marketing, sales and distribution, in particular, clarity on the m7Ps

- Managing manufacturing and product or service deployment

- Building out the team, culture, organisational structure and leadership

- Refining the commercialisation strategy

- Reviewing and refining business models as required.

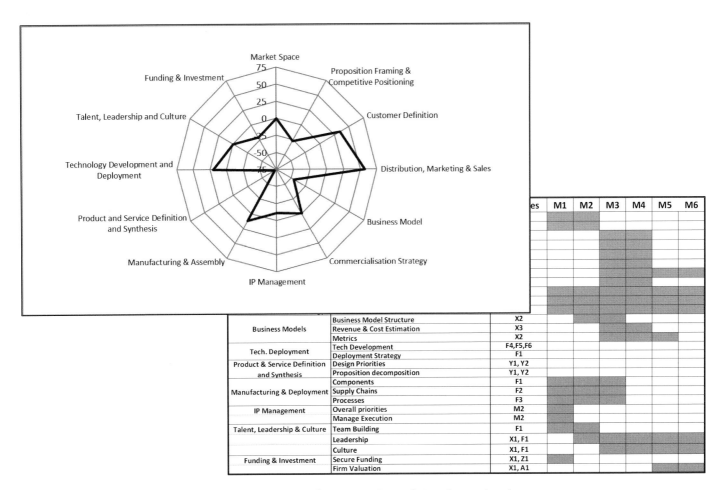

			M1	M2	M3	M4	M5	M6
	Business Model Structure	X2						
Business Models	Revenue & Cost Estimation	X3						
	Metrics	X2						
Tech. Deployment	Tech Development	F4,F5,F6						
	Deployment Strategy	F1						
Product & Service Definition and Synthesis	Design Priorities	Y1, Y2						
	Proposition decomposition	Y1, Y2						
Manufacturing & Deployment	Components	F1						
	Supply Chains	F2						
	Processes	F3						
IP Management	Overall priorities	M2						
	Manage Execution	M2						
Talent, Leadership & Culture	Team Building	F1						
	Leadership	X1, F1						
	Culture	X1, F1						
Funding & Investment	Secure Funding	X1, Z1						
	Firm Valuation	X1, A1						

Figure 17.   Crossing Chasm III — Gap analysis and execution plan.

18.3 Methodology for Multi-product Firms

> **Figure 18 shows the overall methodology for multi-product firms, consisting of the following steps.**

- Articulate your vision
- Define or refine your overall proposition for the whole firm
  - What are your products or services?
  - Who are your target customers?
  - How do your products and services fit into the overall market space(s)?
- *Address each product or service using the approach described for single-product firms*

- *Understand the shape and timing for each of your products and service*
  - *How long will each product journey take?*
  - *Compare the different opportunities?*
- Define your product portfolio and priorities
- Create an aggregate view based on the whole product family
- Create an aggregate Execution Plan for the firm
  - Priority and timing for different products or services?
  - Business models?
  - Resource implications?

> **Figures 19, 20, 21, 22 and 23 illustrate the typical approach for tackling multi-product firms.**

Multi-product Firms						
	Current Product Profile	'Target' Product Profile	The Gap (Target vs Current)	Execution Priorities to tackle the Gap	Execution Plan	The Ultimate Goal
Vision	Define current vision	Define revised vision				The Big Vision?
Market Space & Customer focus	Define portfolio focus	Define portfolio focus				
Product Family	Define current family of products	Define target family of products	Identify New Products			
For each product in the family define						
Maturity Assessment	*Assess your current status*	*Target maturity after next Chasm Crossing*				*Describe future trajectory*
External Vectors	*Assess current status of vectors*	*Define target vector profiles*	*Vector Gaps*	*Define Tasks based on Vectors*		
Internal Vectors	*Assess current status of vectors*	*Define target vector profiles*	*Vector Gaps*	*Define Tasks based on Vectors*		
Composite Vectors	*Assess current status of vectors*	*Define target vector profiles*	*Vector Gaps*	*Define Tasks based on Vectors*		
Strategic Vector Profile	*Current Strategic Vector Profile*	*Target Strategic Profile*	*Define the Vector gap*	*Define Tasks based on Vectors*	*Create Plan at the level of Vectors and sub-vectors*	*Define Final Profile*
Commercialisation Monitor	*Define current CM*	*Define target CM after next Chasm crossing*				
Aggregate Product Family	Build aggregate strategic vector profile	Define aggregate target strategic vector profile	Identify aggregate gaps	Define aggregate tasks		Define Ultimate Family
Critical Aggregate Vectors			Market spaces, Customers, Product synthesis. Others as appropriate	Define key vectors to address aggregate challenges	Creat aggregate plan	
Overall Firm Priorities	Define Strategic vs Financial Goals	Define Strategic vs Financial Goals				Ultimate Firm Goals: Growth vs Exit vs Permanence
Product Portfolio	Define current portfolio	Define target portfolio				Define ideal portfolio

Figure 18. Methodology for multi-product firms.

18.3.1 *What type of multi-product firm are you?*

Define your market space and customer focus for your product portfolio.

Are the products in your portfolio aimed at:

- The same market space and same customers?
- The same market space but different customers?
- Different market spaces and different customers?

Understand how the answer to this question impacts on the 12 vectors.

For each vector, understand where an aggregate view may be required.

- In some cases, the single-product view may be adequate
- In some situations, aggregating multiple views may be required
- In some situations, it may be more appropriate to create a new integrated view, not simply an aggregation.

Vectors	Sub-Vectors	Single-Product Firms	Multiple-Product Firms		
			Same Customers & Same Market Space	Same Market but Different customers	Different Markets and Different Customers
Overall Commercial Summary					
	Commercialisation Monitor for each Product	√	√	√	√
	Maturity Assessment for each Product	√	√	√	√
	Product Portfolio Map	X	√	√	√
External Vectors	**Market Spaces**				
	Define Single Market Space	√	√	√	
	Define Multiple Market Spaces				√
	Proposition Framing, Competition & Regulation				
	Frame Single Proposition	√			
	Frame Multiple Propositions	√	√	√	√
	Customer Definition				
	Define Single Customer	√	√		
	Define Multiple Customers	√		√	√
	Size Aggregate Market	√	√	√	
	Distribution, Marketing & Sales				
	Define m7Ps for single product	√			
	Define m7Ps for mutiple products		√	√	√
	Build Aggregate View of m7Ps		√	√	√
Composite Vectors	**Commercialisation Strategy**				
	Single Strategy	√			
	Multiple Strategies			?	?
	Integrated Strategy		√	?	?
	Business Model Development				
	Single Business Model	√	?	?	
	Multiple Business Models		?	?	√
Internal Vectors	**Technology Development & Contingent Deployment**				
	Single Approach to Deployment	√			
	Multiple Deployment Approaches		√	√	√
	IP Management				
	Narrow focus on IP Management				
	Integrated Approach to IP Management	√	√	√	√
	Product & Service Definition and Synthesis				
	Single Product Focus	√			
	Multiple Product Focus		√	√	√
	Family of Products Approach		√	√	√
	Manufacturing & Deployment				
	Single Product Focus	√			
	Integrated Approach		√	√	√
	Multiple Approaches			?	?
	Talent, Leadership & Culture				
	Firm Level Approach	√	√	√	√
	Funding & Investment				
	Firm Level Approach	√	√	√	√

Figure 19. Defining market space and customer focus of your current portfolio.

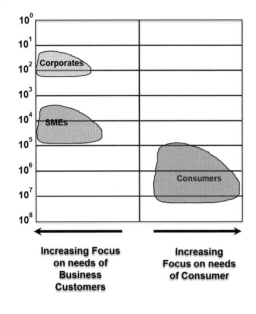

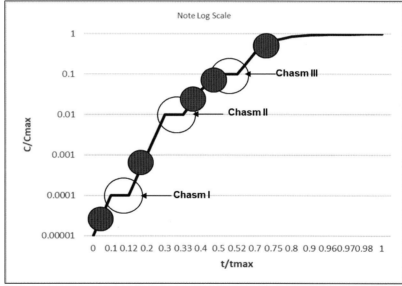

Figure 20. Your product portfolio and customer focus.

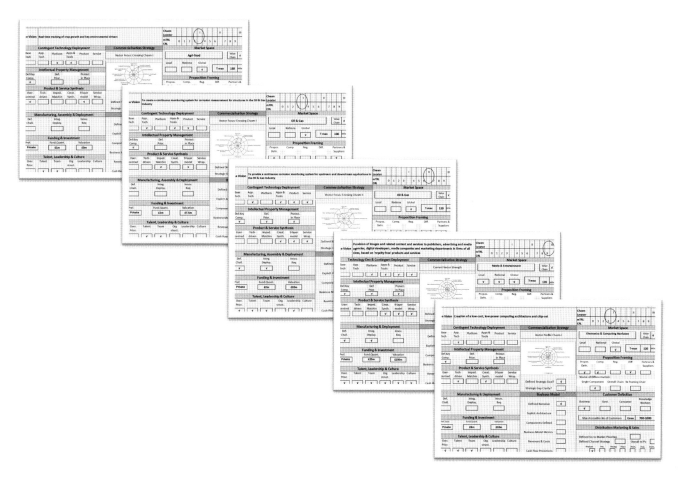

Figure 21. Family of commercialisation monitors.

18.3.2 *What are your portfolio objectives & priorities?*

Articulate your *Strategic Priorities* using weighting criteria for the following variables:

- Market Spaces
- Proposition Framing & Regulation
- Customer Definition
- Distribution, Marketing & Sales
- Commercialisation Strategy
- Business Models
- IP Management
- Manufacturing & Deployment
- Product Definition and Synthesis

- Technology Development and Contingent Technology Deployment
- Human Capital — Talent, Leadership, and Culture

Articulate your *Financial Priorities* using weighting criteria based on the following variables:

- Revenues
- Margins, based on EBITDA
- Investment required
- Time to payback
- Access to investment

Product Portfolio Analysis

	Scoring Logic (0-10)	Relevance Weighting	Product 1 Estimated Perf.	Product 1 Weighted Perf.	Product 2 Estimated Perf.	Product 2 Weighted Perf.	Product 3 Estimated Perf.	Product 3 Weighted Perf.	Product 4 Estimated Perf.	Product 4 Weighted Perf.	Product 5 Estimated Perf.	Product 5 Weighted Perf.
Strategic Impact												
Market Spaces	Market Potential (low to high)	1	5	5	8	8	8	8	8	8	8	8
	Entry Barriers (high to low)	1	2	2	5	5	5	5	5	5	5	7
	Characteristic Time, Tmax (long to short)	1	7	7	5	5	5	5	5	5	5	7
Proposition Framing, Competition & Regulation	Value Chain Impact (narrow to broad)	1	3	3								7
	Competitive Intensity (High to Low)	1	2	2								8
	Regulatory Constraints (High to Low)	1	7	7								7
Customer Definition	Max. No. Customers, Cmax (low to high)	1	5	5								7
	Total Market Size (low to high)	1	6	6								7
Distribution, Marketing & Sales	Distribution Network Maturity (low to hi)	1	8	8								8
	Cost of Marketing & Sales (high to low)	1	3	3								7
	Channel Complexity (High to Low)	1	2	2								6
Commercialisation Strategy	Strategic Clarity (low to high)	1	5	5								8
Business Model Development	Bus Model Innov. Reqd (High to low)	1	6	6								6
	Business Model Complexity (High to Low)	1	3	3								7
IP Management	IP Strength (low to high)	1	3	3								6
Manufacturing & Deployment	Manufacturing Complexity (High to Low)	1	7	7								7
	Supply Chain Complexity (High to Low)	1	3	3								8
Product Definition and Synthesis	Product Complexity (High to Low)	1	5	5								7
Technology Dev. & Contingent Deployment	Tech Deploy. Complexity (High to Low)	1	4	4								8
Human Capital:Talent, Leadership & Culture	Access to Core Comp. (low to high)	1	4	4								6
Total Impact Score				90								142
Normalised Impact Score				**0.45**								**0.71**
Financial Impact												
Funding & Investment	Revenue Potential (low to high)	1	8	8								5
	Margin, EBIT (low to high)	1	8	8								1
	Investment Required (high to low)	1	7	7	2	2	5	5	7	7	1	1
	Time to Payback (long vs short)	1	8	8	6	6	6	6	6	6	2	2
	Access to Investment (low to high)	1	7	7	7	7	7	7	7	7	3	3
Total Impact Score				38		27		29		31		12
Normalised Impact Score				**0.76**		**0.54**		**0.58**		**0.62**		**0.24**

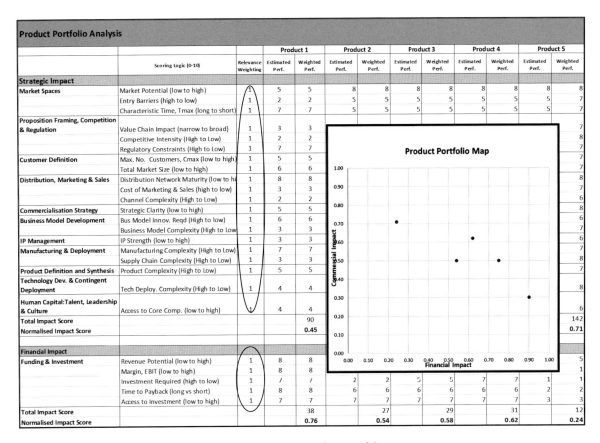

Figure 22. Your product portfolio.

18.3.3 *Build your integrated execution plan*

Your execution plan for a multi-product firm needs to reflect three key areas:

- Profiling the status of each product in the overall portfolio, with an aggregate view of the current portfolio.

- Consolidated forward-looking view which covers the objectives of the multi-product firm.

- An integrated execution plan which covers the activities required to address the gap between the current and target portfolios, based on specific activities identified in the weighted portfolio priorities.

Key Activities	Tasks	Resources	M1	M2	M3	M4	M5	M6	M7	M8	M9
Profile status of Individual Products in Portfolio											
	Collate information on all products	A1, A2	■								
	Assess maturity of all products	A1, A2		■							
	Assess vector profile for each product				■						
	Build Portfolio Map					■					
Consolidated forward-looking view											
	Map Products vs market-space-centric value chain and identify opportunities	A1, B1				■					
	Clarify future Customer Targeting	B1, B2					■				
	Clarify Channels & Partners	B1, B2							■		
	Clarify key enabling technologies and associated IP	C1, C2						■			
	Potential Business Models	A1, D2							■		
Build Integrated basis for excecution plan											
	Shape new Propositions	A1, B1, D1								■	
	Overall Strategic Priorities	A1, B1, X1								■	
	Build Target Portfolio Map	A1, B2, D2								■	■

Figure 23. Your integrated execution plan.

References

1. Phadke, U.P. & Vyakarnam, S. (2017), *Camels, Tigers & Unicorns*, World Scientific Publishing, London.
2. Audretsch, D.B., *Determinants of High-Growth Entrepreneurship: Report Prepared for the OECD/DBA International Workshop on High-growth Firms: Local Policies and Local Determinants*, Copenhagen, University of Indiana, USA, 28 March 2012.
3. Schumpeter, J.A. (2018), *Capitalism, Socialism and Democracy* (2nd ed.), Impact Books, Floyd, VA.
4. Porter, M. (1985), *Competitive Advantage: Creating & Sustaining Competitive Advantage*, Free Press, Simon & Schuster Inc, New York.
5. Mitchell, A., Logothetti, A., Thomas J. & Kantor, R.E. (1971), An approach to measuring quality of life, SRI International Paper.
6. Rogers, E.M. (1983), *Diffusion of Innovations* (3rd ed.), Free Press, New York.
7. Belbin, R.M. (2000), *Beyond the Team*, Elsevier, Butterworth-Heinmann.
8. Nowack, K. (1996), Is the Myers Briggs type indicator the right tool to use? Performance in practice, American Society of Training and Development, Fall, 6.
9. Drath, W.H., McCauley, C.D., Palus, C.J, Van Velsor, E., O'Connor, P. & McGuire, J.B. (2008), Direction, alignment, commitment: Towards a more integrative ontology of leadership, *The Leadership Quarterly*, 19, 635–653.
10. Greiner, L.E. (1998), Evolution and revolution as organizations grow, *Harvard Business Review*, (May–June).
11. Prahalad, C.K. & Hamel, G. (1983), The core competence of the corporation, *Harvard Business Review*, 68(3), 79–91.
12. Teece, D.J. (2010), Business models, business strategy, and innovation, *Long Range Planning*, 43(2–3), 172–194.

13. Burgelman, R. & Grove, A. (2012), Strategic dynamics: three key themes, Stanford Graduate School of Business Research Paper No. 2096, June.

14. Johnson, P. (2007), *Astute Competition: The Economics of Strategic Diversity*, Emerald Group Publishing, UK.

Index

business customers, 76, 80

business model components, 160–161

business model(s), 24, 34, 36, 57, 85, 152, 160

C

case studies, 10, 181, 183

case study coverage, 185

cash flow, 164

C/C-max ratio, 86

changing IP priorities, 116

changing priorities, 46

channels-to-market, 96

channel strategies, 97

characterising the consumer profile, 79

characteristic times for market spaces, 64

charter customers, 84–85

Chasm I, 20, 36, 46

Chasm II, 9, 20, 36, 46

Chasm III, 9, 20, 36

chasms, 8, 14

cloud computing firms, 129

C-max, 86

co-creation, 74

collaborate–compete, 74

collaborators, 66

commercial impact vs the financial impact, 176

commercial integration, 112

commercialisation canvas, 8, 26, 28

commercialisation journey, 40, 46

commercialisation monitor, 167–168

commercialisation readiness level, 22, 32

commercialisation strategy, 24, 34, 36, 152, 154

commercialization readiness, 8

commercial strategies, 57

communications, 140

company valuation, 148

comparative impact assessment, 40

competition, 24

competition & regulation, 66, 68, 70

competitive differentiation, 114

completed commercialisation monitor, 170

completely new markets, 88

composite (trade-off) vectors, 24, 34, 152

consumers, 76, 78

content, 100

contingent, 102

contingent deployment, 106

control systems, 138, 140

copyright protection, 114

core competences, 68, 136

corrosion monitoring system for oil & gas, 206

cost of customer acquisition, 164

creative synthesis, 118, 122–123

CRL, 8

cross-border commercialisation, 9

cross-fertilisation strategy, 128

G

gatekeeper, 82
geographic focus, 86
go-to-market challenges, 90
go-to-market variables, 90
governments, 76
grants, 142
gross margin, 164
growth firms, 4
growth vectors, 32
guidance on scoring, 40

H

healthcare market space, 60
H-form teams, 138
high-performance teams, 138
human capital, 100
hybrid approaches, 137
hybrid groups, 82

I

impact assessment, 40
incubators, 4
industrial bio-tech market space, 62
industry 4.0, 129
industry value chains, 54
innovation agencies, 4
innovators, 4
integrated operations, 126

integrated teams, 138
integration of technology functionality, 112
intellectual property management, 24, 34, 100, 114
internal vectors, 24, 34, 99
internet of things or IoT, 129
intervention agencies, 4
intervention shaping, 51, 99
intervention shaping: *composite* vectors, 151
IP management, 36
IP mapping grid, 114
iterations, 152

J

journey, 28
just-in-time methods, 128

K

key user analysis, 120
knowledge and affinity centric groups, 83
knowledge and expertise-mediated groups, 82
knowledge or affinity-based groups or communities, 76

L

9-layer model, 125
launch teams, 138
leadership, 100, 132, 137
lean manufacturing, 128

Triple Chasm Model, 8, 86
type of customer, 86
types of multi-product firms, 172
typical product portfolio, 178
typical scale-up journey, 45

U
U-form teams, 138
understanding IP, 114
unique value chains, 57
unpacking manufacturing, 126
unpacking market spaces, 57
unregistered, 100
unregistered rights, 114
upfront subscription revenues, 146
user behaviour, 78
user–customer ratio, 85

users, 85
users vs customers, 85

V
valuation, 148
variable costs, 164
VC funds, 144
vector-based approach to multi-product firms, 173
vector impact, 34, 40
vectors, 34
vectors used to define commercialisation strategy, 156
voice-of-the customer, 118
voice of the customer approaches, 120

W
womens' fashion clothing retail & e-commerce, 264